MATHEMATICAL TASKS IN CLASSROOMS AROUND THE WORLD

Mathematical Tasks in Classrooms around the World

Edited by

Yoshinori Shimizu
University of Tsukuba, Japan

Berinderjeet Kaur
Nanyang Technological University, Singapore

Rongjin Huang
Texas A&M University, USA

and

David Clarke
University of Melbourne, Australia

SENSE PUBLISHERS
ROTTERDAM / BOSTON / TAIPEI

A C.I.P. record for this book is available from the Library of Congress.

ISBN 978-94-6091-148-4 (paperback)
ISBN 978-94-6091-149-1 (hardback)
ISBN 978-94-6091-150-7 (e-book)

Published by: Sense Publishers,
P.O. Box 21858, 3001 AW Rotterdam, The Netherlands
http://www.sensepublishers.com

Printed on acid-free paper

DEDICATION

With the greatest respect and affection this book is dedicated to

GODFREY ISHMAEL SETHOLE
25 SEPTEMBER 1967 TO NOVEMBER 16, 2007

Godfrey Sethole was a respected mathematics educator in South Africa. He was an Associate Professor and Head of the Mathematics, Science and Technology Department at the Tshwane University of Technology and played an important role in the development of the Association for Mathematics Education of South Africa (AMESA) in the North West Province. Godfrey was much loved and respected by all those of us who had the privilege (and the fun) of working with him on the LPS project. He will be missed by all who knew him: for his quick intelligence, for his warmth and for his sense of humour. The LPS community is the richer for Godfrey's contribution and we miss him deeply.

SERIES PREFACE

The Learner's Perspective Study provides a vehicle for the work of an international community of classroom researchers. The work of this community will be reported in a series of books of which this is the third. The documentation of the practices of classrooms in other countries causes us to question and revise our assumptions about our own practice and the theories on which that practice is based. International comparative and cross-cultural research has the capacity to inform practice, shape policy and develop theory at a level commensurate with regional, national or global priorities. International comparative research offers us more than insights into the novel, interesting and adaptable practices employed in other school systems. It also offers us insights into the strange, invisible, and unquestioned routines and rituals of our own school system and our own classrooms. In addition, a cross-cultural perspective on classrooms can help us identify common values and shared assumptions, encouraging the adaptation of practices from one classroom for use in a different cultural setting. As these findings become more widely available, they will be increasingly utilised in the professional development of teachers and in the development of new theory.

David Clarke
Series Editor

TABLE OF CONTENTS

ACKNOWLEDGEMENTS

The Editors would like to express their gratitude to Carmel Mesiti for her meticulous work in formatting the chapters in this book and in constructing both the Subject Index and Author Index. This book is very much the result of her efficient organization, her unfailing patience, and her unceasing persistence.

The research reported in this book benefited substantially from funding awarded by the following agencies, centres and universities:

The Australian Research Council
Bank of Sweden Tercentenary Foundation
Centre for Research in Pedagogy and Practice, National Institute of Education, Nanyang Technological University *(Singapore)*
The Collier Charitable Trust *(Australia)*
Committee for Research and Conference Grants, University of Hong Kong, *(Hong Kong SAR, China)*
Czech Science Foundation *(Czech Republic)*
Global Development Network (GDN), World Bank
Japan Society for the Promotion of Science
Mathematics Association of Victoria *(Australia)*
Ministry of Education, Science, Sports and Culture *(Japan)*
Ministry of Education, Youth and Sports *(Czech Republic)*
The Potter Foundation *(Australia)*
Pundasyon sa Pagpapaunlad ng Kaalaman sa Pagtuturo ng Agham, Ink. *(The Philippines)*
Research Commission, Freie Universität Berlin *(Germany)*
Research Grants Council *(Hong Kong SAR, China)*
The Spencer Foundation *(USA)*
Swedish Research Council
The University of Macau, Academic Community *(China)*
The University of Melbourne *(Australia)*

All editors and authors would like to thank the teachers and students, whose cooperation and generous participation made this international study possible.

YOSHINORI SHIMIZU, BERINDERJEET KAUR, RONGJIN HUANG
AND DAVID CLARKE

CHAPTER ONE

The Role of Mathematical Tasks in Different Cultures

THE CENTRALITY OF TASKS IN MATHEMATICS CLASSROOM INSTRUCTION

Mathematics classroom instruction is generally organised around and delivered through students' activities on mathematical tasks (Doyle, 1988). International comparative studies on mathematics classroom instruction tend to report analyses of such students' activities engaged in tasks that occupy various amounts of lesson time in classrooms. Notably, in all of the seven countries that participated in the TIMSS 1999 Video Study, eighth-grade mathematics was most commonly taught by spending at least 80% of lesson time in mathematics classrooms working on mathematical tasks (Hiebert et al., 2003).

Classroom activities are coherent actions shaped by the instructional context, in general, and, in particular, by what is taught through the use of tasks (Stodolsky, 1988). Individual teachers arrange instruction very differently, depending on what they are teaching, and students respond to instruction very differently, depending on the structure and demands shaped by tasks enacted in the classroom. The tasks that teachers assign can determine how students come to understand what is taught. In other words, tasks serve as a context for students' thinking, during and after instruction. Doyle argues the point that

> tasks influence learners by directing their attention to particular aspects of content and by specifying ways of processing information. (Doyle, 1983, p.161)

Mathematics tasks are important vehicles for classroom instruction that aims to enhance students' learning. To achieve quality mathematics instruction, then, the role of mathematical tasks to stimulate students' cognitive processes is crucial (Hiebert & Wearne, 1993).

In summary, the centrality of tasks in mathematics classroom is evident from theoretical perspectives as well as in empirical results from international comparative studies. The role of mathematical tasks provides a key to any attempt to understand teaching and learning in research on classroom practices in mathematics.

Y. Shimizu, B. Kaur, R. Huang and D. J. Clarke (Eds.), Mathematical Tasks in Classrooms around the World, pp. 1–14.
© *2010 Sense Publishers. All rights reserved.*

MATHEMATICAL TASKS AND THE LEARNER'S PERSPECTIVE STUDY

This book is the third in a series arising from the international collaborative project called The Learner's Perspective Study (LPS). The LPS documented sequences of at least ten lessons, using three video cameras, supplemented by the reconstructive accounts of classroom participants obtained in post-lesson video-stimulated interviews, and by test and questionnaire data, and copies of student written material (Clarke, 1998, 2001, 2003). In each classroom, formal data generation was preceded by a one-week familiarisation period in which the research team undertook preliminary classroom videotaping and post-lesson interviewing until such time as the teacher and students were accustomed to the classroom presence of the researchers and familiar with the research process. In each participating country, the focus of data generation was the classrooms of three teachers, identified by the local mathematics education community as competent, and situated in demographically different school communities within the one major city. For each school system (country), this design generated a data set of at least 30 'well-taught' lessons (three sequences of at least ten lessons), involving 120 video records, 60 student interviews, 12 teacher interviews, plus researcher field notes, test and questionnaire data, and scanned student written material. Well-taught, in the context of this study, meant that the teachers in each country were recruited according to local criteria for competence: visibility as presenters at conferences for other teachers, leadership roles in professional organisations, and, acclamation by colleagues and students. It is not surprising, therefore, that the classroom of a competent teacher in Uppsala might look a little different from the classroom of a competent teacher in Shanghai or San Diego. The local construction and enactment of competence was one of the most appealing aspects of this study. Greater detail on data generation procedures is provided in the appendix to this book. Signature elements of the LPS Research Design are (i) the commitment to studying 'competent' teachers as these are locally defined; (ii) the recording of a sequence of at least ten lessons constituting a mathematics topic; and (iii) the use of classroom videos in video-stimulated reconstructive interviews with teacher and students as soon as possible after the recorded lesson. The teacher and student interviews offer insight into both the teacher's and the students' participation in (and reconstruction of) particular lesson events and the significance and meaning that the students associated with their actions and those of the teacher and their classmates.

The classroom use of mathematical tasks has been addressed in previous publications from the Learner's Perspective Study (LPS). For example, the first book in the LPS series (Clarke, Keitel, & Shimizu, 2006) included a chapter on "Setting a Task" (Keitel, 2006) and another on "The Role of the Textbook and Homework" (Kaur, Low, & Seah, 2006), and the second LPS book (Clarke, Emanuelsson, Jablonka, & Mok, 2006) included a chapter on "Learning Tasks" (Mok & Kaur, 2006). It is difficult to imagine any substantial investigation of the mathematics classroom that did not address the tasks that characterise such settings. This book, the third in the LPS series, is devoted entirely to research into the role of mathematical tasks in the classrooms of different countries.

THE NATURE OF MATHEMATICAL TASKS IN CLASSROOMS

A mathematical task has been defined as a set of problems or a single complex problem that focuses students' attention on a particular mathematical idea (Stein, Grover, & Henningsen, 1996). The construct 'task' also includes the intellectual and physical products that are expected of students, such as the operations that students are to use to obtain the desired results, and the resources that are available for students to produce the products (Doyle, 1983). In his elaboration of the construct 'task,' Doyle (1988) included the following components: The product(s), such as numbers in blanks on a worksheet; the operation(s) required to produce the product; the resources drawn upon in completing the task, such as notes from textbook information; and, the significance or 'weight' of a task in the accountability system of a class.

In their critique of 'minimal guidance' instruction, Kirschner, Sweller and Clark (2006) make the insightful observation that

> it may be an error to assume that the pedagogic content of the learning experience is [should be] identical to the methods and processes (i.e., the epistemology) of the discipline being studied. (p. 84)

In particular, their assertion that "The practice of a profession is not the same as learning to practice the profession" (p. 83) highlights a critical issue in the design of instruction in mathematics. How is classroom mathematical activity related to the activity of the mathematician? While we may classify the tasks of the mathematics classroom in a variety of ways, we should not confuse those tasks with the tasks of the mathematician: they are fundamentally different in purpose.

Mathematical tasks employed in educational settings have been variously categorised under designations such as 'authentic,' 'rich' and 'complex.' The classification 'authentic' has particularly emotive overtones – suggesting that some mathematical tasks might be classified as 'inauthentic.' The most common usage of the term 'authentic' in this regard seems to refer to an assumed correspondence between the nature of the task and other mathematical activities that might be undertaken outside the classroom for purposes other than the learning of mathematics. The value attached to 'authentic mathematical tasks' seems to appeal to a theory of learning that measures mathematical understanding by the capacity to employ mathematical knowledge obtained in the classroom in non-classroom ('real-world') settings and which constructs the process of mathematical learning as 'legitimate peripheral participation' (Lave & Wenger, 1991) in the mathematical activities of a community larger than a mathematics class.

To illustrate another classificatory scheme: Williams and Clarke (1997) developed a framework that identified the following forms of task complexity: linguistic, contextual, numerical, conceptual, intellectual, and representational. In her subsequent research, Williams (2000, 2002) identified a phenomenon she called 'discovered complexity.' This research identified situations in which students discovered complexities in the course of attempting a mathematical task posed by the teacher. These discovered complexities in combination with other instructional and learning conditions would stimulate the creation by students of their own mathematical tasks. These student-created tasks provide the focus of Chapter 9.

An academic task can be examined through a wide variety of attributes. When a teacher selects a task for her/his teaching, she/he may think of such task attributes as: context, complexity, degree of openness, form and representation. In the mathematics education research tradition, considerable research has been devoted to task attributes which affect students' mathematical problem solving (Goldin & McClintock, 1984). Each of the attributes just listed has its own structure and variations – as has just been illustrated in the case of complexity.

As these earlier studies pointed out, a systematic analysis of task attributes has direct implications for teaching and learning in mathematics classroom, and particularly for teaching via problem solving. As discussed below, it is especially important that attention be given to the analysis of the cognitive demands enacted by tasks presented in the classroom and to the situated nature of the task as it is enacted by teacher and students in the classroom.

Task attributes need to be considered in relation both to the teacher and the learners in a mathematics classroom as well as in relation to broader contextual influences such as the curriculum, social expectations and so on. Also, considerations of the ternary relations such as Teacher-Task-Learner or Learner-Task-Mathematics are needed to explore fundamental aspects in mathematics teaching and learning (Christiansen & Walther, 1986). Study of the nature of such relations will reflect the choice of theoretical framework.

Although attention to the nature of mathematical tasks is important, attention to the classroom processes associated with mathematical tasks is equally needed. Such student activities as making conjectures, abstracting mathematical properties, explaining their reasoning, validating their assertions, and discussing and questioning their own thinking and the thinking of others do not fit well with the tasks and task use employed in many 'traditional classrooms' (Lampert, 1990). Yet such activities are the explicit goal of many curricular initiatives (for example, NCTM, 1989) and it is mathematical tasks that provide the pretext and the catalyst for such activities.

Any consideration of the nature of mathematical tasks in classrooms must attend to elements such as: task complexity, social participants and the nature of participation, socio-cultural context, and, most importantly, the purpose for which the task has been introduced into the mathematics classroom. Some of the chapters of this book explore such purposes: mathematical tasks as catalysts for student talk (Chapter 3 by Bergem and Klette); the function of mathematical tasks in connecting mathematical ideas (Chapter 5 by Shimizu and Chapter 6 by Novotná and Hošpesová); and the use of mathematical tasks "to scaffold student entry to idiosyncratic exploration" (Chapter 9 by Williams). In Chapter 2, Kaur distinguishes tasks according to their use for learning, review, practice or assessment, and then employs an analytical framework synthesised from other studies to carry out a more fine-grained analysis of task use in three Singapore classrooms.

It is the intention of this book to contribute to the extensive and diverse literature on mathematical tasks in two ways: by examining the classroom use of mathematical tasks from a variety of perspectives; and, by making comparison possible between forms of classroom use of mathematical tasks in different classrooms around the world. Neither approach is intended to be comprehensive, but it is hoped that the chapters that follow, both individually and in combination, will address issues of interest to the mathematics education community internationally. The remainder of this introductory chapter sets out some of the theoretical and contextual considerations that should be taken into account in any reading of this book.

THEORETICAL ALTERNATIVES IN CONSIDERING THE CLASSROOM USE OF MATHEMATICAL TASKS

There are many different theories currently being employed in mathematics education. Activity Theory, for example, is an obvious contender in considering how the classroom use of mathematical tasks might be situated theoretically. Recent developments in the conceptualisation of Activity Theory (eg Engeström, 2001) have increased the breadth of phenomena and contexts able to be addressed using Activity Theory. In particular, mathematical tasks can be situated naturally within the tools available for use in pedagogic activity systems. Our purpose here is not to catalogue all the different theories that might be employed in researching the classroom use of mathematical tasks, but to examine briefly a selection of relevant theories that informed the analytical work of the LPS community represented in the chapters of this book. In this context, Activity Theory serves as a useful example of an eminently eligible theory, used in other LPS publications for consideration of classroom discourse, but which was not explicitly employed in any of the chapters that follow. This example provides an opportunity to re-emphasise the commitment of the LPS community to an inclusive selectivity, by which the theory guiding each analysis is chosen pragmatically for its consistency with the purposes of that analysis.

Gellert (2008) usefully contrasts 'interactionist' and 'structuralist' perspectives on mathematics classroom practice. In the consideration of the classroom use of mathematical tasks, the interactionist perspective offers insight into the negotiative processes that interact with individuals' use in classroom settings for the socially-mediated constitution of learning. Chapters 4 (Gallos Cronberg) and 7 (Mok) report interactionist analyses that emphasise student engagement and mediated learning respectively.

In Chapter 3, Bergem and Klette suggest that greater emphasis be given to mathematical communication in research and theory. They argue that

> cognitive psychology, social constructivism, distributed cognition, semiotics and socio-cultural theory all draw our attention to the essential role that

reflective discourse and discursive practices have for fostering mathematical understanding (p. 36).

For Bergem and Klette, therefore, mathematical conversations and the discourses such conversations might embody warrant close research scrutiny. The situatedness of any such conversations is seen as critical to their realisation in consequent student learning.

The structuralist perspective potentially offers very different insights into the deployment and function of mathematical tasks in classrooms. Focusing attention on differentiated participation, a structuralist analysis aspires to explain such differentiation in terms of hierarchies and power relationships. In the case of mathematical tasks, these hierarchies reflect the enactment of an entrenched social order and the privileging of particular forms of knowledge. Within the structuralist perspective, particular pedagogies can be seen as embodying systems of social and academic privilege (Bernstein, 1996) and in the mathematics classroom it is primarily through the performance of mathematical tasks that these pedagogies are enacted. The chapter by Kaur (Chapter 2) reports an analysis that could be considered structuralist. The analysis differentiates usefully between forms of knowledge and the key resources that structure instruction in the three Singapore classrooms studied.

The chapter by Mesiti and Clarke (Chapter 10) argues that mathematical tasks should only be considered 'as performed,' since the same mathematics problem can provide a vehicle for the realisation of very different social and educational purposes. This performative emphasis is echoed in Chapter 5 by Shimizu, where it is asserted that the functions of mathematical tasks posed in classroom settings need to be considered within the contexts in which they are undertaken.

The *Theory of Didactical Situations in Mathematics* (TDSM) (Brousseau, 1997) is a coherent, well-elaborated instructional theory, capable of supporting the explicit advocacy of particular practices. Within TDSM, Brousseau carefully distinguishes the work of the mathematician, the work of the student and the work of the teacher. Particular attention is given to 'The notion of problem.'

A student isn't really doing mathematics unless she is asking herself questions and solving problems. (Brousseau, 1997, p. 79)

Similar care is given within TDSM to critical considerations such as 'epistemological obstacles' and 'didactic problems.' Novotná and Hošpesová make use of TDSM to theorise about the teacher's scaffolding of linkages between different mathematical concepts and procedures, using specific examples from two mathematics classrooms in the Czech Republic to illustrate the key points.

By way of comparison, Variation Theory is a similarly coherent theory that provides clear criteria for instructional advocacy. Variation Theory privileges constructs such as 'the object of learning' and 'dimensions of variation' (Marton & Tsui, 2004). In Chapter 7, Mok draws attention to one Shanghai teacher's deliberate partial variation of the content and constraints between problems and questions.

The choice of the theoretical lens focuses analytical attention on some aspects of the role of mathematical tasks and ignores others. This is inevitable. It is a strength of the combination of analyses reported in this book that they are not restricted to the application of a single theory. Instead, the tasks of the mathematics classroom are examined from a variety of theoretical perspectives. In several cases, the same tasks occur in different chapters, to be re-examined from the perspective of tasks tasks occur in different chapters, to be examined from the perspective of different theories. The reader is encouraged to compare the treatment of the same task in the different analyses and to reflect on which analysis connects most usefully with the reader's concerns, interests and purposes.

Another entry point for consideration of the theories relevant to the classroom use of mathematics tasks are the three related issues of Abstraction, Context and Transfer. In some discussions, abstract mathematics seems to be treated as simply decontextualised mathematics. Clarke and Helme have argued that there is no such thing as decontextualised mathematics (Clarke & Helme, 1998), since all mathematical activity is undertaken in a context of some sort. If abstraction in mathematics is to have any legitimacy or relevance, then it must reside in some form of generalisability of the mathematical matter under consideration, in the sense that the principle, concept or procedure can be thought of as transcending any particular context or instance. But, to argue that an exercise in Euclidean geometry or in pure number is an abstract task is to deny the social situatedness that has become accepted even from the most cognitivist of perspectives (Lave & Wenger, 1991).

In relation to mathematical tasks, Clarke and Helme distinguished the social context in which the task is undertaken from any 'figurative context' that might be an element of the way the task is posed. In this sense, the task:

> Siu Ming's family intends to travel to Beijing by train during the national holiday, so they have booked three adult tickets and one student ticket, totalling $560. After hearing this, Siu Ming's classmate Siu Wong would like to go to Beijing with them. As a result they buy three adult tickets and two student tickets for a total of $640. Can you calculate the cost of each adult and student ticket? (Shanghai School 3, Lesson 7, Train task)

has a figurative context that integrates elements such as the family's need to travel by train and the familiar difference in cost between an adult and a student ticket. The social context, however, could take a wide variety of forms, including: an exploratory instructional activity undertaken in small collaborative groups; the focus of a whole class discussion, orchestrated by the teacher to draw out existing student understandings; or, an assessment task to be undertaken individually. In each case, the manner in which the task will be performed is likely to be quite different, even though we can conceive of the same student as participant in each setting. The significance of the context in which mathematical tasks are undertaken has been persuasively demonstrated by Nunes, Schliemann, Carraher and their co-workers through the well-known series of studies contrasting the performance of mathematically equivalent tasks in school and everyday settings (Nunes, Schliemann, & Carraher, 1993).

If we take 'transfer' not as a description of a particular cognitive process, but as a metaphor for a skill developed in one context being used in a different context, then it is reasonable to ask, "Under what conditions (and through the instructional use of what tasks) will the likelihood of transfer be maximised?" A cognitivist might direct attention to the selective variation of task attributes with the intention of successively focusing student attention on salient aspects of the mathematical concept or procedure to be learned. Variation Theory (Marton & Tsui, 2004) identifies learning with an increasing capacity to discern relevant attributes in the object of learning. From such a perspective, particular tasks and particular sequences of tasks can be critiqued as more or less conducive to directing student attention appropriately and thereby to the optimal promotion of the discernment that is identified with learning.

Distributed Cognition (Hutchins, 1995) and other theories with a material semiotic character accord significance to artefacts as participating in cognition. Once representational forms are included in the broad class of artefacts, then mathematical tasks cease to be either the objects to which we apply our cognitive tools nor merely the social catalysts for their deployment. Rather, mathematical tasks become the embodiment of performed cognition, integrating, as they do, representational forms, socio-cultural imperatives and mathematical entities. In Chapter 10, Mesiti and Clarke attempt to portray mathematical tasks performatively in order to examine the role each task plays in affording or constraining agency and voice in the social settings in which the tasks are communally performed.

COGNITIVE DEMANDS OF DIFFERENT TASKS FOR DIFFERENT LEARNERS

Selecting and setting appropriate tasks is key to the success of teaching mathematics (Doyle, 1988; Hiebert & Wearne, 1993; Stein & Lane, 1996; Martin, 2007). Tasks can vary not only with respect to mathematics content but also with respect to the cognitive processes involved in working on them. Worthwhile tasks are those that offer students the opportunity to extend what they know and stimulate their learning.

Doyle (1988) argues that tasks with different cognitive demands are likely to induce different kinds of learning. Tasks that require students to solve complex problems can be considered to be cognitively demanding tasks. In contrast, cognitively undemanding tasks are those that give less opportunity for the students to engage in high-level cognitive processes. Thus, the nature and the role of tasks that entail different types of cognitive demand are key to students' opportunities for learning. Chapter 8 by Huang and Cai compares the cognitive demands of the mathematical tasks used in the US and Chinese classrooms. In this chapter, reference is made to 'declining cognitive demand' and the important point is introduced that the cognitive demand of a task depends not just on the mathematical form of the initial task, but on the manner in which the task is enacted in the classroom.

The cognitive demands of mathematical tasks can change as tasks are introduced to students and/or as tasks are enacted during instruction (Stein, Grover, & Henningsen, 1996). The progression of mathematical tasks can be modeled by identifying the phases of enactment from their original form as they appear in the pages of textbooks or other curriculum materials to the tasks that teachers actually provide to students and then to the tasks as enacted by the teacher and students in classroom lessons (see Figure 1).

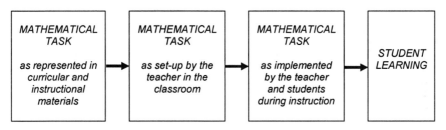

Figure 1. Progression of mathematical tasks (adapted from Stein, Grover, & Henningsen, 1996)

The first two arrows in the diagram identify critical phases in the instructional life of tasks at which cognitive demands are susceptible to being altered. The tasks, especially as enacted, have consequences for student learning of mathematics, as is shown by the third arrow in the figure. The features of an instructional task, especially its cognitive demand, often change as a task passes through these phases (Stein, Grover, & Henningsen, 1996).

In order to track changes in cognitive demand, tasks can be classified at different levels of cognitive demand. Implementing cognitively challenging tasks in ways that maintain students' opportunities to engage in high-level cognitive processes is not a trivial endeavour (Henningsen & Stein, 1997). In the TIMSS 1999 video study, the ability to maintain the high-level demands of cognitively challenging tasks during instruction was the central feature that distinguished classroom teaching in different countries (Hiebert et al., 2003). One of the questions addressed in several of the chapters in this book is whether it is useful or even feasible to classify a task as cognitively challenging, independent of the manner in which it is performed in the classroom. Instead, the progression in task form and demand as depicted in Figure 1 resembles the distinction made by Variation Theory between the intended object of learning, the enacted object of learning, and the experienced object of learning. The TIMSS 1999 Video Study sensibly distinguished between the potential demands of a task and the extent to which those demands were realised in the actual practice of the classroom. As can be seen, there is a strong convergence of view towards seeing mathematical tasks as performatively defined rather than as static objects enshrined in text.

DISTINGUISHING BETWEEN THE USE OF MATHEMATICAL TASKS FOR INSTRUCTION AND ASSESSMENT

If the use of a mathematical task is intended to promote the student's learning of mathematics, that use can reasonably be designated *instructional*. If the use of a mathematical task is intended to generate information about student learning or, relatedly, about the effectiveness of instruction, then we can characterise that use as being for the purposes of assessment. Of course, the same task can serve both purposes, even at the same time, as is evident from the extensive literature on formative assessment (Wiliam & Black, 1996). It does not necessarily follow, however, that a given task (or task type) is equally effective when used for instructional purposes or assessment purposes. This distinction must be seen as indicative rather than definitive. It can be argued that all tasks constitute assessment in as much as all tasks reveal information regarding any students' attempts at the task (particularly given the contemporary prioritisation of formative assessment). Equally, even test items can be instructional, serving to convey messages about what is and what is not correct and valued mathematical performance.

The chapter by Kaur (Chapter 2) classifies tasks as learning, review, practice and assessment tasks. The distinction between the instructional and assessment uses of mathematical tasks in the classrooms studied draws attention to the lack of alignment of the espoused curricular goals with either instructional or assessment practices in the three Singapore classrooms.

Earlier, reference was made to the designation 'rich mathematical tasks.' One context in which this characterisation of tasks has been used is assessment. In that context, 'rich' is taken to signify a task of sufficient complexity as to admit a variety of approaches and therefore to have the capacity to reveal differences in student conceptions of relevant mathematical concepts and procedures.

Assessment tasks should be sufficiently open to invite a range of responses from students and so allow students to disclose their level of competence and understanding at a number of levels. Such rich assessment tasks:

- connect naturally with what has been taught
- address a range of outcomes in the one task
- allow all students to undertake the activity
- can be successfully undertaken using a range of methods or approaches
- encourage students to disclose their own understanding of what they have learned
- allow students to show connections they are able to make between the concepts they have learned
- are themselves worthwhile activities for children's learning
- draw the attention of teachers to important aspects of mathematical activity

- help teachers to decide whether it is appropriate to move on for most students and what specific help others may require. (Clarke, 1996, pp. 361-362)

There is no question that many of the tasks discussed in this book are 'rich tasks' by the criteria just listed. Whether a particular task should be categorised as an instructional task or an assessment task or as both depends on the way in which the task was utilised by the particular teacher. Certainly, it is clear in several chapters that teachers made use of the information provided by many tasks to guide their instruction.

The premise of Kaur's chapter is an important one: however we might classify tasks (whether as serving instructional or assessment purposes), a crucial consideration is the coherence with which valued mathematical performance is nurtured, promoted, revealed, evaluated and acknowledged in the classroom and it is through our choice and use of mathematical tasks that this coherence is displayed and communicated.

THE FOCUS AND THE STRUCTURE OF THIS BOOK

The following chapters in this book explore and discuss the nature and roles of mathematical tasks in LPS classrooms with a focus on their impact on students' learning. It is an essential theme of the Learner's Perspective Study that international comparative research offers unique opportunities to interrogate established practice, existing theories and entrenched assumptions (Clarke, Emanuelsson, Jablonka, & Mok, 2006; Clarke, Keitel, & Shimizu, 2006). In this book, focusing on the nature, role and implementation of mathematical tasks, we offer the reader a variety of images of classrooms from the countries participating in the Learner's Perspective Study.

It was of interest in the development of this book whether the enactment of mathematical tasks observed in the classrooms of one country showed consistency of form and purpose, sufficiently different from other classrooms, such as to suggest a culturally-specific character. Because of the highly selective nature of the classrooms studied in each country, no claims can be made about national typification of practice, however any regularities of practices sustained across thirty lessons demand some consideration as to the possible causes of such consistency. Whether or not such identifiable characteristics in the treatment of tasks exist as cultural traits, the Learner's Perspective Study was predicated on a belief that international comparative studies are likely to reveal patterns of practice less evident in studies limited to a single country or community.

'Teaching' is not only about teaching what is conventionally called content, but also teaching what a lesson is and how to participate in it. Students learn not only what the answer is to a task but also how to approach academic tasks. The performative nature of tasks and the nature of student participation in the classroom activities catalysed by mathematics tasks are explored in many different ways in the chapters that follow.

This book includes chapters with very different approaches, such as: comparisons of the features of tasks within a lesson sequence in different cultures, the cognitive demands of different tasks for different learners, mathematical tasks as experienced from the learner's perspective, the role of tasks as vehicles for interaction among classroom participants, or the analysis of particular emphases within tasks: representations, real-world contexts, proof, problem solving, or types of reasoning and argumentation. The chapters have been organised as a progression from the consideration of mathematical tasks in the classrooms of single countries to comparative analyses across classrooms situated in several countries. While each individual chapter rewards careful reading, it is our hope that in combination the different perspectives on the classroom use of mathematical tasks will provide insights through differences in the settings in which the tasks are performed, differences in ways in which classroom participants are positioned in relation to the tasks, and profound differences in how each teacher utilises mathematical tasks, in partnership with their students, to create a distinctive form of mathematical activity.

REFERENCES

Bernstein, B. (1996). *Pedagogy, symbolic control and identity: Theory, research, critique.* London: Taylor & Francis.

Brousseau, G. (1997). *Theory of didactical situations in mathematics.* (N. Balacheff, M. Cooper, R. Sutherland, V. Warfield, Eds. & Trans). Dordrecht: Kluwer.

Christiansen, B., & Walther, G. (1986). Task and activity. In B. Christiansen, A. G. Howson, & M. Otte (Eds.), *Perspectives on mathematics education* (pp. 243-307). Dordrecht: Reidel.

Clarke, D. J. (1996). Assessment. In A. Bishop (Ed.), *International handbook of mathematics education* (pp. 327-370). Dordrecht: Kluwer Academic Publishers.

Clarke, D. J. (1998). Studying the classroom negotiation of meaning: Complementary accounts methodology. In A. Teppo (Ed.), *Qualitative research methods in mathematics education.* Monograph Number 9 of the *Journal for Research in Mathematics Education.* Reston, VA: NCTM, 98-111.

Clarke, D. J. (Ed.) (2001). *Perspectives on practice and meaning in mathematics and science classrooms.* Dordrecht: Kluwer Academic Publishers.

Clarke, D. J. (2003). International comparative studies in mathematics education. In A. J. Bishop, M. A. Clements, C. Keitel, J. Kilpatrick, & F. K. S. Leung (Eds.), *Second international handbook of mathematics education* (pp. 145-186). Dordrecht: Kluwer Academic Publishers.

Clarke, D. J., & Helme, S. (1998). Context as construction. In O. Bjorkqvist (Ed.), *Mathematics teaching from a constructivist point of view* (pp. 129-147). Vasa, Finland: Faculty of Education, Abo Akademi University.

Clarke, D. J., Emanuelsson, J., Jablonka, E., & Mok, I. A. C. (Eds.) (2006). *Making connections: Comparing mathematics classrooms around the world.* Rotterdam: Sense Publishers.

Clarke, D. J., Keitel, C., & Shimizu, Y. (2006). The learner's perspective study. In D. J. Clarke, C. Keitel, & Y. Shimizu (Eds.), *Mathematics classrooms in twelve countries: The insider's perspective* (pp. 1-14). Rotterdam: Sense Publishers.

Doyle, W. (1983). Academic work. *Review of Educational Research, 53,* 159-199.

Doyle, W. (1988). Work in mathematics classes: The context of students' thinking during instruction. *Educational Psychologist, 23,* 167-180.

Engeström, Y. (2001). *Expansive learning at work. Towards an activity-theoretical reconceptualisation.* London: Institute of Education, University of London.

Gellert, U. (2008). Validity and relevance: Comparing and combining two sociological perspectives on mathematics classroom practice. *ZDM- International Journal on Mathematics Education, 40*, 215-224.

Goldin, G. A., & McClintock, C. E. (Eds.) (1984). *Task variables in mathematical problem solving.* Philadelphia: Franklin Institute Press.

Henningsen, M. A., & Stein, M. K. (1997). Mathematical tasks and student cognition: Classroom-based factors that support and inhibit high level mathematical thinking and reasoning. *Journal for Research in Mathematics Education, 8,* 524-549.

Hiebert, J., Gallimore, R., Garnier, H., Givvin, K. B., Hollingsworth, H., Jacobs, J., Chui, A. M. Y., Wearne, D., Smith, M., Kersting, N., Manaster, A., Tseng, E., Etterbeek, W., Manaster, C., Gonzales, P., & Stigler, J. W. (2003). *Teaching mathematics in seven countries: Results from the TIMSS 1999 video study.* Washington, DC: NCES.

Hiebert, J., & Wearne, D. (1993). Instructional tasks, classroom discourse, and students' learning in second-grade arithmetic. *American Educational Research Journal, 30,* 393-425.

Hutchins, E. (1995). *Cognition in the wild.* Cambridge, Mass: MIT Press.

Kaur, B., Low, H. K., & Seah, L. H. (2006). Mathematics teaching in two Singapore classrooms: The role of the textbook and homework. In D. J. Clarke, C. Keitel, & Y. Shimizu (Eds.), *Mathematics classrooms in twelve countries: The insider's perspective* (pp. 99-115). Rotterdam: Sense Publishers.

Keitel, C. (2006). 'Setting a task' in German schools: Different frames for different ambitions. In D. J. Clarke, C. Keitel, & Y. Shimizu (Eds.), *Mathematics classrooms in twelve countries: The insider's perspective* (pp. 37-57). Rotterdam: Sense Publishers.

Kirschner, P. A., Sweller, J., & Clark, R. E. (2006). Why minimal guidance during instruction does not work: An analysis of the failure of constructivist, discovery, problem-based, experiential, and inquiry-based teaching. *Educational Psychologist, 41*(2), 75-86.

Lampert, M. (1990). When the problem is not the question and the solution is not the answer: Mathematical knowing and teaching. *American Educational Research Journal, 27,* 29-63

Lave, J., & Wenger, E. (1991). *Situated learning: Legitimate peripheral participation.* Cambridge: Cambridge University Press.

Martin, T. S. (2007). *Mathematics teaching today: Improving practice, improving student learning* (2nd ed.). Reston, VA: National Council of Teachers of Mathematics.

Marton, F., & Tsui, A. (2004). *Classroom discourse and the space of learning.* Mahwah, N. J.: L. Erlbaum Associates.

Mok, I. A. C. & Kaur, B. (2006). 'Learning task' lesson events. In D. J. Clarke, J. Emanuelsson, E. Jablonka, & I. A. C. Mok (Eds.), *Making connections: Comparing mathematics classrooms around the world* (pp. 147-163). Rotterdam: Sense Publishers.

National Council of Teachers of Mathematics (NCTM) (1989). *Curriculum and evaluation standards for school mathematics.* Reston, VA: NCTM.

Nunes, T., Schliemann, A., & Carraher, D. (1993). *Street mathematics and school mathematics.* Cambridge: Cambridge University Press.

Stein, M. K., Grover, B. W., & Henningsen, M. A. (1996). Building student capacity for mathematical thinking and reasoning: An analysis of mathematical tasks used in reform classrooms. *American Educational Research Journal, 33,* 455-488.

Stein, M. K., & Lane, S. (1996). Instructional tasks and the development of student capacity to think and reason: An analysis of the relationship between teaching and learning in a reform mathematics project. *Educational Research and Evaluation, 2,* 50-80.

Stodolsky, S. (1988). *The subject matters: Classroom activity in math and social studies.* Chicago: The University of Chicago Press.

Wiliam, D., & Black, P. (1996). Meanings and Consequences: A basis for distinguishing formative and summative functions of assessment. *British Educational Research Journal, 22,* 537-48.

Williams, G. (2000). Collaborative problem solving and discovered complexity. In J. Bana & A. Chapman (Eds.), *Mathematics education beyond 2000* (pp. 656-663). Perth, Australia: Mathematics Education Research Group of Australasia.

Williams, G. (2002). Developing a shared understanding of task complexity. In L. Bazzini & C. Whybrow Inchley (Eds.), *Proceedings of CIEAEM53: Mathematical Literacy in the Digital Era, 263-268.*

Williams, G., & Clarke, D. J. (1997). The complexity of mathematics tasks. In N. Scott & H. Hollingsworth (Eds.), *Mathematics: Creating the future* (pp. 451-457). Melbourne, Australia: AAMT.

Yoshinori Shimizu
Graduate School of Comprehensive Human Sciences
University of Tsukuba
Japan

Berinderjeet Kaur
National Institute of Education
Nanyang Technological University
Singapore

Rongjin Huang
Department of Teaching, Learning and Culture
Texas A&M University
USA

David Clarke
International Centre for Classroom Research
Melbourne Graduate School of Education
University of Melbourne
Australia

BERINDERJEET KAUR

CHAPTER TWO

A Study of Mathematical Tasks from Three Classrooms in Singapore

INTRODUCTION

The basic aim of a mathematics lesson is for learners to learn something about a particular topic that the teacher has planned. To do this the teacher engages them in mathematical tasks during the lesson. Mathematical tasks in this context refer to what the students are asked to do, be it computations to be performed, symbols to be manipulated, diagrammatic representations to be made or translations of word problems into mathematical statements or models (Mason & Johnston-Wilder, 2006). Experiences gained by students (through the mathematical tasks that teachers engage them in to actualise the intended curriculum) form the bedrock of their knowledge and perception of mathematics. Therefore the nature and source of the tasks are important contributors to the pedagogical goals of the lessons in which they are enacted. In this chapter we examine the source and nature of tasks used by three competent mathematics teachers in grade eight classrooms from Singapore schools.

This study has emerged from two main considerations, namely the source and nature of mathematical tasks, which specifically are learning, review, practice and assessment tasks used by the three teachers to implement the intended curriculum and the link between the tasks and the primary goal of the school mathematics curriculum, that is, mathematical problem solving (Ministry of Education, 2006). A learning task (Mok, 2004) is an example the teacher uses to teach the students a new concept or skill. A review task is a task used by the teacher to review previously learnt concepts and/or skills so as to facilitate the learning of new concepts and skills. Practice tasks are tasks used during the lesson to either illuminate the concept or demonstrate the skill further and the teacher asks students to work through tasks during the lesson either in groups or individually or during out of class time. Assessment tasks are tasks used to assess the performance of the students. Based on these considerations, we have attempted to examine the tasks used by the teachers, in particular the source of the tasks and aspects of the demands the tasks make on the learners.

Y. Shimizu, B. Kaur, R. Huang and D. J. Clarke (Eds.), Mathematical Tasks in Classrooms around the World, pp. 15–33.

RESEARCH FRAMEWORK

Stein and Smith (1998) in their framework of mathematical tasks clarified the multiple roles of tasks that may be available in curricular instructional materials such as textbooks. These tasks may be set up by teachers during their instruction as learning tasks to introduce new concepts and skills, make connections between old and new concepts or skills, or illustrate the application of concepts in problem solving. Such tasks may also be set up by teachers as review tasks to review past knowledge. Lastly, tasks from such materials may also be used as practice and assessment tasks. Practice and assessment tasks are completed or implemented by students with no interjections from the teacher. The purpose of assessment tasks is evaluation, be it formative or summative. In all of the above instances, the teacher's goal for setting the tasks is student learning.

Mathematical tasks can be examined from a variety of perspectives including the demands of the tasks and the presentation of the tasks. However it is not always possible to subject all the tasks to the same type of analysis. As learning tasks, taken from textbooks or other sources, are set up for specific goals of instruction during the instructional cycle, these tasks cannot be treated in the same vein as review, practice and assessment tasks because the corresponding classroom discourse has a lot to do with how the pupils engage with it. Drawing on the framework for the analysis of learning task lesson events proposed by Mok and Kaur (2006), three levels of the first aspect, differentiation of the learning process, namely

Level 1:   introducing new concepts and skills

Level 2:   making connections between new and old concepts or skills

Level 3:   introducing knowledge or information beyond the scope
         of the curriculum requirement or textbook

were found relevant to the present study.

Koh and Lee (2004) as part of a core project of the Centre for Research in Pedagogy and Practice (CRPP) at the National Institute of Education (NIE) in Singapore created and validated a set of standards for scoring teacher assignments[i] (practice tasks) and assessment tasks in languages (English, Chinese, Malay and Tamil), mathematics, science, and social studies. Six standards were selected to analyse the practice and assessment tasks used by the teachers in the study. The first standard, depth of knowledge, is about the type of knowledge the task requires. The second standard, knowledge criticism, is about what students are required to do with the knowledge. The third standard, knowledge manipulation, is about the nature of thinking skills the task requires students to engage in. The next three standards: supportive task framing, clarity and organisation, and explicit performance standard or marking criteria are about the form of the tasks. Details of the standards are shown in Table 1.

Table 1. Relevant standards and dimensions (Koh & Lee, 2004)

Standard 1 - Depth of knowledge

- Dimension 1 – factual knowledge

Possible indicators are tasks that require students to recognise mathematical terms; state concepts, facts or principles; identify objects, patterns, or list properties; recall rules, formulae, algorithms, conventions of number, or symbolic representations; describe simple mathematical facts and computational procedures and perform routine arithmetic operations.

- Dimension 2 – procedural knowledge

Possible indicators are tasks that require students to know how to carry out a set of steps; use a variety of computational procedures and tools; perform strategic or non-routine arithmetic operations and manipulate the written symbols of arithmetic.

- Dimension 3 – advanced knowledge

Possible indicators are tasks that require students to expand definitions; relate facts and concepts; make connections to other mathematical concepts and procedures; explain one or more mathematical relations; understand how one major math topic relates to another and understand how a mathematical topic relates to other disciplines or real world situations

---

Standard 2 – Knowledge criticism

- Dimension 1 – presentation of knowledge as truth or given

Possible indicators are tasks that require students to accept or present ideas and information as truth or affixed body of truths; perform a well-developed algorithm; follow a set of preordained procedures and perform a clearly defined series of steps.

- Dimension 2 – comparing and contrasting information or knowledge

Possible indicators are tasks that require students to identify the similarities and differences in observations, data and theories; classify. Organise, and compare data, and develop heuristics to identify, organise, classify, compare and contrast data, observations or information.

- Dimension 3 – critiquing information or knowledge

Possible indicators are tasks that require students to comment on different mathematical solutions, theories, and procedures; discuss and evaluate approaches to mathematics-related problems; make mathematical arguments, and pose and formulate mathematical problems.

Standard 3 – Knowledge manipulation

- Dimension 1 – reproduction

Possible indicators are tasks that require students to reproduce facts or procedures; recognise equivalents; recall familiar mathematical objects and properties; perform a set of preordained algorithms; manipulate expressions containing symbols and formulae in standard form; carry out computations; apply routine mathematical procedures and technical skills, and apply mathematical concepts and procedures to solve simple and routine problems.

- Dimension 2 – organisation, interpretation, analysis, synthesis or evaluation

Possible indicators are tasks that require students to interpret given mathematical models (equations, diagrams, etc); organize, analyse, interpret, present or generate data or information; interpret tables, graphs and charts; predict

---

mathematical outcomes from the trends in the data; interpret the assumptions and relations involving mathematical concepts and consider alternative solutions or strategies.

- Dimension 3 – application or problem solving

Possible indicators are tasks that require students to apply mathematical concepts and processes to solve non-routine problems; apply the signs, symbols and terms used to represent concepts and use problem-solving heuristics for non-routine problems.

- Dimension 4 – generation or construction of knowledge new to students

Possible indicators are tasks that require students to come up with new proofs or solutions to a mathematical problem; generalize mathematical procedures, strategies and solutions to new problem situations and apply modelling to new contexts.

Standard 4 – Supportive task framing
The task provides students with appropriate framing or scaffolding (written or graphic guidance in view of the students' skill levels and prior knowledge) in order to support them to complete the task given

- Dimension 1 – content scaffolding
- Dimension 2 – procedural scaffolding
- Dimension 3 – strategy scaffolding

Standard 5 – Clarity and Organisation
The task is framed logically and has instructions that are easy to understand.

Standard 6 – Explicit performance standard or marking criteria
The task is provided with the teacher's clear expectations for students' performance and the marking criteria are explicitly clear to the students.

Aspects of Stein and Smith's (1998) task analysis guide were also drawn on to establish the cognitive demands of the tasks used by the teachers in their classrooms. A brief outline of Stein and Smith's guide with adaptations made by the author for the analysis of data presented in this chapter is shown in Table 2.

Table 2. Levels of cognitive demand

Levels of cognitive demand	Characteristics of tasks
Level 0 – [Very Low] Memorisation tasks	- Reproduction of facts, rules, formulae - No explanations required
Level 1 - [Low] Procedural tasks without connections	- Algorithmic in nature - Focussed on producing correct answers - Typical textbook word - problems - No explanations required
Level 2 [High] Procedural tasks with connections	- Algorithmic in nature - Has a meaningful / 'real-world' context - Explanations required
Level 3 – [Very High] Problem Solving / Doing Mathematics	- Non-algorithmic in nature, requires understanding of mathematical concepts and application of - Has a 'real-world' context/a mathematical structure - Explanations required

Hence, appropriate aspects of the works of Stein and Smith (1998), Mok and Kaur (2006) and Koh and Lee (2004) contributed towards the analytical framework used for the analysis of learning tasks, practice tasks, and assessment tasks. However, the framework was not able to provide for the analysis of the review tasks, which were a part of the data analysed and presented in this chapter.

METHOD

Source of Data

Three competent mathematics teachers participated in the study and their competence was locally defined by the community in which they worked. Data was collected in accordance with the protocol set out in the Learner's Perspective Study (LPS) (Clarke, 2006). Teacher 1 (T1) from school 1 (SG1) was a female with 21 years of teaching experience and taught a class of 37 students. Teacher 2 (T2) from school 2 (SG2) was also a female with 27 years of teaching experience and taught a class of 40 students and Teacher 3 (T3) was a male with 15 years of teaching experience and taught a class of 40 students. For each teacher, 10 consecutive grade eight mathematics lessons, L01–L10, were observed and video-taped by the researchers. For the purpose of this chapter, a topic of a particular textbook chapter that the teachers taught during the 10-lesson period was selected for study. The topic was defined by a sequence of lessons that captured the curricular coherence between lessons. For all the three teachers, the topic selected was made up of learning tasks, review tasks and practice tasks. As assessment tasks were only administered during class tests we have included these 'test items' in our analysis

19

to represent assessment tasks. Studying the tasks used in a topic would help us to document how students' learning is developed through the use of different tasks from the introductory level to the application level. In addition, this would allow us to see the kind of opportunity that existed for students to engage in problem solving by applying the skills they have acquired. From the corpus of data of schools SG1, SG2 and SG3, the source of data was primarily the lesson tables. A lesson table is a chronological narrative account of activities that take place during the lesson. This table also details all the tasks (learning, review, practice and assessment) that the teacher used during the lesson, and their source.

Content and Lessons

Table 3. Content of lessons

SG1-T1	SG2-T2	SG3-T3
Topic: Power of Ten and Standard Form	Topic: Algebraic Manipulation and Formulae	Topic: Pythagoras' Theorem
Part I [L01] – ordinary notation and power of ten Part II [L02] – standard form and the use of calculator Part III [L03] – Continuation of the use of calculator	Part I [L02] – simplification of algebraic fractions Part II [L03] – More methods of simplifying algebraic fractions Part III [L04] – multiplication and division of algebraic fractions Part IV [L05] – Addition and subtraction of algebraic fractions Part V [L06] – Changing the subject of a formula	Part I [L02] – introduction of Pythagoras' theorem Part II [L04] – application of Pythagoras' theorem Part III [L05] – continuation of application of Pythagoras' theorem
Class test [L06] – power of ten, standard form and problem solving strategies	Class test [L07] – power of ten, standard form and expansion and factorisation of algebraic expressions	Class test [L03] – linear graphs and their applications

Each topic comprised several lessons and during a lesson a part of the topic was covered. Every part contained some of the following tasks: learning tasks, review tasks and practice tasks. The lesson during which the class test was administered or discussed contained all the assessment tasks. Table 3 shows the overview of the main content of a specific topic covered by each teacher and the class test topic/s being tested during the class test lesson in each school. For SG1, the topic on power of ten and standard form was chosen and T1 took three lessons to complete this topic. For SG2, we selected the topic on algebraic manipulation and formulae and this topic was covered by T2 over five lessons. For T3 the topic on Pythagoras' theorem was selected and it took three lessons to complete. In general, during the lessons, learning tasks were used to introduce new knowledge, review tasks to recall prior knowledge and practice tasks were given to the students to practice during the lesson either in groups or individually or at home after each part of the topic was covered.

The tests were the only source of assessment tasks. For all three schools during the ten-lesson period of observation and videotaping, only one class test was administered or reviewed. For SG1, a test was conducted during L06. For SG2, the corrections of a test administered during the assessment week were reviewed during L07. For SG3, a test was conducted during L03. For both SG1 and SG2, the tests contained the respective topics selected for the analysis in this chapter, but for SG3 this was not the case, as the test was on a topic taught just before the start of the observation and videotaping period of SG3.

Data Analysis

All the tasks from the selected lessons were compiled and their sources traced, that is, where they were taken from. Next the tasks were analysed using appropriate frameworks elaborated in the first part of the chapter. The match of frameworks and task types was as follows:

- framework proposed by Mok and Kaur (2006) was used to ascertain the role of the learning tasks in the learning process differentiated by levels
- framework of Koh and Lee (2004) was used to examine against selected standards and their corresponding dimensions the nature of practice and assessment tasks
- framework of Stein and Smith (1998) was used to establish the cognitive demands of the practice and assessment tasks.

As none of the frameworks were suitable to characterise the review tasks an exploration of these tasks was carried out to develop a possible framework.

Using the appropriate frameworks, the author and a research assistant analysed all the learning, practice and assessment tasks independently. The overall rate of agreement was 80%. Next, they jointly examined the 'disputed tasks' and after extensive discussion reached consensus on them. The review tasks were analysed differently. The purpose of each review task was examined by referring to the lesson during which it was enacted as well as the lesson prior to it.

FINDINGS

Number and Sources of Tasks

Table 4. Number and sources of review, learning, practice and assessment tasks

School-Lesson	Review tasks Source		Learning tasks Source		Practice tasks Source		Assessment tasks Source	
	Text book	Other	Text book	Other	Text book	Exam Papers	Text book	Exam Papers
SG1-L01	-	-	3	2	6	-	-	-
SG1-L02	-	2	1	2	5	1	-	-
SG1-L03	-	-	-	-	5	2	-	-
SG1-L06*	-	1	-	-	-	-	-	7
Total	-	3	4	4	16	3	-	7
SG2-L02	-	-	3	1	6	1	-	-
SG2-L03	-	-	1	-	2	-	-	-
SG2-L04	1	-	1	-	5	-	-	-
SG2-L05	-	-	1	-	4	-	-	-
SG2-L06	-	-	1	-	4	-	-	-
SG2-L07**	-	-	-	-	-	2	-	9
Total	1	-	7	1	21	3	-	9
SG3-L02	-	-	-	5	1	1	-	-
SG3-L03*	-	-	-	-	-	-	-	4
SG3-L04	-	-	1	-	2	-	-	-
SG3-L05	-	-	-	-	1	-	-	-
Total	-	-	1	5	4	1	-	4

*   class was having a test
** teacher went through the test corrections

Table 4 shows the number and sources of review, learning, practice and assessment tasks. From the table, it is apparent that T3 used less tasks in total compared to both T1 and T2. It must be noted that all the lessons of both T1 and T2 that contribute towards the data of this chapter were an hour in duration, while that of T3 were only 35 minutes in duration. The purpose of this table is not to provide any comparison between numbers of tasks used by the teachers but rather to explore the sources of the tasks. Only T1 and T2 used review tasks in their lessons. Review tasks used by T1 were non-textbook materials, real-life objects such as the Russian dolls and cutlery, which were collections of similar solids and self-made simple mathematical tasks, such as, "How would you write the number 392.5 in standard form?" and common factors, for example, $5x + 10y = 5(x + 2y)$, $4ab + bc = b(4a + c)$. The only review task T2 used was taken from the textbook that both the students and teacher of SG2 used for their mathematics lessons. It was "Find the Highest Common Factor (HCF) and Lowest Common Multiple (LCM) of $3a^2b$ and $4ab^2$," which led to a review of the three methods: prime factorisation, division and inspection that may be used to find the HCF and LCM of two or more algebraic polynomials.

As for learning tasks, T1 used both the textbook and herself as a source, while T2 relied mainly on the textbook for tasks, while T3 used mainly non-textbook sources such as the internet and self. For all three teachers, the textbook was their main source for practice tasks. The assessment tasks were sourced from past school and national examination papers. The textbook appears to be a significant source of learning and practice tasks (Kaur, Low, & Seah, 2006), while past school and national examination papers appear to be a significant source of the assessment tasks. This alignment suggests that to a large extent the textbook tasks drive the implementation of the school curriculum, while the "collection of past examination tasks" assists teachers in assessing the performance of their students benchmarked against "examination standards."

Learning Tasks

Table 5. Learning tasks and their levels

SG1	Level			SG2	Level			SG3	Level		
Tasks	1	2	3	Tasks	1	2	3	Tasks	1	2	3
T1-L01-L1	√	√		T2-L02-L1	√			T3-L02-L1			√
T1-L01-L2	√	√		T2-L02-L2	√			T3-L02-L2	√		
T1-L01-L3	√			T2-L02-L3	√			T3-L02-L3	√		
T1-L01-L4	√			T2-L02-L4	√			T3-L02-L4	√		
T1-L01-L5	√			T2-L03-L1	√			T3-L02-L5			√
T1-L02-L1	√			T2-L04-L1	√			T3-L04-L1	√		
T1-L02-L2	√			T2-L05-L1	√						
T1-L02-L3	√			T2-L06-L1	√						

Legend
Level 1: introducing new concepts and skills
Level 2: making connections between new and old concepts or skills
Level 3: introducing knowledge or information beyond the scope of the curriculum requirement or textbook

Table 5 shows the purpose of the learning tasks used by the three teachers, as defined by Mok and Kaur (2006). It appears that all the learning tasks used by T1 and T2 were of level 1 type, that is, used to introduce new concepts and skills as stipulated by the curriculum guides. However, this was not the case for T3, as two of his six learning tasks were of level 3 type, that is, used to introduce knowledge or information beyond the scope of the textbook requirement. As an introductory task, T3-L02-L1 (Teacher 3, Lesson 2, Learning Task 1) for the topic Pythagoras theorem, T3 used the internet and showed the students the portrait of Pythagoras and also his contribution in the field of mathematics. The other level 3 type of learning task used by T3 (T3-L02-L5) introduced students to two algebraic methods of finding the Pythagorean triplets. The first was $\{ 2m, m^2 - 1, m^2 + 1$ for integer values of $m > 1\}$ and the second $\{ 2pq, p^2 - q^2, p^2 + q^2$ for integer values of p and q where $p > q > 1\}$. Using algebraic methods to list Pythagorean triplets is beyond the scope of the grade eight mathematics curriculum, but T3 has certainly shown the students that the Pythagorean triplets are not random and can be generalised. Two of the learning tasks used by T1 were of both levels 1 and 2 as they were used to bridge the past knowledge of students, for example, multiplication of 10^3 and 10^4 using ordinary notation [T1-L01-L1], division of 10^6 by 10^4 using ordinary notation and also the introduction of the laws of indices: $a^m \times a^n = a^{m+n}$ and $a^m \div a^n = a^{m-n}$. None of the learning tasks used by T2 and T3 were of level 2 and this is perhaps due to the nature of the topics T2 and T3 were teaching, as students are introduced to algebraic fractions and transformation of formulae and also Pythagoras theorem for the first time in grade eight.

Review Tasks

Table 6. Review tasks and their purposes

Task	Purpose (Teacher's goal)
T1-L02-R1[1]	Recall prior knowledge
T1-L02-R2	Recall prior knowledge
	Make connection between newly acquired and past knowledge
	Provide procedural scaffolding for subsequent tasks
T1-L06-R1	Relate newly acquired mathematical concepts to real life examples
T2-L04-R1	Recall prior knowledge

[1] Teacher 1, Lesson 2, Review Task 1

Table 6 shows the review tasks and the corresponding teacher's goals. It is apparent that T1 used review tasks to help her students recall prior knowledge, provide procedural scaffolding for later work during a lesson, connect newly acquired and past knowledge, and relate newly acquired mathematical concepts to real life examples. T2 used only one review task and it was to help her students recall prior knowledge while T3 used none. Based on this small sample of review tasks, which T1 and T2 used during the teaching of a topic each, a preliminary framework for the analyses of review tasks may be proposed as follows:

Type 1:   recall of prior knowledge

Type 2:   provide scaffolding for subsequent tasks

Type 3:   connect newly acquired knowledge with past knowledge

Type 4:   relate newly acquired knowledge to real life examples

Practice Tasks

Table 7. Standards and dimensions of practice tasks

Task	S1			S2			S3				S4			S5	S6
	1	2	3	1	2	3	1	2	3	4	1	2	3		
T1-L01-P1-2	√			√			√							√	
T1-L01-P3	√				√			√			√			√	
T1-L01-P4	√			√			√							√	
T1-L01-P5-6		√		√			√							√	
T1-L02-P1-6		√		√			√							√	
T1-L03-P1-4		√		√			√							√	
T1-L03-P5-7		√		√			√							√	
T2-L02-P1-7	√			√			√							√	
T2-L03-P1-2		√		√			√							√	
T2-L04-P1-5		√		√			√							√	
T2-L05-P1-4		√		√			√							√	
T2-L06-P1		√		√			√					√		√	
T2-L06-P2-4		√		√			√							√	
T2-L07-P1-2		√		√			√							√	
T3-L02-P1	√			√				√						√	
T3-L02-P2		√		√			√							√	
T3-L04-P1		√		√			√							√	
T3-L04-P2		√		√			√							√	
T3-L05-P1		√		√					√					√	

Legend

S1- Depth of knowledge
  1- factual knowledge
  2- procedural knowledge
  3- advanced knowledge

S2 - Knowledge criticism
  1- presentation of knowledge as truth or given
  2- comparing and contrasting information or knowledge
  3- critiquing information or knowledge

S3 - Knowledge manipulation
  1- reproduction
  2- organisation, interpretation, analysis, synthesis or evaluation
  3- application or problem solving
  4- generation or construction of knowledge new to students

S4 - Supportive task framing
  1- content scaffolding
  2- procedural scaffolding
  3- strategy scaffolding

S5 - Clarity and organisation

S6 - Explicit performance standard or marking criteria

The analysis of the practice tasks using Koh and Lee's (2004) framework is presented in Table 7, which shows the standards and dimensions of the tasks used by the three teachers during their course of teaching a topic each. Only three of the tasks used by all the three teachers dealt with factual knowledge, while the rest dealt with procedural knowledge. None of the tasks were about advanced knowledge. All except one of the tasks were about the presentation of knowledge as truth.

Complete the table:

10 000	=	10^4
1000	=	10^3
100	=	10^2
10	=	10^1
1	=	$10^?$
$0.1 = \dfrac{1}{10} = \dfrac{1}{10^1}$	=	$10^?$
$0.01 = \dfrac{1}{100} = \dfrac{1}{10^2}$	=	$10^?$
$0.001 = \dfrac{1}{1000} = \dfrac{1}{10^3}$	=	$10^?$
$0.0001 = \dfrac{1}{10000} = \dfrac{1}{10^4}$	=	$10^?$
$0.00001 = \dfrac{1}{100000} = \dfrac{1}{10^5}$	=	$10^?$

Figure 1. Task T1-L01-P3

PQRS is a rectangle in which PQ = 9 cm and PS = 6 cm. T is a point on PQ such that PT = 7 cm and RV is the perpendicular from R to ST. Calculate ST and RV.

Figure 2. Task T3-L05-P1

Make 'a' the subject by completing the following:

$$e = \sqrt{(5a - 8)}$$
$$\sqrt{(5a - 8)} = e$$
$$(5a - 8)^{\frac{1}{2}} = e$$
$$\dotfill$$
$$\dotfill$$

Figure 3. Task T2-L06-P1

Generate Pythagorean triplets (a, b, c)
Such that $a^2 + b^2 = c^2$

Figure 4. Task T3-L02-P1

The exception was a task given by T1 to her students to compare and contrast factual knowledge. The task, T1-L01-P3 (Teacher 1, Lesson 1, Practice Task 3), shown in Figure 1 required students to analyse the facts presented and predict the missing bits of information. It was framed to provide content scaffolding and was clearly presented in an organised manner. All except three of the tasks demanded the lowest level of knowledge manipulation, that is, reproduction. Of the three non-reproduction type of tasks, two required students to analyse, predict and evaluate knowledge while one (T3-L05-P1 shown in Figure 2) required students to apply their conceptual knowledge to solve a mathematical problem. The only task that provided students with procedural scaffolding was T2-L06-P1 shown in Figure 3. All the practice tasks given by the three teachers to their students were clearly presented, but students were not given any explicit performance or marking criteria along with the tasks.

Table 8. Levels of cognitive demand of practice tasks

Task	Levels of cognitive demand			
	Level 0	*Level 1*	*Level 2*	*Level 3*
T1-L01-P1-2	√			
T1-L01-P3			√	
T1-L01-P4-6	√			
T1-L02-P1-5	√			
T1-L02-P6		√		
T1-L03-P1-4	√			
T1-L03-P5-7		√		
T2-L02-P1-7	√			
T2-L03-P1-2	√			
T2-L04-P1-5	√			
T2-L05-P1-4	√			
T2-L06-P1-4	√			
T2-L07-P1-2	√			
T3-L02-P1			√	
T3-L02-P2	√			
T3-L04-P1-2	√			
T3-L05-P1		√		

Legend
Level 0 - Memorisation tasks
Level 1 - Procedural tasks without connections
Level 2 - Procedural tasks with connection
Level 3 - Problem solving / Doing mathematics

Table 8 shows the cognitive demands of the practice tasks according to Stein and Smith's (1998) task analysis guide. All except five of the tasks were of memorisation type [level 0], that is, they required of students to reproduce facts, rules and formulae without any explanations. Of the five non-memorisation type of tasks, three were of the procedure without connections type [level 1], that is, they required students to use algorithms to do typical textbook type of exercises, which contextualise concepts and skills taught. Figure 2, shows an example of one such task, which is classified as an application of knowledge type of task according to the standards and dimensions analysis using Koh and Lee (2004) framework. The two tasks that were of the procedures with connections type are shown in Figures 1 and 4. Both these tasks required the students to do mathematics in meaningful and mathematically rich contexts.

Assessment Tasks

Table 9. Standards and dimensions of assessment tasks

Task	S1			S2			S3				S4			S5	S6
	1	2	3	1	2	3	1	2	3	4	1	2	3		
T1-L06-A1-4	√			√			√							√	√
T1-L06-A5-6	√			√			√					√		√	√
T1-L06-A7	√			√					√					√	√
T2-L07-A1-5	√			√			√							√	√
T2-L07-A6-7								√							
T2-L07-A8-9							√								
T3-L03-A1	√			√			√							√	√
T3-L03-A2	√			√			√							√	√
T3-L03-A3	√			√				√						√	√
T3-L03-A4	√			√				√				√		√	√

Legend
S1- Depth of knowledge
  1 - factual knowledge
  2 - procedural knowledge
  3 - advanced knowledge
S2 - Knowledge criticism
  1 - presentation of knowledge as truth or given
  2 - comparing and contrasting information or knowledge
  3 - critiquing information or knowledge
S3 - Knowledge manipulation
  1 - reproduction
  2 - organisation, interpretation, analysis, synthesis or evaluation
  3 - application or problem solving
  4 - generation or construction of knowledge new to students
S4 - Supportive task framing
  1 - content scaffolding
  2 - procedural scaffolding
  3 - strategy scaffolding
S5 - Clarity and organisation
S6 - Explicit performance standard or marking criteria

The analysis of the assessment tasks using Koh and Lee's (2004) framework is presented in Table 9 which shows the standards and dimensions of the tasks that were given to the students as part of their mathematics assessment. All the tasks tested procedural knowledge. All the tasks also required students to present knowledge as truth rather than as comparing and contrasting knowledge or critiquing knowledge. All except five of the tasks required students to reproduce facts or procedures; manipulate algebraic expressions; carry out computations and apply mathematical concepts and procedures to solve simple and routine problems. Of the five non-reproduction type of tasks, four required students to analyse information given and use it to carry out a computation or interpret the data given, make a graphical representation and find the solution. Three such tasks, which also had procedural scaffolding, are T3-L04-A4 (Teacher 3, Lesson 4, Assessment Task 4) shown in Figure 5, T2-L07-A6 shown in Figure 7 and T2-L07-A7 shown in Figure 8. The only task, T1-L06-A7, that required students to engage in problem solving is shown in Figure 6. This was a 'non-routine' task for the students. All the tasks were clearly presented in an organised way showing the marks allocated to each or parts of it.

Table 10 shows the cognitive demands of the assessment tasks according to Stein and Smith's (1998) task analysis guide. All except eight of the tasks were of memorisation type [level 0], that is, they required students to reproduce facts, rules and formulae without any explanations. The eight non-memorisation types of tasks were of the procedures without connections type [level 1]. These tasks were algorithmic in nature and required students to apply facts, rules and formulae to standard textbook type of problems. Figures 5, 7 and 8 show three examples of such tasks.

Table 10. Levels of cognitive demand of assessment tasks

Task	Levels of cognitive demand			
	Level 0	*Level 1*	*Level 2*	*Level 3*
T1-L06-A1-4	√			
T1-L06-A5-7		√		
T2-L07-A1-5	√			
T2-L07-A6-7		√		
T2-L07-A8-9	√			
T3-L03-A1	√			
T3-L03-A2-4		√		

Legend
Level 0 - Memorisation tasks
Level 1 - Procedural tasks without connections
Level 2 - Procedural tasks with connection
Level 3 - Problem solving / Doing mathematics

The whole of this question must be answered on a single sheet of graph paper.
On a Saturday, Ahmad left home on his bicycle at 8 a.m. and travelled 4 km at a speed of 8 km/h directly to his school. After staying in school for CCA for 2 hours, he returned home by the same route in 20 minutes.

(a) Use a scale of 2 cm to represent 20 minutes for the time taken from 08 00 to 11 00 on the horizontal axis and 2 cm to represent 1 km for the distance on the vertical axis, and draw the travel graph.   [3 marks]

(b) From the graph, find
  (i) the time at which Ahmad arrived home   [1 mark]
  (ii) the speed at which he travelled on the retuned journey.   [1 mark]

Figure 5. Task T3-L03-A4

> 12 chickens took 5 days to eat 3 bags of corn. How many days will 10 chickens take to finish 4 bags of corn? [3 marks]

Figure 6. Task T1-L06-A7

> If $10^x = 3$, find the value of 10^{3x+1} [2 marks]

Figure 7. Task T2-L07-A6

> Given that $(x+y)^2 = 36$ and $xy = 4$, find the value of
> (a) $x^2 + y^2$ [1 mark]
> (b) $(3x - 3y)^2$ [2 marks]

Figure 8. Task T2-L07-A7

DISCUSSION

Figure 9 shows the framework of Singapore's school mathematics curriculum, the primary goal of which is *mathematical problem solving* (Ministry of Education, 2006). As shown in the figure the development of mathematical problem solving ability is stated to be dependent on five inter-related components, namely, Concepts, Skills, Processes, Attitudes and Metacognition. The findings from the study of the tasks used by the three teachers who participated in the study will be examined in relation to three components, namely concepts, skills and processes of the framework.

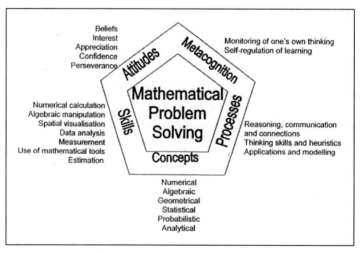

Figure 9. Framework of school mathematics curriculum

Learning tasks used by the teachers either introduced new concepts and skills, made connections between new and old concepts or skills, or introduced students to knowledge or information that might excite them (example T3 showing them the history of Pythagoras via the internet) or explained some of their observations (example T3 working through the generalised representations of Pythagorean triplets). These tasks were either taken from the textbook or sourced by teachers from their personal resources. A closer examination of the learning tasks showed that the tasks were used for dissemination of knowledge via teacher talk. In other words the only activity the tasks led to were teacher–whole class discourse that culminated with teacher telling and showing. None of the tasks were exploratory, that is, allowing students to engage in some activity before conjecturing and finally making knowledge one's own.

Also the significantly large number of practice tasks that preceded a learning task showed that there was great emphasis on 'practice makes perfect'. Most of the practice tasks were taken from the textbook and were procedural in nature. The textbooks used in the three classrooms adopted the exposition-examples-exercises model (Love and Pimm, 1996) and therefore the exercises of the textbook for the relevant topic formed the bulk of the practice tasks. These tasks were mainly procedural and algorithmic in nature. The few tasks that were word problems contextualised in some 'real-world' context also failed to provide students with the experience of applying their knowledge to solve novel problems, as the deictic relation of mathematics textbook questions to the real world is a highly problematic one (Love and Pimm, 1996). Only two tasks, T1-L01-P3 (shown in Figure 1) and T3-L02-P1 (shown in Figure 4), provided students with opportunities to engage in thinking skills such as comparing, inductive reasoning and systematic listing.

It may be said that in all the three classrooms, concepts and skills were developed during the mathematics lessons but the range of processes that students were given opportunities to engage in were limited. The scope of the term 'processes' in the framework shown in Figure 9 is

> skills involved in acquiring and applying mathematical knowledge. This includes reasoning, communications and connections, thinking skills and heuristics, and application and modelling. (Ministry of Education, 2006, p. 4)

The assessment tasks were taken from past examination papers. These tasks mainly tested the reproduction of facts or procedures, manipulation of algebraic expressions, computations and application of mathematical concepts and procedures to solve simple and routine problems. Bearing in mind the limitations of pencil-paper tests, these items appeared to largely test for concepts and skills. The task T1-L06-A7 is noteworthy as it attempted to engage grade eight students, who have not worked with complex variation tasks, to attempt it using problem solving heuristics. The assessment tasks were to a large extent aligned to the practice tasks and it may be claimed that the nature of assessment tasks push textbook writers to mould their exercises accordingly and teachers to provide their students with purposeful practice!

CONCLUSIONS

The data analysed and presented in this chapter were part of the LPS data from Singapore. Three grade eight mathematics teachers who were deemed competent by their local community participated in the LPS from Singapore. The goal of this chapter was to study the source and nature of mathematical tasks, specifically the learning, review, practice and assessment tasks used by the three teachers to implement the intended curriculum and ascertain the extent of the link between the tasks and the primary goal of the school mathematics curriculum, in other words, mathematical problem solving (Ministry of Education, 2006). The questions that may be answered by the data and analysis in this chapter are:

"What drives the classroom instruction?" and
"Is mathematical problem solving the end goal of both the instructional and assessment practice in the three classrooms?"

The source of the learning tasks shows that teachers draw on both the textbook and personal resources where appropriate, to assist students with the learning of concepts and skills. This is followed by practice, which is mainly driven by the textbook that is used by both the teacher and students. With the exception of the two practice tasks that engaged students in more than algorithmic and procedural activity, it may be said that most of the practice tasks were textbook exercises to hone skills and application of concepts in simple routine tasks. The assessment tasks were closely aligned with the practice tasks, and it appears that the assessment tasks influence the textbook exercises. The marks for each part of the assessment tasks were clearly indicated, but no other explicit marking criteria, for example the tension between product and process were given. Hence it may be claimed that in these three classrooms the instruction was driven mainly by the textbook and somewhat by the teachers' personal resources. Although textbooks used in Singapore schools must have the approval from the Ministry of Education and satisfy the curriculum content requirements, they have their limitations too. The data presented in this chapter shows that although problem solving is the official end goal of both instruction and assessment as stipulated by the framework for the school mathematics curriculum, the instructional practice and assessment practice of the three classrooms appear to be poorly aligned with this goal.

This chapter has also made a contribution towards a framework for the analysis of review tasks. An analysis of the purpose of the review tasks used by the three teachers has resulted in a preliminary framework for the analysis of such tasks. This framework, which comprises the following types:

Type 1:   recall of prior knowledge
Type 2:   provide scaffolding for subsequent tasks
Type 3:   connect newly acquired knowledge with past knowledge
Type 4:   relate newly acquired knowledge to real life examples

will be used to analyse more review tasks from the corpus of LPS data in Singapore to test for its validity and expansion where feasible.

NOTES

[i]Teacher assignments – this term is coined and means written assignments given by teachers to their students for either in class or out of class follow-up work subsequent to a lesson.

ACKNOWLEDGEMENTS

This chapter is based on the funded project, CRP 3/04 BK, at the Centre for Research in Pedagogy and Practice, National Institute of Education, Nanyang Technological University, Singapore. The contribution of Low Hooi Kiam, research assistant attached to the project, towards the preparation of this chapter is acknowledged.

REFERENCES

Clarke, D. J. (2006). The LPS research design. In D. J. Clarke, C. Keitel, & Y. Shimizu, (Eds.), *Mathematics classrooms in twelve countries* (pp. 15-29). Rotterdam: Sense Publishers.

Kaur, B., Low, H. K., & Seah, L. H. (2006). Mathematics teaching in two Singapore classrooms: The role of the textbook and homework. In D. J. Clarke, C. Keitel, & Y. Shimizu, (Eds.), *Mathematics classrooms in twelve countries* (pp. 99-116). Rotterdam: Sense Publishers.

Koh, K. H., & Lee, A. N. (2004). *Technical report: Manual for scoring teacher assignments or assessment tasks.* Singapore: National Institute of Education, Centre for Research in Pedagogy and Practice.

Love E., & Pimm, D. (1996). 'This is so': A text on texts. In A. J. Bishop, M. A. Clements, C. Keitel, J. Kilpatrick, C. Laborde (Eds.), *International handbook of mathematics education* (pp. 371-409). Dordrecht: Kluwer Academic Publishers.

Mason, J., & Johnston-Wilder, S. (2006). *Designing and using mathematical tasks.* St Albans, UK: Tarquin Publications.

Ministry of Education. (2006). *A guide to teaching & learning of 'O' level mathematics 2007.* Singapore: Curriculum Planning and Development Division, Ministry of Education.

Mok, I. A. C. (2004, April). *Learning tasks.* Paper presented at the Annual Meeting of the American Educational Research Association, San Diego, CA.

Mok I. A. C., & Kaur, B. (2006). 'Learning task' lesson events. In D. J. Clarke, J. Emanuelsson, E. Jablonka, & I. A. C. Mok (Eds.), *Making connections: Comparing mathematics classrooms around the world* (pp. 147 – 164). Rotterdam: Sense Publishers.

Stein, M. K., & Smith, M. S. (1998). Mathematical tasks as a framework for reflection: From research to practice. *Mathematics Teaching in the Middle School, 3*(4), 268-275.

Berinderjeet Kaur
National Institute of Education
Nanyang Technological University
Singapore

OLE KRISTIAN BERGEM AND KIRSTI KLETTE

CHAPTER THREE

Mathematical Tasks as Catalysts for Student Talk:
Analysing Discourse in a Norwegian Mathematics Classroom

INTRODUCTION

The focus of this chapter is to discuss tasks, thematic patterns and types of discourses involved when students use issues from everyday and real-world contexts as a basis for learning mathematics. The study draws its empirical evidence from video observations and interviews from lower secondary mathematics classrooms in Norway, and is based on sequences where newspapers are used as devices to develop mathematical understanding. An important aim in this chapter is to present different aspects of the observed classroom discourses, and to discuss if and how these discourses can contribute to the development of mathematical reasoning and understanding among secondary level students. The aim of the analysis is thus to inform our understanding of how participation in a discourse related to mathematical tasks can foster student learning in mathematics.

To be able to relate mathematical learning and teaching inside schools to mathematical learning based on real life experience has been a major challenge in mathematical education for years (see for instance Gravemeijer, 1994; and Blum, Galbraith, Henn, & Niss, 2007). More recently, mathematical understanding understood as discursive competence, that is to say, being able to take part in mathematical discourses and express oneself through the use of mathematical signs, symbols and representations, has been emphasised (Cobb, Boufi, McClain, & Whitenack, 1997; Cobb, 2007; Gravemeijer, Cobb, Bowers, & Whitenack, 2000; Lerman, 1996; Sfard, 2000; Steinbring, 2005; Yackel, 1995). How schools can succeed in enabling students to participate in central mathematical discourses, with a capacity to use mathematical reasoning in practical problem solving, is a key challenge. This is also a central concern within the academic discipline of mathematics education as well as in studies with a broader educational agenda; see for instance PISA (OECD, 2000, 2003, 2006). A central concept that is used to describe this kind of competence is *mathematical literacy*.

Scholars and theorists have argued that learning in mathematics should be based on the understanding of fundamentals in a structured pattern linked to everyday mathematical situations. This is to nurture *relational* reasoning; knowing what to do and why, and *instrumental* reasoning; knowing what to do or the possession of a

Y. Shimizu, B. Kaur, R. Huang and D. J. Clarke (Eds.), Mathematical Tasks in Classrooms around the World, pp. 35–62.

rule and ability to use it (see for example Hiebert et al., 1997). Such learning is also supposed to facilitate transfer, and secure mathematical reason and mathematical literacy in a life-long learning perspective.

Over the decades we can identify several initiatives aimed at bridging mathematical reasoning inside schools with that of mathematical reasoning in out-of-school settings. The work of Lave (1988) on grocery shopping, Scribner's (1984) study of packing crates in dairies, and Saxe's (1991) study on selling candies in the streets document how people develop significantly different forms of mathematical reasoning as they participate and move between different cultural practices and contexts. All of these studies document how contrasting forms of reasoning inherent in the different cultural practices bear directly on issues of equity in students' access to significant mathematical ideas.

More recently, equity issues in students' access to mathematical ideas have been closely linked to the access to rich mathematical conversation and discussions. To be exposed to, and take part in, rich mathematical conversations which give the students the possibility to discuss connections between mathematical ideas and concepts, are held to promote mathematical understanding. Different camps within the field of mathematical education, such as cognitive psychology, social constructivism, distributed cognition, semiotics, and socio-cultural theory, all draw our attention to the essential role of reflexive discourses and communication in fostering mathematical understanding. Since the early 90s there seems to be a strong consensus among educators about the merits in stimulating students' ability to talk mathematics (Bauersfeld, 1995; Cobb, 1995; Ernest, 1991; Yackel, 1995). Niss (2007), however, points to the lack of congruence among the different camps, and claims that a convergent and overarching unified framework, agreed upon by all researchers, is still not in sight. Changing mathematical classrooms into 'discursive communities of learners' has, moreover, proven to be challenging. This is because the changes require more than just adopting a new set of practices or curricula. They must also include a change in teachers' and students' patterns of interaction, and more importantly, a broader repertoire of communicative skills and capacities when talking in and about mathematics. Recent research underscores the nature and quality of the discourses around mathematical problem solving as critical to learning (Cobb, Yackel, & McClain, 2000; Sfard & Kieran, 2001). The teachers' ability to design and skilfully structure the learning situations is also crucial. Learning mathematics through conversations requires that the teachers know about their students' thinking and can support their development of mathematical proficiency. Therefore the ability to turn mathematical conversations into 'discursive communities of learners' require teachers that are equipped with adequate didactical tools, and who above all are able to support student verbal reasoning in a way that promotes mathematical understanding.

In this chapter we will argue that 'talking mathematics' as a theory of mathematical instruction and didactic template is underdeveloped. As a tool for learning it must be backed up and supported with *how*-related remedies, recipes and procedures. Sfard (Sfard, Nesher, Streefland, Cobb, & Mason, 1998, p. 1) questions the inherent qualities in mathematical discourses when she rather rhetorically asks: "Learning mathematics through conversations: Is it as good as they say?" Sfard points out that scholars worldwide agree on the great potential in mathematical conversations as a tool for learning, yet on the other hand, only certain types of conversation are likely to bring this potential to fruition. To follow up on this critique, we would like to point out that theories of learning are often poorly aligned with theories of instruction. Consequently many questions about student learning, vital to any pedagogic decision, remain unanswered.

Research Questions

The following analyses draw on video observations of two consecutive mathematics lessons in a 9th grade classroom in Norway where newspaper articles were used to discuss mathematical issues. The instructional design of the teacher was constructed around mathematical conversations as a central learning device. After working in pairs with the real-life mathematical tasks in the first lesson, the students were, in the second lesson, invited to participate and contribute in whole-class discussion. The newspaper session, as a learning sequence, pulled together some of the more central ideas surrounding mathematics education of today. It linked mathematical reasoning in the classroom with mathematical reasoning outside the school context and supported infrastructures that emphasise learning mathematics through talking mathematics. The research questions we are advancing are the following:

- What sort of mathematical reasoning takes place when students are engaged in talking mathematics through discursive tasks derived from everyday settings?
- How do students perform, negotiate and stabilize the distributed expertise among the involved participants?
- What is the nature and the scope of the mathematical tasks involved?
- How does the teacher's support influence the mathematical relevance of the classroom discourse?

All the four research questions are quite generally formulated, and will be discussed in the light of analyses of actual dialogues and actions from the two mathematical lessons. The discussion will also be related to relevant theory within mathematics education.

THEORETICAL PERSPECTIVES

Views of Communication in Mathematics

Researchers and theorists alike are calling for increased focus on mathematical communication. Since the early 90s there has been a strong consensus among educators about the need to promote students' ability to talk mathematics. The TIMSS video study (Hiebert et al., 2003) enclosed features of pedagogical scripts of mathematical lessons from different parts of the world. In US classrooms, for example, it was reported that students had little opportunity to develop mathematical reasoning and discuss connections among mathematical ideas or to reason about mathematical concepts. A number of studies support the TIMSS report, and the consensus is that currently many mathematics classrooms do not provide sufficient opportunities for students to develop mathematical understanding. It is pointed out that students are not trained to talk *in* and *about* mathematics through discursive practices in mathematics classrooms. This is in spite of many national curriculum documents stating that students' should not only have the opportunity to write, but also read and discuss ideas in mathematics classrooms, and that oral forms of working should be given high priority (KUF, 1996; K, 2005; LP, 1994; NCTM, 1989).

Different camps within the field of mathematical education, such as cognitive psychology, social constructivism, distributed cognition, semiotics and socio-cultural theory, all draw our attention to the essential role that reflective discourse and discursive practices has for fostering mathematical understanding. The mathematical philosopher Paul Ernest (1993) claims for example that:

> ... mathematics is dialogical and (that) conversation permeates mathematics in deep and multiple ways. The underpinning metaphor of conversation stresses dialogic, comprising alternating voices in a shared quest for understanding, based on the logic of question and answer, and on uncertainty. (p. 3)

Despite theoretical differences all camps consider communication, discursive skills and communicative practices as essential for mathematical understanding and they all paraphrase versions of the 'communicative, and reflective, turn' within the field of mathematics education.

How communication is defined and which aspects of communication are most valued varies. Some researchers highlight communication as a process of creating publicly shared knowledge (Carpenter, Fennema, Franke, Levi, & Empson, 1999; O'Connor 1998), others emphasise the opportunities it provides for participation (Bauersfeld, 1995; Lampert, 1990; Nunes, 1999), while still others see communication as a way to further develop the practices of mathematics through explanations, descriptions, and arguments (Boaler, 2002; Silver & Smith, 1996). Some researchers focus on students that share their solutions and their ideas surrounding those solutions (Hiebert et al., 1997), while others focus on the development of mathematical arguments through conversation (Sfard, 2001). What most have in common is the Vygotskyan confidence in the advantages of interaction between students with differing knowledge and skills and more knowledgeable others, and a general belief in communication and communicative skills as essential for student learning in mathematics (Vygotsky, 1978). This is often underpinned by references to empirical and theoretical evidence showing the beneficial effects of students verbalising their mathematical thinking. However, these views have recently been challenged by several educational researchers. Cazden (2001), Nemirovsky (2005), Sfard and Kieran (2001) and others argue that teachers need to apply a didactical repertoire when engaging students in mathematical conversations. They also argue the need to be able to consider how different kind of contexts may afford and constrain the potential learning value of conversations, and maybe most importantly; that teachers must know how to support a variety of classroom discourses. Cobb et al. (1997) underscore the *quality* of conversation as central for student learning. A pressing question is therefore: What characterizes conversations that support student participation and learning in mathematics? Furthermore; how can teachers provide opportunities for participation in mathematical conversations in ways that benefit students' learning?

Cobb et al. (1997) argue that reflective discourse and collective reflection constitutes conditions for the possibility of mathematical learning. Participation in reflective discourse is considered to enable and constrain mathematical development, but not to determine it. The teacher's role in this process is to initiate shifts in the discourse that ensure that the topics in question are explicitly focused on mathematics. With regard to classroom conversations, Cobb, in his contribution to a co-authored article (Sfard et al., 1998), points out that it is crucial that we base our theoretical discussions about this issue on empirical data. He insists that researchers, through experiments and observation of student participation in classroom discourses, should investigate what students actually learn in the course of that participation. Cobb criticizes the view that classroom discourses *per se* should be a goal in mathematics education, and argues that what matters is whether the students are learning aspects of mathematics worth knowing. He also stresses the important role that the teacher plays in initiating, guiding and monitoring classroom discussions. It is the teacher's responsibility to help students realize what kind of statements is acceptable within a mathematical discourse and to stimulate the students to take part in rich mathematical discussions. Mason, contributing to Sfard et al. agrees with these views, arguing that a critical component of effective discussion is the presence of an expert, and that most students will not be able to reconstruct the central and important ideas of mathematics without guidance from such an expert. In a school context this is most likely to be the teacher. Conversation and classroom discussions should therefore not uncritically be considered positive elements of the teaching and learning of mathematics; their value will depend on the quality of the discourse, the commitment of the participating individuals and the composition of the group. Sfard et al. also point to the important role of the teacher in directing and orchestrating meaningful classroom discussions. She sums up the critique of the naïve views of the unquestioned value of classroom discussions about mathematics by stating that:

> There are many ways to turn classroom discussion or group work into a great supplier of learning opportunities; there are even more ways to turn them into a waste of time, or worse than that – into a barrier to learning. (p. 50)

Sfard et al. concede that to initiate and orchestrate meaningful mathematical discussions is an extremely demanding and intricate task for teachers. They also run a great risk of being unsuccessful in accomplishing this if they take for granted that the students already know how to mathematically express their views and intentions to others.

The Ability to Talk in and about Mathematics – Required Communicative Skills

Within socio-cultural theory, learning is viewed as becoming a participant in a certain discourse, or as expanding ones' discursive participation, in which discourse is broadly defined as the totality of communicative activities practiced within a given community (Van Oers, 2001; Sfard & Kieran, 2001). The mathematical community can in this theoretical tradition be characterised by its different discourses. Sfard (2000) claims that one of the strengths of this view of learning is that knowledge is seen as a human construction, and not as a disembodied, impersonal set of propositions. Assigning central importance to discourse also precludes the possibility of viewing learning as a predominantly individual endeavour and ensures its social situatedness. Sfard (2000) argues that connecting learning to discourse makes the inclusion of *meta-discursive rules* relevant for the analysis taking place within mathematics education.

> Meta-level rules are those that speak of mathematical utterances, of their structures, and of relations between them, as well as those that deal with producers of the utterances, that is, interlocutors. (p. 167)

These rules cannot be accounted for completely and are first and foremost learned through practice. They do not take the form of explicit prescriptions, but have a normative impact on discourse participants. Yackel and Cobb (1996) argue, using the adjacent concept of *socio-mathematical norms*, that these norms have an emergent status in the mathematical classroom and that they are interactively constituted through negotiations between the participants of the mathematical discourse. Sfard and Kieran (2001) make use of the concept *meta-discursive rules* when in their analysis of classroom conversations they distinguish between object rules and meta rules. While the former are connected to the cognitive intentions of solving a particular mathematical problem, the latter are related to various aspects of the social interaction *per se*, for instance attempting to manage and renegotiate social positions. *Meta level rules* refer to general discursive rules – that is; rules that "regulate the flow of exchange", whilst *object level rules* refer to "rules that govern the content of the exchange" (Sfard, 2000, p. 161). Sfard and Kieran argue that students generally will be put under a lot of pressure because they are forced to handle these rules simultaneously during classroom dialogues, that is to say; they are simultaneously involved in a number of object-level and meta-level tasks. This can be quite strenuous and often students' attention will be drawn away from the mathematical tasks. Based on longitudinal observations and analysis of student dialogues, Sfard and Kieran claim that in order for student conversations to be effective mediators for the growth of mathematical knowledge, the interlocutors' intellectual resources must be saved for the major, object-level tasks. Sfard and Kieran therefore challenge both the common belief that working together always has a positive synergetic effect and the Vygotskian 'theorem' that working with a more knowledgeable other necessarily leads to increased learning.

Sfard (2000) further questions the presumed benefits for mathematical reasoning when moving between everyday discourse and modern mathematical discourse.

The tendency to always look for real-life situations and to avoid or minimize dealing with abstract mathematics is very much in the spirit of everyday discourses, but it contradicts what is often believed to be the very essence of *mathematisation*. After all, "mathematising is almost synonymous with 'flying high' above the concrete and about classifying things according to features that cut across contexts", Sfard argues (p. 181). For mathematicians, the inner consistency and overall coherence of mathematics is the ultimate source of its justification. For these reasons, we could argue that 'rich mathematical discourses' could be evaluated on the basis of how well defined and focused, intrinsically coherent, and convincing the conversations that take place turn out to be.

The Construction and Experiences of Meaning

Wenger (1998) uses the concepts *participation* and *reification* in his discussion of the construction and experiences of meaning. The term participation is used to describe:

> the social experience of living in the world in terms of membership in social communities and active involvement in social enterprises. (Wenger, 1998, p. 55)

What characterizes *participation* is the possibility of mutual recognition and of developing an identity constituted through relations of participation. Wenger states that this concept is meant to capture the profoundly social character of our experiences in life. *Reification* is, on the other hand, used by Wenger (1998) to mean: "giving form to our experience by producing objects that congeal this experience into thingness" (p. 58). Reification is central to all forms of practice, any community of practice reifies some aspects of that practice in a congealed form, be it abstractions, symbols, terms, or concepts. The products of reification are reflections of these practices, "tokens of vast expanses of human meanings" (p. 61). Wenger claims that these two concepts, participation and reification, are both distinct and complementary and that used in various combinations they give rise to a variety of experiences of meaning. These complementary concepts are used to secure some continuity of meaning across time and space within communities of practice. What makes these two concepts particularly relevant in the discussion in this chapter is Wenger's explanation that when too much reliance is placed on one of these concepts at the expense of the other, "the continuity of meaning is likely to become problematic in practice" (p. 65). If participation prevails at the expense of reification, this may lead to confusion, to an experience of meaninglessness. Participation must be balanced with reification in order to anchor the processes of meaning in actual, socially established discourses. Wenger (1998) sums up the consequences for pedagogical practice as follows:

> An excessive emphasis on formalism without corresponding levels of participation, or conversely a neglect of explanations and formal structure, can easily result in an experience of meaninglessness. (p. 67)

To sum up the above discussion; mathematical discourse closely tied to real life mathematics may turn out to be quite different from the professional discourse of the working mathematician. If the students are to be *'legitimate peripheral participants'* (Lave & Wenger, 1991) in mathematical discourses, it seems vital that participation is not prioritised on the expense of reification. This is may be particularly important when the tasks involved are from real life, where there is a somewhat peripheral, and for many students rather unclear relation to mathematics.

Challenges for the Teacher

One obvious challenge for teachers is to bridge the gap between mathematical discourse and everyday discourse that the students already are engaged in. How should classroom conversations be designed in order to promote mathematical understanding and reasoning? Based on the above-mentioned overview, we would like to draw attention to the following four features:

Firstly, teachers' and students' communication skills regarding *object-level rules* and *meta-level rules* - that is, their ability to talk in and about mathematics as well as general communication skills – are of utmost importance.

Secondly, how well *defined* and focused, intrinsically coherent and generally convincing the mathematical discourse (and tasks) turn out to be, has been proposed as criteria for judgement.

Thirdly, the teachers' careful orchestration of classroom talk is vital. Franke, Kazemi and Battey (2007), for example, point out that the teachers' active and deliberate use of revoicing can increase students' learning from mathematical conversations. Revoicing – that is to re-utter – serves to clarify or amplify an idea. It allows the teacher to substitute everyday words with mathematical vocabulary or vice versa, and it also allows the teacher to redirect the conversation. Revoicing gives teachers the opportunity to communicate new ways of thinking and doing mathematics while simultaneously paying attention to student ideas and encouraging student involvement. Revoicing is thus a tool teachers can use to frame the discussions about content and renegotiate the social roles of the students.

Fourthly, the *nature* of the tasks involved has a huge impact on how and what students learn from talking about mathematics. The nature of the tasks that the students' undertake defines the nature of the subject matter involved and contributes significantly to the quality of their mathematical reasoning and understanding. Silver and Smith (1996) define worthwhile mathematical tasks as problems that engage students in thinking and reasoning about important mathematical ideas. From their perspective, worthwhile mathematical tasks are ones that can be solved in multiple ways that involve multiple representations and require students to justify, make conjectures, and interpret the different approaches. Stigler, Gallimore and Hiebert (2000) link worthwhile mathematical tasks to their mathematical importance (with an emphasis on mathematical rather than other aspects of the situation) along with how the tasks make use of knowledge student already possess. Furthermore, Sfard and Kieran (2001) draw our attention to focus and coherence as criteria for evaluating the quality of mathematical conversations.

Consequently tasks should be designed in a way that makes such conversations possible. "Although too much rigor is paralysing", Sfard (2000, p. 173) argues, "so is a complete lack thereof."

Object-level Skills and Discursive-level Skills

The instructional design and the activities surrounding the mathematical tasks the students worked on in our study, put emphasis on the students' discursive opportunities and their capacity to talk *in* and about mathematics as tools for developing understanding of mathematical reasoning. Inspired by Sfard and her colleagues' distinction between *object-level rules* and *meta-level rules*, we will use *object-level skills* (understood as the capacity to talk in and about mathematics), and *discursive-level skills* (understood as general communicative skills such as negotiating, positioning, repair work and models of division of labour) as analytical devices to analyse the different mathematical sequences. The role of the expert other – and especially the role of the teacher as a more competent and didactically equipped expert – will also be considered.

SAMPLE, METHOD AND TASKS

Sample and Method

The analysis in this chapter is based on empirical data from a 9th grade mathematics classroom where newspapers were used as learning tools to develop mathematical insight. The 9th grade class observed had 18 students, 11 girls and 7 boys, and according to the mathematics teacher, the proficiency level in mathematics in this class could be described as average in relation to national standards. The teacher of this class was certified as a teacher a few years ago and in addition to this she had recently completed a one year study in mathematics education. According to Norwegian standards, she therefore is well qualified as a teacher in mathematics. The school is situated in a suburban area outside of Oslo that is characterised by being ethnically homogenous and socio-economically middle-/upper middle class.

The study of this mathematics class is part of a broader classroom video study of mathematics, science and reading conducted in six classes located at different schools in Oslo and adjacent areas. It also is a part of The Learner's Perspective Study (Clarke, Keitel, & Shimizu, 2006; Clarke, Emanuelsson, Jablonka, & Mok, 2006), an international classroom study in mathematics. The video material from the present study has been analysed using Videograph[i] both across the different subjects, using theory based categories developed in this same study (Klette et al., 2005), and using subject-dependent categories, also developed by researchers participating in this study (Arnesen & Ødegaard, 2005). Only a few of the results from the Videograph analysis of the mathematics classes will be used in this chapter.

The subsequent analysis is based on a sequence of two consecutive mathematics lessons from one single classroom in our sample that:

- used mathematical discussions systematically for the learning of mathematics
- linked inside school mathematics with out-of-school mathematics in an elaborated and systematic way.

In the first of these lessons all the students worked in pairs. Two students, referred to as Joe and Jim, were video-recorded during this group work and equipped with small microphones. The dialogue between these two students was later transcribed and analysed. After the first lesson these two students were interviewed, and so was the teacher a few days later.

The second lesson was a teacher-led, whole-class discussion based on the pair work from the previous day. These two different discursive settings are analysed in this chapter. Mathematical conversations in pairs serve as one setting of discursive mathematical practice. The teacher-led whole-class discussion serves as a second setting for analysing the observed students' engagement with talking mathematics as a tool for learning mathematics. Our analysis is based on a qualitative review of the observed data and serves as a first step in investigating how different discursive practices in classrooms support mathematical understanding.

Criteria for Selection of this Particular Sequence

Videograph analysis conducted on all the six mathematics classrooms in our study revealed that generally very little time was used on non-conventional problems (Klette et al., 2008). Our analysis indicated that the typical pattern in most of these classrooms was that the students would work on quite conventional tasks from the textbook. The sequences used for analysis in this chapter were thus quite untypical in our sample of mathematics lessons. Our criteria for selecting the actual sequences were therefore not based on their typicality, but were chosen because the teacher involved was regarded as a competent teacher, with a genuine interest in mathematics and mathematics education. She led the class through a quite interesting learning sequence, using various discursive working methods that are strongly recommended in the literature within the field. Through the use of empirical data from these sequences, we will try to discuss some of the upsides and downsides of these recommended discursive methods of teaching.

Mathematical Tasks Involved

The teacher began the first lesson by giving instructions about the tasks that the students were going to work on. These problems were a combination of open-ended and structured tasks, referred to as Task 1 and Task 2. Task 1 consisted of two open-ended cases while Task 2 consisted of four (see Appendix). All the tasks were related to a real-world context. In Task 1, the students were asked to find material in the newspaper that was made relevant through the use of mathematical representations. They were told that they in principle could choose anything they liked, but challenged to try to find examples that were not too elementary. Additionally, they were instructed to not use too much time on this first task. In Task 2, the students were asked to comment upon four cases reported in the newspapers. One was about smoking and cancer, one was related to average income in the county where the students lived, one was about medication and healing rates, and the last one was about the increase in tuberculosis in Norway. These cases were selected by the teacher, presumably because of their relevance to the theme in this lesson, photocopied and distributed to the students. Task 2 was thus more structured than Task 1 and the students were asked to critically comment on the way mathematics was being used.

This first lesson lasted for 43 minutes and the students were told that they had to finish the tasks at home if they were not able to complete them all during the lesson.

The second lesson took place the day after the group work. At the beginning of this lesson the teacher told the students that they were collectively to discuss the work from the previous day. She asked them to pull up a chair in the middle of the classroom and to bring their written answers from the group work. After a short introduction by the teacher, where she briefly repeated what kind of tasks the students worked on the day before, they started discussing the different tasks and issues. It all took place in a very quiet and comfortable atmosphere where all contributions were valued, albeit some more than others, depending on the content of the statements. Another general point worth mentioning is that the teacher consistently used expressions and formulations that the students seemed to understand.

MATHEMATICAL TALK IN THE CLASSROOM

Positioning in the Group

As previously mentioned, the two video-filmed students were two boys, Joe and Jim. Joe reported in the follow-up interview that he was getting 4 in mathematics, which is a little above average in Norway. Jim did not disclose his grade, but his statements made it reasonable to infer that his grade was a little below average. Their positioning during group work reflected that they recognised that there was some difference in mathematical proficiency between the two of them. This was revealed by the fact that Jim throughout the interview on various occasions asked Joe for help and assistance, while Joe took on a leading role in the group, particularly through structuring their work towards producing answers to the given tasks. Even if this seemed to be a quite dominant pattern, Jim also occasionally contributed to the discussion by suggesting certain solutions.

Mathematical Talk in the Dyadic Student Group

The teacher used about six minutes to start the first lesson and introduce the tasks. During the next minute the teacher handed out the sheets, simultaneously answering student inquiries. While the students were working on these non-conventional problems in pairs, the teacher walked around between the groups and gave additional support, guided the students and explained the core meanings of the tasks. She seemed to be allocating support according to how well the student-groups were working; spending most time with the groups that expressed that they had problems interpreting the tasks.

The two male students in our focus group started to read the tasks 7 minutes into the lesson. Joe read aloud, while Jim immediately began to ask Joe questions about what they were supposed to do. Here is an excerpt from this situation:

```
JOE:    [Reads silently from the task-sheet]
JIM:    That means that we are supposed to do what?
JOE:    Wait a second. [Reads aloud] Well, I guess we have to go and
        get some newspapers.
        [After Joe was back with the newspapers, they hesitated a
        moment, then decided to get sheets to write their answers on.]
JOE:    I think maybe we should get sheets to write the answers on,
        before we get started.
JIM:    Yeah, I write, you fetch. (Grabs the newspaper from JOE)
JOE:    [A bit aggressively] You can go and fetch it, you don't
        understand anything anyway.
JIM:    [laughs] Well, that's true.
```

Key to symbols used in transcripts in this chapter
[text]   Comments and annotations, often descriptions of non-verbal action
<u>text</u>   Underlined text indicates emphasis added by the authors.

As can be seen from this episode, the students negotiated (in a boyish way) how to organise the work. Jim was trying to take command of the situation, but this was quite fiercely contested by Joe, who indirectly referred to his superior academic proficiency to resume his position as the leader of the group. Jim immediately recognised this claim as reasonable and accepted his academic inferiority. After this episode, Jim never challenged his internal social positioning in the group.

Later in the lesson Joe and Jim were discussing what piece of information from the newspaper they should use for Task I, and the following dialogue took place:

```
JIM:    And the answer is?
JOE:    [Gives JIM the newspaper, a little annoyed] Look here and then
        you will see what to do.
JIM:    The question is?
JOE:    We are supposed to use the newspaper and then find examples.
JIM:    Yes.
JOE:    It's not difficult. And then we have to write the answers
        here. Then we are supposed to figure out the meaning and write
        down what they use.
JIM:    What they use? What's that stuff called?
JOE:    We call that a pie-chart.
JIM:    And bar chart.
JOE:    No, that's here, but we won't use them.
```

After being interrupted by the teacher who asked if they needed more paper, Joe and Jim went on to discuss what the pie chart showed (it was about political parties). They had difficulties interpreting it and decided to use a different example, but they did come back to the first pie chart a little later. Very little was said explicitly about mathematical issues in this part of the group work. A lot of attention was paid to non-mathematical issues, which seemed to have little relevance for mathematical knowledge production. Both students used quite some time to draw the pie chart. After twenty minutes of the lesson had passed, the teacher came over and told the two students to just write down how the pie chart was being used in the paper. This information seemed to have a structuring effect on the two boys and they were then able to come up with a reasonable answer to this task.

JOE: Let's write that Daily News shows the different political fractions by using a pie chart.

In both the statement above and on various other occasions, Joe clearly assumed a large degree of responsibility for the work the two students were supposed to accomplish. He seemed to be oriented towards producing results and several times in the dialogue with Jim he explicitly stated that they should write down their answers, and get the work done.

The Importance of the More Knowledgeable Other – Five Illustrations

Illustration one After following up on Joe's recommendation to write down their answers, the students paused a little, but then decided to try to look for the final example. (*Twenty-two minutes of the lesson had now passed.*) They discussed a few very simple alternatives, for instance to use telephone numbers, before finally deciding to go for soccer tables.

JOE: Let's write; In Daily News there is a table which shows…What are you doing now?
JIM: Just fooling around
JOE: [Repeats aloud what he has already said in order for JIM to be able to copy him]
JIM: What does it show then? Premier League men, or?
JOE: It shows the position of many teams that is in Premier League for men.
JIM: Premier League men positioned??? [His utterance does not make sense]
JOE: No, no.
JIM: Are positioned.
JOE: Yes. Then we have to write: It shows the goal difference and how many points they have.
JIM: I don't know anything about football.

Once again, it can be observed that Joe tried to assume responsibility by declaring that they should write down their answers. By doing this he was also structuring their work according to general schoolwork expectations, where writing down your answer is both an implicit and often explicit rule of action. The students were to a very small extent able to relate their discussion around this task to mathematics, so they seemed to structure their work in relation to meaningful actions within the school context. To use Wenger's demand of a needed balance between participation and reification, the two students seemed to mainly be involved in a discourse related to participation. The connection with reification processes of mathematical concepts, and with any social established mathematical discourse, appeared to be rather vague.

After twenty-eight minutes the students finished this part of the task. Generally, very little mathematics or mathematical concepts were discussed explicitly, especially when the students worked on their own, without any interference from the teacher. The students seemed to have problems relating the tasks to relevant mathematical discourse. However, when the teacher intervened by giving them a clearer interpretation of the task, the students were able to come up with a reasonable answer in relation to the first example they were using. The teacher intervention seemed to be quite decisive and to play an important role in structuring the students' conversation. On the other hand; left alone the students' were scarcely able to produce statements that had potential mathematical value. Neither seemed in discussion to have contributed to a development of an extended discursive repertoire in mathematics among the two. It therefore seems reasonable to conclude that this part of the group work had limited value for the students as regards mathematical learning through the training of their *object-level skills*. Only after the teacher's intervention was Joe able to formulate a statement that can be considered to relate to this kind of skill. One reason for this might be that the gap between the actual tasks the students were given and the mathematical discourse they have participated in throughout their entire school career, and thus were acquainted with, was too large. They were therefore unable to bridge this distance when left on their own and consequently the dialogue between them was very loosely connected to any mathematical discourse. The students' *discursive-level skills* have, on the other hand, been challenged through these tasks. Joe and Jim were able to communicate successfully and they both suggested solutions to this first task, although parts of their work and their final answers had little substantial reference and limited mathematical value.

Illustration two Joe and Jim now began to work on the next set of mathematical tasks, Task 2. As previously mentioned, these tasks were also based on information mediated through newspapers, and the teacher had made the selection with a clear didactical purpose based on mathematical relevance of the information presented. This is how the teacher, in a later interview, formulated her general thoughts about this specific lesson:

T: I wanted them to practice on expressing what they found (in
        the newspaper), to make them realize what they know and that
        they need to know mathematics outside of school. That
        mathematics can be used, that they need this knowledge.

Joe and Jim started discussing Task 2a (about smoking). Here is an excerpt from this discussion:

JIM: It's only about the means [seems to be reading from the next
        task]
JOE: It's only something that is claimed, it's not sure it's like
        that.
JIM: Yeah, it's only claimed. It could be true though; there are
        people who smoke that don't… [Interrupted by JOE]
JOE: Yeah, but it's not. Smoking is no good anyway.
JIM: Anybody who smokes doesn't stay healthy, if they smoke a lot.
JOE: Let's write that then. [Both students start to write down this
        answer. After a few seconds JOE starts to read aloud what he

```
              is writing down] Some manage to smoke without getting cancer,
              but others don't.
JIM:          [Also reads aloud what he writes down] Let's say that the
              majority die of cancer.
```

What primarily characterizes this dialogue is that none of the students are able to build their arguments on any kind of statistical or mathematical concepts. No reference whatsoever is made to statistics, even if this task obviously invites the students to use their pre-knowledge about these matters. By failing to relate the task to statistical discourse, only to normative views of smoking, the dialogue seems to have little value from a mathematical perspective. Once again it can be observed that the *object-level skills* of the students are not activated and trained. This also reveals the potential danger of using small-scale group work in mathematics. The necessary competence for solving the task is not available among the group members in this group, or at least it is not made relevant. In a larger group one runs a smaller chance of experiencing this. On the other hand; the two students seem on this occasion to have a "true dialogue" (Lemke, 1990), they both contribute in the conversation on apparently equal terms and both students seem to appreciate the others' statements. Their *discursive-level skills* are thus trained through this interaction. Unfortunately, none of them are able to bring in the relevant subject knowledge needed to make the dialogue mathematically fruitful.

Illustration three   In the next task that the students worked on, Task 2b, the dialogue had a quite different pattern. Here the students were supposed to comment on a newspaper text which revealed that the average income in the county where they live was 380 000 NOK. After reading the task, they started discussing this issue:

```
JIM:          I didn't understand that.
JOE:          There's nothing to understand. Some people have very high
              incomes.
JIM:          Yes, but some have very low, and...[Gets interrupted by JOE]
JOE:          Yes, but then we have to write that down. Not everybody earns
              that much.
JIM:          No, it's not. Someone makes more.
JOE:          And someone makes less.
JIM:          But it's just the mean.
JOE:          Yes, then we write that. [They both write for a few seconds,
              and then JOE continues to talk] We write that this is the mean
              income, but it is still a lot of people that don't make that
              much yet.
JIM:          And a lot that earn more.
JOE:          Many that earn more and many that earn less.
JIM:          Many earn a lot more and this makes the mean income higher.
```

In this dialogue, one of the students, Joe, was able to use his *object-level skills*, by bringing forward relevant statistical content knowledge which made the discussion meaningful from a mathematical perspective. Jim expressed in the beginning of this dialogue that he did not understand this task. Joe tried to explain what it was all about by interpreting the given information. In order to succeed in this, Joe had to apply both his *discursive-level skills* and his *object-level skills*. Soon Jim got involved in a meaningful statistical dialogue. This probably would not have

49

happened if Joe had not provided the necessary mathematical knowledge at the beginning of the conversation. The above dialogue can therefore serve as an example of how a student can broaden his discursive mathematical repertoire through the help of a more knowledgeable other in a group work context, through the latter person's capacity to make relevant and apply his *object-level skills*.

Illustration four   Task 2c contained the next issue the students were discussing. It was about a survey conducted by a pharmaceutical company. The students were informed that 80% of the people that used this drug recovered. Joe started by reading the text loudly and the dialogue went like this:

```
JIM:    But it's still only 80%.
        [They both seem a little bored and start to discuss how much
        time is left of the lesson.]
JIM:    Are we going to write about what happens or the statistics?
JOE:    We'll just write; we'll just write that not everything is
        true, or, it's true but it's not; here for instance it's 20%
        that's not healed.
JIM:    Yes, 20%.
JOE:    So it is two out of ten that didn't recover. But it is eight
        out of ten that recovered.
JIM:    It is not always like that. Maybe suddenly one day it's the
        other way around.
JOE:    Yes, yes.
JIM:    Because if it is 20%; 20 that didn't recover, then soon it
        is...
JOE:    We should write that down then. That's what we are supposed to
        write down.
        [They both start to write down their answer.]
JIM:    [Loudly while he writes] But it may soon change.
```

The above dialogue provides an example of how the students were able to apply and train their *discursive-level skills*, but not their *object-level skills*. While they communicated well socially, the conversation between the two students were not that useful from a mathematical point of view. Joe was able to relate his argumentation somewhat to mathematical concepts by reasoning in percent about how many persons recovered and how many did not. He stated that 20% did not get well and had obviously subtracted 80% from 100%. In addition to this he was able to infer that this meant that statistically two out of ten did not recover. He thus managed to use parts of his prior knowledge to comment on the issues in this task. A major problem, however, is that that he did not manage to use his *object-level skills* to instigate a mathematically relevant dialogue. Understanding per cent is a prerequisite, but not sufficient for being able to comment on this task in a mathematically meaningful way. Other, more sophisticated mathematical and statistical concepts would have had to be introduced and made relevant. As neither Joe nor Jim were capable of doing this, and with no help from more knowledgeable others, the conclusions that were drawn at the end of this dialogue seemed rather out of place, if not completely irrelevant, from a mathematical perspective.

Another point worth noticing is that contrary to what happened in the previous dialogue about mean income, where Jim through the help of Jim got to be involved in a mathematically relevant discussion, things did not seem to get clearer for Jim here. Even if Joe related the information given in this task to his prior knowledge about percent, this was not sufficient for them to be able to formulate any adequate statements in which they succeeded in evaluating the given information in this task.

Illustration five   Finally, in Task 2d, our two students were supposed to comment upon the way a newspaper reported about tuberculosis. In a headline, a newspaper claimed that there had been a doubling in the number of cases of tuberculosis in Norway the last year. Later in the article it was revealed that only six people had been diagnosed with this sickness, as compared with just three the year before. Jim and Joe read the task aloud, but seemed to be insecure of how to make any comments. After forty minutes of the lesson had passed, especially Jim appeared tired and uninspired. He yawned and moaned quite demonstratively. This dialogue took place:

```
JIM:    The last one is?
JOE:    It's... [Pauses a few seconds]
        [The teacher passes by and Joe asks her about the task]
JOE:    What's this one about, this one? What are we supposed to do
        here? Six persons got tuberculosis, as compared with three
        last year.
T:      If you came to buy the newspaper one day and this was the top
        headline: Tuberculosis doubles in one year! What would you
        think about that?
JOE:    That a lot of people die, a lot would get it. But it's only
        six persons, is that what you're saying?
JIM:    (Quite eagerly) It's only six persons, it's a big headline.
        You would think it was a hundred or so!
        [The teacher walks away and there is a short pause. Then Jim
        starts talking]
JIM:    Gets what? [JOE gives no response]
JIM:    I'll just argue that... [Still no response from JOE]
JIM:    I could really need some help, you see.
JOE:    [Annoyed] You've got to think just a little bit then.
JIM:    Yes, but if I... [Gets interrupted by JOE]
JOE:    You've done the same on all the tasks. What are you supposed
        to figure out here?
JIM:    Why, what, what then?
JOE:    No, I really won't bother helping you. Now you got to figure
        it out yourself.
JIM:    Now I'm completely lost, I'm completely lost.... Ok, then. [Both
        write on their sheets until the teacher calls the end of the
        lesson after 43 minutes]
```

By this time, approximately forty minutes into the lesson, Jim seemed tired and unmotivated. Even if both the students expressed confusion about how to answer this last task, the dialogue revealed that Joe took an initiative to ask the teacher for help. The teacher answered the call by prompting the students about their likely reactions if confronted with these headlines in a real life situation. By giving this support the teacher seemed to inspire the students' interest in the actual issue and their replies revealed that they were both able to rationally relate to the task. The teacher seemed to make a positive assessment of these statements, which must be interpreted as a sign of approval of these kinds of comments, even if they were very implicit as regards mathematically relevant concepts. In this way the teacher signalled that she did expect the students to be able to relate to the presentation of statistical data in media, but that it was acceptable to do this without referring to statistical concepts explicitly. She apparently did not consider it necessary for the students to link their comments to any concepts of this kind. The talk in this dialogue could thus be characterised as being about mathematically relevant issues, but with a loose connection to a more explicit mathematical discourse. In relation to the relatively broad definition that was given of *object-level skills* earlier in this chapter, it would be reasonable to claim that the teacher wanted to encourage the students to apply their *object-level skills* in their discussion of this task, and that they in fact managed do this after being supported by the teacher in interpreting it.

Another interesting matter that is revealed in this dialogue is the difference in social positioning according to the presence of the teacher. As long as the teacher was with them, both students seemed to participate in the discussion on equal terms. Jim was particularly eager when the teacher was present and made several relatively valuable comments. As soon as the teacher had gone away, however, he seemed to become quite confused and started to question Joe about how to go on. Joe got annoyed by what he probably experienced as obnoxious behaviour from Jim, and in the last part of this dialogue communication about the mathematical task has broken down completely. The social positioning has been re-established with Joe being in command and with Jim placed in an inferior position.

Fostering Mathematical Reasoning – Looking across the Tasks

In Table 1, a summary of our findings, related to the skills involved when working with the referred mathematical tasks, is presented. While the students used their *discursive-level skills* in different ways throughout the discussions of all the actual mathematical tasks, this was not the case with their *object-level skills*. Only in Task 2b were they able to apply their object-level skills without getting any outside support. In both Tasks 1a and 2d was this skill activated only after an intervention by the teacher (this is why these cells in the table have a somewhat ambiguous notation: No-Yes). In Tasks 1b, 2a, and 2c they did not succeed in using their *object-level skills* at all and the mathematical value of the dialogues that took place in connection to these tasks was, as previously pointed out, therefore minimal.

Table 1. Skills used in dyadic group work

Tasks	A. Object-level skills (talk in and about mathematics)	B. Discursive-level skills
Task 1a Finding examples of applied mathematics in the newspaper	No-Yes	Yes
Task 1b Finding examples of applied mathematics in the newspaper	No	Yes
Task 2a Smoking and Cancer	No	Yes
Task 2b Mean Income	Yes	Yes
Task 2c Pharmaceutical Company	No	Yes
Task 2d Doubling of Tuberculosis	No-Yes	Yes

Mathematical Talk in the Whole-Class Discussion – The Role of the Teacher

In the mathematics lesson the day after the group work the teacher started out by asking about Task 1, where the students were supposed to find examples of use of mathematics in the newspaper. Many students raised their hands and a multitude of different answers were produced. Most of them were characterised by being quite simple, mentioning telephone numbers, weekdays, recipes, etc. The teacher accepted all the answers. Some students also suggested tables and pie charts and the teacher then asked the students to explain what a pie chart is. Jim raised his hand and answered this question. The answer was not very precise, but was accepted by the teacher as adequate. In asking for this kind of definition the teacher was able to make mathematical knowledge relevant for the understanding and interpretation of information presented in media. By stating this kind of questions the teacher made it clear that the students were not only expected to be able to talk about mathematics and statistics, but also to provide definitions of certain concepts. The students were thus being trained in using their object-level skills in mathematics.

Another method that the teacher used throughout the entire whole-class discussion sequence was revoicing – to personally re-utter some of the verbal formulations of the students, in order both to recognise the mathematical importance of their suggestions and to ensure that a mathematical perspective was made explicit. By doing so she was also able to connect their collective discussion to a mathematical discourse, actualising and reifying central mathematical concepts. In this way she managed to balance participation and reification to make this session quite meaningful for the students involved, judged by their clear participation in the discussion.

Many of the 18 students had by now already contributed to the discussion. By being able to involve almost everybody in the discussion, the teacher assured that they were also being trained in using their *discursive-level skills*, such as turn taking. The teacher summed up this part by saying that it is important both to know how to interpret tables and diagrams, and to be able to evaluate the way information is being presented in media by the use of these artefacts. By drawing this conclusion the task was made relevant for the students in a real life setting.

Now the class went on to talk about the other issues from the group work. They started with Task 2a, about smoking/cancer. As previously discussed, Joe and Jim did not manage to relate their solution to a mathematical discourse by bringing in relevant statistical concepts. The teacher opened up for debate and again many students contributed. However, most of the suggested answers were of the kind that Joe and Jim came up with, fundamentally normative, with little relevance within a mathematical discourse. After a while the teacher asked the class if they thought it was acceptable to take a stand on smoking based on the information given in this article. One student answered that smoking is not good for you anyway. Then a second student started introducing statistical notions by saying that it is not "exact" when only one person is used. This was followed up by a third student who managed to add on to this by stating that to base this kind of study on just one person is not acceptable, one has to use a lot more. The teacher immediately made a very positive assessment of this last statement and then summed up the discussion by saying that the essence here was that it is not possible to draw any conclusions on the basis of such a small sample.

Even if no precise statistical concepts were introduced in this discussion, the teacher succeeded in making statistical knowledge relevant in relation to this task. She did this by first eliciting student responses, and when these comments seemed to be rather displaced, she asked questions that made the dialogue more mathematically relevant. In this way the students were guided by the teacher in a certain direction, and she supported them in order to ensure that their statements became relevant within a mathematical discourse. In other words, she succeeded in anchoring the discussion in a mathematical discourse using *object-level skills* prevalent in student contributions.

Linking Students' Utterances to Mathematically Relevant Interpretations

In Task 2b the reader was informed that the mean income in Hill County was 380 550 NOK. To get the discussion started, the teacher asked the students if anyone could explain the concept of *a mean value*. One student tried, but his formulations were somewhat unclear. The teacher then commented that it is often difficult to explain mathematical concepts to others in words even if one understands it and is able to use it properly. Another student succeeded quite well in explaining this concept. A third student brought up, on his own accord, the concept *median*, and the teacher asked the students to explain this new concept and to give comments upon the differences in the use of mean value and median. Once again the first definition of the *median* that was presented was rather weak, but a second student came up with a quite precise definition of this concept. A third student answered that when using the *median* one got rid of the ones that earn most and the ones that earn least. As can be observed, this student referred to the task in question when explaining the use of the concept. The teacher made a positive comment to this last contribution, and summed up this part of the whole-class discussion by stating that in the actual task about *mean* income in Hill County it might have been better to give information about the *median*. She supported her argument by claiming that one knew that in Hill County a lot of people have very high incomes and that there always will be people that make very little. One student raised his hand and commented that it would be very difficult to list all incomes in a county in order to find the *median*. The teacher responded briefly by saying that there are certain methods available for doing this. However, after observing this discussion one wonders if all students were able to understand how to choose between these two concepts, the *mean value* and the *median,* in reporting from a survey. It seems that the differences between these statistical concepts were not elaborated upon sufficiently during this whole-class discussion for the students to get a grip of when to apply the one or the other.

By first asking the students to define *the mean value* and later *the median*, and then using follow up questions to stimulate and ensure student understanding, the teacher assumed responsibility for keeping the discussion within a mathematical discourse. She quickly gave positive responses to contributions that she apparently found valuable, and then added relevant information about the mathematical issues in question. Her method led to high student involvement and ensured that the class was introduced to specific mathematical concepts within a more general mathematical discourse. The students' *object-level skills* were here again stimulated and made relevant.

Task 2c was the next one discussed. It was about a survey conducted by a pharmaceutical company (see Appendix). After reading the task aloud, the teacher asked for comments. One student claimed that you often get well anyway, without using any medication. The teacher responded affirmatively and went on to ask the students if they could think of anything else that they would have liked to investigate in order to believe in the results with this medicine. Another student stated that a large part of the group did not recover. The teacher nodded, but then prompted the students to think about other things that would have been interesting to know about this survey. When no one answered this call, she gave them additional cues. This dialogue then took place (S1, S2 and S3 are different students, T is the teacher):

```
T:    How much is eighty per cent?
S1:   Eight out of ten.
T:    Or? Eighty per cent can be a lot, can't it?
S2:   Yes.
T:    Depending on what? (With a smile) What do you all think I'm
      after?
S3:   If you ask ten persons and eight of them answer yes, then that
      is eighty per cent.
```

```
T:        Yes, but then you can ask a hundred. The more you ask, the
          better reasons to believe in the results of this survey. If
          you ask just a few, then there are hardly grounds for drawing
          any conclusions. It usually says how many people have been
          asked.
```

Apparently the teacher on this occasion did not succeed in eliciting the answers she had in mind from the students. It might be mentioned that she got a quite precise answer to her first question and that the second question was rather obscure. Anyway, when no acceptable answer was received, the teacher herself complemented the students' statements by saying that the more people you ask, the better reasons to believe in the results of a survey. Even if more advanced statistical concepts was not introduced at this level, it seems reasonable to conclude that the teacher did succeed in relating the discussion to the mathematical discourse by referring to the need for a certain number of people in a survey sample. The *object-level skills* of the students were once again trained and broadened. This contrasts sharply with the way this same task was discussed by Joe and Jim during group work. As previously mentioned, they were not able to relate their arguments to any statistical concepts at all, except percent. This illustrates the need for a knowledgeable other in guiding the students' attention towards the mathematically relevant aspects of the information in a task.

Finally, the class discussed the issue in Task 2d, about increase in cases of tuberculosis (see Appendix). The following dialogue took place (T is the teacher, S1, S2, S3 are three students):

```
T:        If you read the paper one day and it tells you that the number
          of cases of tuberculosis has doubled in one year. Then some
          readers probably will be scared if they don't continue
          reading. Or what?
S1:       It's probably only coincidental.
T:        Well, that's what you would have figured, that it is only
          coincidental.
S2:       Some people just read the headlines, they don't go further.
T:        And if they only read the headlines here; what do you think
          they would figure?
S3:       That it was a lot.
T:        Maybe someone would believe it was an epidemic and that a lot
          of people would have to see a doctor, but if we read further
          down then it says?
S2:       Doubling from three to six
T:        Exactly; then maybe it's not so dramatic anyway - as one
          should think from the headline.
S2:       It's like he (S1) said, very coincidental, really, when the
          figures are that small. If one only reads the headline…
T:        Yes, one doesn't really know the number until one starts
          reading further down the page. Any other comments?
```

The teacher used the same introductory question to this task in the whole-class setting as she did when talking with Joe and Jim during group work. She wanted the students to relate the text to their own experience, to how they would think and feel if confronted with this kind of information, and the students did not have any difficulties relating this story to their personal experience. Anchoring the story to the students' daily life and to their own experiences apparently made it easier for them to comprehend the issue at hand. The teacher did not introduce any explicit statistical or mathematical concepts, in fact the mathematics involved in this task can be considered to be quite implicit. She did, however, manage to keep the dialogue within what can be labelled an extended or comprehensive mathematical discourse, where critical thinking and talking about how mathematical concepts are used in real life settings were assigned an important value. These kinds of skills are central elements in definitions of mathematical literacy (OECD, 2000) and it seems reasonable to infer that the teacher of this mathematics class, through managing the discourse the way it is described above, succeeded in training the *object-level skills* of the students.

Summing up this sequence, which lasted a little less than 20 minutes; it seems clear that even if a lot of students participated in this classroom discussion around mathematical tasks, the teacher played a very important and major role in ensuring that the talk was closely related to mathematical and statistical concepts and issues. She managed to do this partly by asking the students mathematical relevant questions, but also by revoicing student suggestions and giving very positive evaluations to the student contributions that she regarded as particularly important or interesting from a mathematical perspective. In this way, the quality of the discussion was quite high, especially as compared with the corresponding dialogue during group work. By introducing relevant mathematical and statistical concepts and inquiring about their definitions, by bringing in perspectives on how to critically relate to the use of these concepts in media, and by giving the students the opportunity to talk about these issues in whole-class discussions, the teacher actively ensured the mathematical relevance of the whole-class discussion. Applying these kinds of methods she made sure that the students, through the work with these mathematical tasks, were trained to participate in mathematical discourses in a socially acceptable manner. As opposed to what happened in the previously referred student dialogue about these same issues, illustrated in Table 1, we can observe that in this whole-class sequence the students were trained in using both their *object-level skills* and their *discursive-level skills* across all the tasks involved.

CONCLUSION

In this chapter we have, through the analysis of talk around mathematical real-life tasks in two different settings, small-scale group work and whole-class discussion, argued that from a mathematical perspective the value of this talk is dependent upon various contextual factors. Viewing mathematical learning according to socio-cultural theory as a process of expanding ones' participation in mathematical discourses, we have pointed out that small-scale group work seems to be a method of working that stimulates broad participation, but where the anchoring of the discussion to a mathematical discourse is often weak and tenuous. Using Wenger's (1998) complementary concepts to describe the processes taking place in this method of work, participation seems to be prioritised at the expense of reification. Many reasons for this could certainly be listed. Inspired by Sfard's and Kieran's (2001) distinction between *object-level rules* and *meta-level rules,* we have used the concepts *object-level skills* and *discursive-level skills* to analyse the actual content of the group dialogue. *Object-level skills* are here understood as the capacity to talk in and about mathematics, while *discursive-level skills* are seen as general communicative skills. Analysis of the talk taking place during group work reveals that the students, when left on their own, seem to have difficulties relating their mathematical knowledge to the real-life tasks they are working on. They very easily get involved only in everyday discourses, which have very little mathematical relevance. According to our observations the students succeeded in bringing in relevant mathematical information only in one of the six actual tasks, without outside support. Their *object-level skills* were not activated and trained when working on their own on the five remaining tasks, only after teacher intervention were these skills made relevant in two of these. The students did on the other hand manage to apply their general communicative skills, their *discursive-level skills*, throughout most parts of the group work.

In the sequence with the teacher-led whole-class discussion, we observed a different pattern. By personally revoicing student utterances, by giving immediate positive evaluations to valuable student contributions, and by posing questions that connected the real life tasks to a mathematical discourse, the teacher managed to make the students *object-level skills* relevant in the discussion of the tasks. Through the use of these measures, she seemed to succeed in balancing participation and reification and connect the processes of meaning to a social established mathematical discourse.

Why do talk about the same tasks turn out so differently in these two contexts? In addition to the arguments made above, we would like to point out that the small scale group is dependent on some of its participants managing to make their *object-level skills* relevant in order for the group to succeed in relating its discussion to a mathematical discourse. A group with only two members is very vulnerable in this respect. There are very few individuals to rely on and on many occasions relevant *object-level skills* will not be activated. As Sfard et al. (1998) formulate it, this kind of group work can most aptly be described as a waste of time. During whole-class discussion, it seems that more students will participate and contribute to the collective discourse, and there is a greater chance that some will be able to use their *object-level skills* and bring forward relevant mathematical content knowledge. This was observed in the discussion of the smoking/cancer task where several students in the beginning made quite irrelevant comments before one student was, finally, able to relate the task to significant statistical notions. The teacher's role in the whole-class discussion was also quite decisive. While the teacher evidently will experience problems in trying to assist a whole number of different groups simultaneously during group work, she will, in monitoring and orchestrating whole-class discussions, have the opportunity to ensure that the discussion is related to a mathematical discourse. In other words, just putting students in groups and/or asking them to talk and reflect on the bases of mathematical tasks involved, does not lead to the development of mathematical understanding as such (see also Stigler & Hiebert, 1999; Webb, 2006). *How* teachers and students engage in these discourses and the quality of the tasks involved is of vital importance for the possible development of their mathematical reasoning.

APPENDIX

Tasks for group work (pairs)

Do your best to answer these tasks. You are to discuss some of these problems in both mathematics class and social studies class this week. When you're done; remember to put the tasks and the answers in your blue workbook.

Task 1

We live in an information age, and very often numbers and mathematics are used to inform us. In our democracy it is important that everybody can understand and evaluate information from different sources, for instance newspapers, TV, journals, commercials and advertising, political meetings and debates. Use the newspapers at school to find examples where numbers and mathematics are used for information purposes.

Task 2

When numbers, calculations and statistics are used, we easily believe that what is being said has to be true. Study the cases below. What kind of impact do you think the numbers have on people? What kind of information is given? Give your comments and explain different interpretations of these cases.

- <u>Task 2a</u> Henry (smoking manly): "That smoking is dangerous is just a bunch of crap. My grandfather smoked two packs of cigarettes daily. He was never sick and passed away at 87."
- <u>Task 2b</u> The mean income in Hill County is 380550 NOK.
- <u>Task 2c</u> A pharmaceutical company has presented a study of the healing effect of a cold medicine. 80 % of the people that used this medicine recovered within a week. On the grounds of this study, the use of this medicine is recommended.
- <u>Task 2d</u> Big headline in the paper: "Tuberculosis doubles in one year". In the text below is added "this year six people got tuberculosis as compared with three last year."

The students got three additional tasks, but as our focus students did not work on those during the video filmed mathematics class, the other tasks were not discussed in this paper.

NOTES

[i] Videograph ® is a computer software programme developed at IPN, Kiel, http://www.ipn.uni-kiel.de/aktuell/videograph/htmStart.htm

REFERENCES

Arnesen, N., & Ødegaard, M. (2005). *Categories for video analysis of science classroom activities.* Oslo: University of Oslo.

Bauersfeld, H. (1995). Language games in the mathematics classroom: Their function and their effects. In P. Cobb, & H. Bauersfeld (Eds.), *The emergence of mathematical meaning* (pp. 271-291). Hillsdale, NJ: Lawrence Erlbaum Associates.

Blum, W., Galbraith, P. L., Henn, H.-W., & Niss, M. (Eds.) (2007). *Modelling and applications in mathematics education. The 14th ICMI study.* New ICMI Studies Series Vol. 10. New York: Springer.

Boaler, J. (2002). *Experiencing school mathematics: Traditional and reform approaches to teaching and their impact on student learning.* Mahwah, NJ: Lawrence Erlbaum Associates.

Carpenter, T. P., Fennema, E., Franke, M. L., Levi, L. W., & Empson, S. B. (1999). *Children's mathematics: Cognitively guided instruction.* Portsmouth, NH: Heinemann

Cazden, C. B. (2001). *Classroom discourse: The language of teaching and learning.* Portsmouth, UK: Heinemann.

Clarke, D. J., Emanuelsson, J., Jablonka, E., & Mok, I. A. C. (Eds.) (2006). *Making connections: Comparing mathematics classrooms around the world.* Rotterdam: Sense Publishers.

Clarke, D. J., Keitel, C., & Shimizu, Y. (Eds.). (2006). *Mathematics classrooms in twelve countries: The insider's perspective.* Rotterdam: Sense Publishers.

Cobb, P. (1995). Mathematical learning and small-group interaction: Four case studies. In P. Cobb, & H. Bauersfeld (Eds.), *The emergence of mathematical meaning* (pp. 25-129). Hillsdale, NJ: Lawrence Erlbaum Associates.

Cobb, P. (2007). Putting philosophy to work. Coping with multiple theoretical perspectives. In F. K. Lester (Ed.), *Second handbook of research on mathematics teaching and learning* (pp. 3-38). Charlotte, NC: National Council of Teachers of Mathematics, Information Age Publishing.

Cobb, P., Boufi, A., McClain, K., & Whitenack, J. (1997). Reflective discourse and collective reflection. *Journal for Research in Mathematics Education, 28*(3), 258-277.

Cobb, P., Yackel, E., & McClain, K. (Eds.) (2000). *Symbolizing and communicating in mathematics classrooms: Perspectives on discourse, tools, and instructional design.* Mahwah, NJ: Lawrence Erlbaum Associates.

Ernest, P. (1991). *The philosophy of mathematics education.* Hampshire, UK: The Falmer Press.

Ernest, P. (1994). Conversation as a metaphor for mathematics and learning. *Proceedings of the British Society for Research into Learning Mathematics Day Conference (BSRLM), Nottingham, 13*(3), 58-63.

Franke, M. L., Kazemi, E., & Battey, D. (2007). Mathematics teaching and classroom practice. In F. K. Lester (Ed.), *Second handbook of research on mathematics teaching and learning* (pp. 225-256). Charlotte, NC: National Council of Teachers of Mathematics, Information Age Publishing.

Gravemeijer, K. (1994). *Developing realistic mathematics education.* Utrecht: CD-β Press.

Gravemeijer, K., Cobb, P., Bowers, J., & Whitenack, J. (2000). Symbolizing, modeling and instructional design. In P. Cobb, E. Yackel, & K. McClain (Eds.), *Symbolizing and communicating in mathematics classrooms* (pp. 225-273). Mahwah, NJ: Lawrence Erlbaum Associates.

Hiebert, J., Carpenter, T. P., Fennema, E., Fuson, L., Human, P., Murray, H., Olivier, A., & Wearne, D. (1997). *Making sense: Teaching and learning mathematics with understanding.* Portsmouth, NH: Heineman.

Hiebert, J., Gallimore, R., Garnier, H., Givvin, K. B., Hollingsworth, H., Jacobs, J., Chui, A. M. Y., Wearne, D., Smith, M., Kersting, N., Manaster, A., Tseng, E., Etterbeek, W., Manaster, C.,

Gonzales, P., & Stigler, J. W. (2003). *Teaching mathematics in seven countries: Results from the TIMSS 1999 video study.* Washington, DC: NCES.

K (2005). *Kunnskapsløftet. Læreplan for grunnskolen.* (Knowledge promotion: Curriculum for elementary and lower secondary school in Norway). Oslo: Norwegian Ministry of Education and Research.

Klette, K., Lie, S., Anmarkrud, Ø., Arnesen, N., Bergem, O. K., Ødegaard, M., & Zachariassen, J. R. (2005). *Categories for video analysis of classroom activities with a focus on the teacher.* Oslo: University of Oslo.

Klette, K., Lie, S., Ødegaard, M., Anmarkrud, Ø., Arnesen, N., Bergem, O. K., & Roe, A. (2008). *PISA+: Lærings- og undervisningsstrategier i skolen.* (PISA+: Learning- and teaching strategies in school). Oslo: The Research Council of Norway.

KUF (1996). *Læreplanverket for den 10-årige grunnskolen* (Curriculum for primary and lower secondary school in Norway). Oslo: Nasjonalt læremiddelsenter.

Lampert, M. (1990). When the problem is not the question and the solution is not the answer: Mathematical knowing and teaching. *American Educational Research Journal, 27*(1), 29-63.

Lave, J. (1988). *Cognition in practice: Mind, mathematics and culture in everyday life.* Cambridge: Cambridge University Press.

Lave, J., & Wenger, E. (1991). *Situated learning: Legitimate peripheral participation.* Cambridge: Cambridge University Press.

Lehmke, J. (1990). *Talking science: Language, learning, and values.* Norwood, NJ: Ablex/Elsevier.

Lerman, S. (1996). Intersubjectivity in mathematics learning: A challenge to the radical constructivist paradigm? *Journal for Research in Mathematics Education, 27*(2), 133-150.

LP (1994). *Läroplan för det Obligatoriska Skolväsenet* (Curriculum for primary and secondary school in Sweden). Stockholm: Utbildningsdepartementet.

NCTM (1989). *Curriculum and evaluation standards for school mathematics.* Reston, VA: National Council of Teachers of Mathematics.

Nemirovsky, R. (Ed.). (2005). *Everyday matters in science and mathematics: Studies of complex classroom events.* Mahwah, NJ: Lawrence Erlbaum Associates.

Niss, M. (2007). Reflections on the state of and trends in research on mathematics teaching and learning. In F. K. Lester (Ed.), *Second handbook of research on mathematics teaching and learning* (pp. 1293-1312) Charlotte, NC: National Council of Teachers of Mathematics, Information Age Publishing.

Nunes, T. (1999). Mathematics learning as the socialization of the mind. *Mind, Culture, and Activity, 6*(1), 33-52.

O'Connor M. C. (1998). Language socialization in the classroom. In M. Lampert, & M. L. Blunk (Eds.), *Talking mathematics in schools: Studies of teaching and learning* (pp. 15-55). Cambridge, UK: Cambridge University Press.

OECD (2000). *Measuring student knowledge and skills – The PISA 2000 assessment of reading, mathematical, and scientific literacy.* Paris: OECD Publications.

OECD (2003). *The PISA 2003 assessment framework.* Paris: OECD Publications.

OECD (2006). *Assessing scientific reading and mathematical literacy. A framework for PISA 2006.* Paris: OECD Publications.

Saxe, G. B. (1991). *Culture and cognitive development: Studies in mathematical understanding.* Hillsdale, NJ: Lawrence Erlbaum Associates.

Scribner, S. (1984). Studying working intelligence. In B. Rogoff, & J. Lave (Eds.), *Everyday cognition: Its development in social context* (pp. 9-40). Mass.: Harvard University Press

Sfard, A. (2000). On reform movement and the limits of mathematical discourse. *Mathematical Thinking and Learning, 2*(3), 157-189.

Sfard, A. (2001). There is more to discourse than meets the ears: Looking at thinking as Communicating to learn more about mathematical learning. *Educational Studies in Mathematics, 46*(1), 13-57.

Sfard, A., Nesher, P., Streefland, L., Cobb, P., & Mason, J. (1998). Learning mathematics through conversation: Is it as good as they say? *For the Learning of Mathematics, 18*(1), 41-51.

Sfard, A., & Kieran, C. (2001). Cognition as communication: Rethinking learning-by-talking through multi-faceted analysis of students' mathematical interactions. *Mind, Culture and Activity, 8*(1), 42-76.

Silver E. A., & Smith, M. S. (1996). Building discourse communities in mathematics classrooms: A worthwhile but challenging journey. In M. J. Kenney & P. C. Elliott (Eds.), *Communication in mathematics, K-12 and beyond* (pp. 20-28). Reston, VA: National Council of Teachers of Mathematics.

Steinbring, H. (2005). *The construction of new mathematical knowledge in classroom interaction. An epistemological perspective.* New York: Springer.

Stigler, J. W., & Hiebert, J. (1999). *The teaching gap: Best ideas from the world's teachers for improving education in the classroom.* New York: The Free Press.

Stigler, J. W., Gallimore, R., & Hiebert, J. (2000). Using video surveys to compare classrooms and teaching across cultures: Examples and lessons from the TIMSS Video Studies. *Educational Psychologist, 35*(2), 87-100.

van Oers, B. (2001). Educational forms of initiation in mathematical culture. *Educational Studies in Mathematics, 46*(1-3), 59-85.

Webb, R. (Ed.). (2006). *Changing teaching and learning in primary school.* Buckingham, UK: Open University Press.

Wenger, E. (1998). *Communities of practice, learning, meaning, and identity.* New York: Cambridge University Press.

Yackel, E. (1995). Children's talk in inquiry mathematics classroom. In P. Cobb, & H. Bauersfeld (Eds.), *The emergence of mathematical meaning* (pp. 131-162). Hillsdale, NJ: Lawrence Erlbaum Associates.

Yackel, E., & Cobb, P. (1996). Sociomathematical norms, argumentation and autonomy in mathematics. *Journal for Research in Mathematics Education, 27*(4), 458-477.

Vygotsky, L. S. (1978). *Mind in society: The development of higher psychological processes.* Cambridge, MA: Harvard University Press.

Ole Kristian Bergem
Faculty of Education
University of Oslo
Norway

Kirsti Klette
Faculty of Education
University of Oslo
Norway

FLORENDA GALLOS CRONBERG

CHAPTER FOUR

Engaging Students with Mathematical Tasks in a Large Class

INTRODUCTION

In the Philippine public secondary schools it is common to see a class size of sixty. The resources available are the basic ones such as blackboard and chalk, with the teacher dominating the class discussion (Carteciano, 2005; Gordon, 2008; Pascua, 1993). Despite the enthusiasm for group work as an instructional practice in other parts of the world, group mathematical activities are infrequent in Philippine classrooms. Given this, it may be valuable to look more deeply into the observable practices on those infrequent occasions when students are supposed to be engaged in mathematical tasks in groups. In particular, consideration should be given to the role and nature of these tasks and the interactions of the learners. This chapter aims to describe a large class at times when the students were supposed to be engaged in mathematical tasks in groups. In particular, the analysis examines those students' practices evident when the teacher delegates to students the production of actions, formulations and validations without intentional teacher intervention. These occasions, when the students are expected to work independently of the teacher, are considered by Brousseau (1997) as adidactical situations. Also, the kind of tasks given to the students on such occasions will be described. This chapter then attempts to answer these two questions:

What do students in a large class in the Philippines do when they are supposed to be engaged in group tasks, and

What do these mathematical tasks demand from the students, especially if these tasks involve geometric proofs?

The discussions in this chapter are partly guided by the conceptual framework on the construct of a mathematical task by Henningsen and Stein (1997). The use of the Studiocode software aided the processing and analysis of data, for it facilitates the recording, collating and coding of video data.

The class being studied is the 21st class out of 43 classes of Second Year High School (Year 8) and composed of 57 students. The first five classes are grouped homogeneously in terms of academic ability while this class being studied as well as the remaining classes is heterogeneously grouped. The bases for discussion in

Y. Shimizu, B. Kaur, R. Huang and D. J. Clarke (Eds.), Mathematical Tasks in Classrooms around the World, pp. 63–86.

this chapter are the ten videotaped lessons, video-stimulated interviews with the teacher and the students and collected copies of the teacher daily lesson plans. The topics covered here were on triangle congruence and properties of quadrilaterals.

SOME VIEWS

Certainly, there is an abundance of reading material that relates to students doing mathematical tasks, either individually or in groups; about mathematical proofs, particularly tasks on geometric proofs, which is the focus in this chapter and; episodes of particular lessons that are of interest to the mathematics teachers, educators, researchers and the like. Hence for this chapter, some views on these areas will be discussed in the sections to follow.

Mathematical Tasks

Allowing students to engage in worthwhile mathematical tasks is considered by the National Council of Teachers of Mathematics (NCTM) as one of the elements of effective teaching (NCTM, 2000). If well chosen, these tasks could provide a good basis for discussing important mathematical ideas and to engage and challenge students to do mathematics. More so if the tasks are designed in such a way that students can do it in more than one method it would cater to students with varied prior knowledge and experiences. Also mentioned in this NCTM document, the vision of school mathematics should be that

> students confidently engage in complex mathematical tasks chosen carefully by teachers. They draw on knowledge from a wide variety of mathematical topics, sometimes approaching the same problem from different mathematical perspectives or representing the mathematics in different ways until they find methods that enable them to make progress. (p. 3)

It is also worth noting that the documents also mentioned that when providing mathematical tasks for students it is important to decide how to organise and orchestrate the work of the students and how to support students without taking over the process of thinking for them and thus eliminating the challenge.

In the study of Henningsen and Stein (1997), they identified the classroom-based factors that support and inhibit high-level mathematical thinking while students were doing worthwhile mathematical activities. They found that to maintain students' engagement to do the tasks, five prime influences were identified: those tasks that build on student's prior knowledge, appropriate amount of time, sustained pressure for explanation and meaning, scaffolding, and modeling of high-level performance. The last three factors are clearly based on teaching behaviors, hence another confirmation that the teacher is a great influence on students' performance. In the case of the factors that inhibit students to do worthwhile mathematical tasks they had identified three patterns for the decline. The first one relates to decline into using procedures without meaning and understanding. Another is when the task is defined by the solution, or its completeness or accuracy of answers rather than the thinking process entailed in reaching the solution, then this resulted to a decline in engagement. And the third one was a decline into unsystematic exploration. These researchers claimed that the major factor that occurred across these three patterns of decline was the inappropriate amounts of time allotted to the tasks.

In the framework used by Henningsen and Stein (1997), one of the dimensions being looked at is the cognitive demand of the tasks. They refer this to the kind of thinking processes involved in doing the tasks as assumed by the teacher and the thinking processes used by the students. These thinking processes could be classified as knowing facts, procedures and concepts; applying knowledge and conceptual understanding; and reasoning (Mullis, Martin & Foy, 2005). The cognitive demand of the tasks is also one area of interest to look into, especially its workability in a large class.

Geometric Proofs

Geometry is one of the important topics in mathematics secondary curriculum. The main reason is the richness of concepts it comprises (Burger & Culpepper, 1993). So it is not surprising that research on geometry instructions is a popular area of investigation. Some of these research results provided useful ideas and have been applied in the classrooms, such as the study on geometric reasoning based on van Hieles theory (Crowly, 1987; Senk, 1989). In the Philippines, the studies of Asuncion (1981) and Campita (1981) may have contributed ideas on how teaching of geometry may be improved. They revealed that the teachers perceived doing geometric proofs as difficult to teach and that majority of the students were not prepared for this subject. And indeed, much of the learning of geometric concepts has been rote (Clements & Battista, 1992). But up until recently, it is apparent that it has remained so (Herbst, 2002; Knipping, 2004). The Philippines is not spared, as the results of TIMSS, Regionwide Assessment in Mathematics, Science and English (RAMSE) and yearly achievement tests revealed their low performance in Mathematics, in particular when it involved reasoning, an important aspect on geometric proofs (Basic Education Assistance for Mindanao [BEAM], 2004-2007; Mullis et al., 2005; National Statistics Coordination Board [NSCB], 2007). The findings of Burger and Culpepper (1993) could partly explain why this is so. They mentioned that many students find the conceptual and problem-solving aspects of geometry stimulating and useful, but the formal study on mathematical structure is mysterious and frustrating and that, only those students possessing abstract thinking skills were most likely to succeed in doing proofs. Yet, regardless of students' varied thinking skills there is still the expectation that all students do geometric proofs.

In the Principles and Standards of School Mathematics document of the United States of America, it is expected that the instructional programs from Kindergarten to Year 12 should enable all students to develop and evaluate mathematical arguments and proofs and also to select and use various types of reasoning and methods of proofs (NCTM, 2000). They elaborated that students should be able to produce logical arguments and present formal proofs that effectively explain their reasoning, whether in paragraph, two-column, or some other form of proof. In the Philippines, there is no doubt that this is also an expectation for students. For example, in the Philippine Secondary School Learning Competencies (PSSLC) document for Year 8 students, for the on topic triangle congruence, one of the competencies listed is for students to demonstrate the ability to analyse, verify and prove theorems and properties (Department of Education [DepED], 1998). This appears to have been retained in the proposed mathematics curriculum (Philippine Council of Mathematics Teacher Educators [MathTEd], 2007); emphasis is still placed upon constructing proofs. This latest document states that Year 8 students are expected to use geometric proofs to develop higher order thinking skills. Moreover, a suggestion was that formal proofs including conditional/bi-conditional statements, logic, using postulates, proving theorems and corollaries be introduced in Grade 6 and be reviewed, reinforced and enriched in Grade 7 and Grade 8 so that by Grade 9 and beyond students have acquired mastery of proofs. It can be said then that despite the problems encountered by students in the development of proof, it remains a part of the geometry curriculum and may be introduced in the lower year levels. Hence, it is still important to have a closer look, this time with the aid of technology to assist in analysing the data, at how students tackle geometric proofs by themselves.

Doing Group Tasks

Several research studies about group work had been conducted and usually have positive impact on the classroom climate. Davidson (1990) reviewed research reports in this area and found that the results were mainly positive. The studies of Ferido (1999), Leiken and Zaslavsky (1997) and Webb (1991) that focused on analysing students' interactions and collaborations during group work also affirmed the significance of students' achievement. In a geometry class, Walmsley and Muniz (2003) found that cooperative learning has many positive effects in the mathematics classroom, if it is properly implemented. These included enjoyment and improving mathematical abilities of students.

In the Philippines, providing group tasks to students has been encouraged for quite some time. Findings though have shown that attempts to use group work in the classrooms have mainly resulted in superficial outcomes (Pascua, 1993). Thus, in an effort to address the needs of teachers conducting group tasks, the Philippines-Australia Science and Mathematics Education Project (PASMEP) developed teacher resource books to provide teachers with resource materials that included a chapter on cooperative learning (PASMEP, 1992; PASMEP, 1993). The writing team, composed of teachers themselves, was aware of the issues in the classrooms and so suggestions on how to organise group tasks in a large class size and with limited resources, as well as samples of group mathematical tasks, were included. In addition, continuous encouragement to conduct mathematical tasks in groups was seen in documents such as the Philippines Secondary School Learning Competencies (DepED, 1998) and the Science and Mathematics Educational

Manpower Project (National Institute for Science and Mathematics Education Development [NISMED], 1998) sourcebooks. The SMEMDP sourcebooks provided samples of teaching plans that integrated the use of group tasks. Also, in the PSSLC, it was mentioned that students should manifest the personal characteristics of curiosity, self-expression, self-criticism and cooperative work with others.

In the study of Cuevas (1990), he suggested small group discussions should enable students to hold discussions in their native language. Since the Philippine population speaks different languages, with Filipino as the national language and mathematics taught in English, it could be important to find out how students negotiate by themselves in doing geometric proofs in the classroom. With large class size and limited resources in most public schools, it would be interesting to see how it is done in such a situation and could assist teachers in promoting learning in this area in the future.

Adidactical Situations

Part of the discussions of Brousseau (1997) on didactical situations in mathematics concerns adidactical situations. He described this as the situation

> between the moment the student accepts the problem as if it were her own and the moment she produces her answer, the teacher refrains from interfering and suggesting the knowledge that she wants to see appear. (p. 30)

This would partly explain why he described teaching as the delegation to the student of an adidactical, appropriate situation and that learning is the student's adaptation to this situation. These situations should really require students to be doing mathematics, which he meant that students should really be dealing with unfamiliar situations. He elaborated that one would be doing mathematics only if one is dealing with problems. He also mentioned that doing mathematics is primarily a social activity, and not just an individual one. It is clear here that doing mathematical tasks should really involve interactions, with the teacher or among students hence, group work could be encouraged. It is also apparent here that the teacher is given the responsibility in providing students the appropriate mathematical situations or tasks so that learning will take place. In this case, a teacher could resort to what Brousseau (2006) called didactical engineering. This didactical engineering should produce situations or problems and also experimental designs that could be useful in didactical situations. In some ways this is similar to the lesson study in Japan where a group of teachers are actively involved in experimenting with ways of improving the teaching and learning of mathematics (Stigler & Hiebert, 1999). Their outputs are sets of documented researched lessons which other teachers can use as well.

Brousseau (1997) also mentioned that there are three types of adidactical situations: the action pattern, communication pattern and explicit validation pattern. Based on the descriptions of each type, it is apparent that the aim of every teacher should be the attainment of a pattern of explicit validation where students are interacting with each other in the form of exchanging judgements through assertions and proofs, not just actions and not without discussions. Again, equipping students for doing proofs is undoubtedly given importance here. In Brousseau's terms, this is the attitude of proof, where a student has the skills on using mathematics to provide a reason for accepting or rejecting a proposition, strategy or model. He added that this attitude of proof is not innate; it is developed and sustained by particular didactical situations. So he suggested that proofs should be done collaboratively and be written for easy comparison to other written proofs of the same situation. And unquestionably, when students have developed this attitude of proof, doing proofs should not require much effort; it is a habit of the mind.

The class considered in this study appeared to have been provided with adidactical situations. It was thus worthwhile to investigate what really went on while the students were in these situations. With the aid of technology, data difficult to gather in the past, such as conversations, has been captured in this study. Hence, an in-depth look into what went on, particularly in their conversations to arrive at the geometric proofs, can be examined. Results of this study would provide ideas on designing adidactical situations so that time spent on mathematical tasks, especially on geometric proofs could be optimised. In addition, since it is rare to have studies on large class sizes, particularly those with an average of sixty students, results of this investigation could be a revelation to some and beneficial to others; especially those handling large classes.

SOME RESULTS

This study shows that doing mathematical tasks in groups is one of the practices of this class. Eight of the ten video-taped lessons included this practice. The only times they did not do this was when they had a test and when they had a whole class activity on filling in the cells for some mathematical terms. Of the eight group tasks, four involved proving propositions on triangles and quadrilaterals while the remaining ones were exercises on measures of lengths and angles in a given triangle. These group tasks generally occurred at the practice and consolidation stage, and once on introducing the new lesson. It was also found that on average about 19% of the class time was allotted to group tasks. With sixty minutes of the class time, this meant almost twelve minutes was spent on group tasks. On the next page is a graph summarising the time spent on group tasks on proofs and non-proofs. The time spent on group tasks are subdivided into organising the group to do the tasks, the group engaging in mathematical work and when the group are off-task.

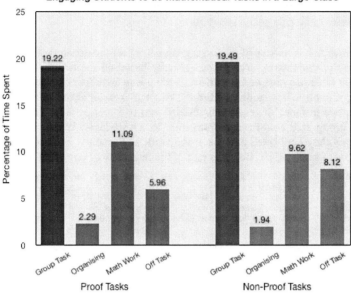

Figure 1. Summary of time spent on group tasks

From Figure 1 it is evident that whether the group is doing a proof or non-proof task, about one-fifth of the class time was spent on these group tasks, with most part of the time students doing the tasks. It is worth noting too that the time spent on off task is higher when the students were doing non-proof tasks. Hence, it would be worthwhile to discuss in more details these two areas:

What do students in a large class do when they are supposed to be engaged in group tasks?

What do these mathematical tasks demand from the students, especially if these tasks involve geometric proofs?

From here, it would be probable to see if the time allotted was appropriate, what students have really been doing and if indeed these tasks demand students to think and work collaboratively. Thus, a more in-depth analysis was made, and the discussions that follow describe some of the results.

What Students Do When Given Group Tasks

It was apparent that the students have established practices and these were noticeable once they were provided opportunities to do group tasks. These practices appeared to have resulted from teacher's instructions or the students

69

themselves have developed these practices. What follows then are the detailed discussions elaborating these noticeable practices when students were given the opportunities to be engaged in group tasks.

Interact with few members of the large group.   In all the group tasks, the teacher organised the students in large groups, usually based on the table where they sat. Since each table has nine or ten students, each group is about this size and at times may even double when students from the two tables were asked to merge as one group. In one instance the class was divided into two groups only. Thus, it can be said the group size could range from nine to 29 students. When students were interviewed they confirmed that the group work is a practice in class and that the group size is usually large. Below is part of the interview of one of the students:

```
Researcher:   Gaano kalaki talaga ang group nyo? (How large really
              is your group?)
Ram:          Ma'am, gaano? (Ma'am, how?)
Researcher:   Gaano kadami kaya? (How many are there?)
Ram:          Mga nine or ten. (About nine or ten.)
```

Key to symbols used in transcripts in this chapter
...   A pause of one second or less
(*text*)   English translations of colloquial language
[text]   Comments and annotations, often descriptions of non-verbal action

Once the task has been set and the materials provided, each group starts to answer the question. It was noticed though that there were no preliminary interactions on how to go about the tasks, despite encouragement from the teacher as captured in one of his statements right after the group task was set: "Huwag kayong sulat ng sulat dahil wala na kayong masusulatan. You should think, isipin. Mag isip muna kayo. (*Don't keep on writing for you'll end up no space to write. You should think, think. Think first.*)". But what was apparent then was that someone acted as a leader and one or two other students tried to contribute in providing answers. This was what happened in Lesson 15 when the group was supposed to prove that the given quadrilateral is a parallelogram. The problem is given in Figure 2.

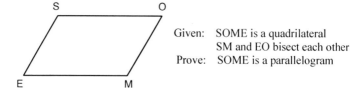

Given: SOME is a quadrilateral
         SM and EO bisect each other
Prove: SOME is a parallelogram

Figure 2. A task in Lesson 15

The conversations of the group went on like this:

```
35:06 Ram:    Ano (What), SOME is a quadrilateral.
```

```
35:12 Ail:      Taasan mo (A bit higher). SOME is a quadrilateral.
35:18 Ail:      Uy, ano ka ba!  Mali 'to!  (Hey, what's the matter!
                This is wrong!)
35:20 Mich      Sorry!
35:21 Teacher:  Uhm. Yung given na yon almost pareho lang dun sa isa,
                di ba?  Yung binigay ko.  Yung two pairs of opposite
                sides congruent.  (Uhm [an expression].  That given one,
                it's almost the same as the other one, right?  The one
                I gave. That two pairs of opposite sides congruent.)
35:36 Ail:      SM.  And EO.  Bisect each other.  Bisect.
35:55 Ail:      Given, given lang naman yan eh. (Given, it's just
                given)
35:21 Mich:     Lagay mo na lang given. (Just write given)
36:01 Ail:      Dapat ito dito. (This one needs to be here) [then said
                something inaudible]
36:45 Mich:     [Scans her notes; shows to Ail]
36:51 Ail:      [Nods] Eh angle yung atin eh.  Tingnan mo. (Well ours
                is on angle. You see.)
```

As noted in this transcript, the interaction is only between the three students. Viewing the remaining portion of the video on this particular group task revealed that this was indeed what happened all throughout, with Mark joining in. Mich attempted to lead the group but again in the later part of the task the ideas came mainly from Ram and Mark. The group is composed of around twenty-seven students and thus only about 15% of the group members were actively participating. The remaining members appeared to be just observing while others had their attention elsewhere.

It was also clear in the above transcript that there was interaction between students and the teacher while group task was going on. Here, the teacher appeared to have them recall what was discussed previously and hence provided a scaffold and encouraged students to proceed with the tasks. In other lessons, it was found that it was a practice of the teacher to move around, at times discussing with the groups.

Indeed, in most lessons only a few members were participating. The students themselves in the interviews confirmed this. Some students even appeared to be doing dual roles while the majority were doing nothing, as documented in this video-stimulated interview:

```
Researcher:     Pag nag gu-group work na makikita dyan ikaw ang
                nagsusulat…Ah, ano talaga ang ginagawa mo pag nag gu-
                group work kayo? (When it's already group work it's
                shown there that you're the one writing… Ah, what are
                you really doing during group work)
Mar:            Wala po, yung parang nag-iisip po yung kung ano po
                yung dapat gawin kung… ako rin po yung nagsusulat eh.
                (Nothing, thinking what is supposed to do… I'm also
                the one writing, see?)
Researcher:     Ikaw ang nag-iisip ikaw pa ang nagsusulat? (You're the
                one thinking and still the one writing?)
Mar:            Kasi po yung iba eh ayaw mag-participate. (Because
                others wouldn't like to participate.)
Researcher:     O, sino sa inyo dyan ang nagpa-participate? (Who among
                you there are participating?)
Mar:            Ma'am, kami pong apat. (Ma'am, the four of us.)
```

Again with so many members in every group, it is clear that only a few were participating. Also, the one acting as group leader always provides the solutions to the problems. Sher, when asked who thinks of the solution when they do group work, her immediate response was, "lagi pong leader" (*always the leader*). Evidently, as shown on video, at most times the same students acted as the leader and that these were the same students who were involved in producing the group's outputs.

Despite most students not participating in group tasks, it appeared to be preferred by them over individual work. Students' interviews revealed that doing tasks in groups has indeed encouraged them to interact with their classmates. In Ram's response to the question on what should happen for the lesson to be considered to a good lesson, his reply was: "pag may group activity, dapat po nakikipagtulungan" (*when there is group activity; there's a need to collaborate*). Mar has a similar reply when asked which part of the lesson is important to him and why. He said: "dahil po yung, sama-sama ho kami tapos, yung, parang teamwork po yung ginagawa po namin kaya po maganda" (*because that, we're together then, that, we did like a teamwork, that's why it was good.*). Even Angie who was not actively participating in group tasks surprisingly appeared to value it as well for when asked which part of the lesson is important to her, she replied: Yung nag gru-group work po kami (*When we're doing group work*).

Furthermore, there were members in the group that were found to have the capability to supplement the teacher's discussions. Sher is one of them for she was captured talking to her seatmates, imitating the expository style of the teacher. Apparently, she is aware of this for in the interview about her personal goal for every mathematics lessons she said:

```
Sher          Sana po na, nakatatak na sa isip ko yung ano yung-yung
              pinag-aralan po namin kanina para halimbawa po may
              magtanong sa akin, at tama po ako, at least tama po
              yung naibigay na impormasyon kaysa po dun sa mali,
              nakakahiya… kasi ako din po yung leader, inaasahan po
              dapat po mas matutunan ko yon dahil sa 'kin po sila
              aasa.  Kailangan po maipakita ko po na tama po yon (I
              hope, it stuck into my mind those we studied a while
              ago so that for example, one will ask me, and I'm
              right, at least I gave the right information, rather
              than a wrong one, shameful…You see I'm also the
              leader, they expect that I learned it because they
              rely on me. I should be able to show the right one.)
```

In a large class size such as in this case, this setup has apparently benefited other students.

Write outputs on manila paper. Every time there is group task, each group is provided with a one piece of manila paper, about 1 m x 1.5 m in size, and a pentel pen. Most of the times the manila paper is bare and the group is supposed to write their outputs on it with letter size large enough to read when posted at the front. At times, the problem is already written on this paper but a space where the answers would be written is provided. This appeared to have facilitated the presentation of the group's output. As Brousseau (1997) had suggested, proofs should be written and presented so as those students doing the same problem can compare their answers. In this aspect, this practice of the class to write their answers on a manila paper appeared to be commendable. In addition, the teacher collected these manila papers because they could be useful later to reflect on the students' outputs, although this area was not pursued in the interviews.

Use mixed language   The group tasks were expected to generate discussions among members of the group. It was captured on video that the students used a mix of the English and the Filipino language, as the above transcripts attest. When they provided answers to the tasks, they mainly used the English language, this language being required by the Department of Education as the medium of instruction in mathematics. Otherwise, they used the Filipino language and code-switched it with the English language.

To recap on what students do when given group tasks, it is apparent that in a large class as this, engaging students to do mathematical tasks in groups has its benefits and concerns. It was clear that students liked to do group tasks for they were free to talk using their preferred language and able to show their outputs to the whole class. However, it was obvious that the majority of the students did not actively participate so it is questionable as to how these students benefited from the allotted time for group tasks, which was found to have consumed about one-fifth of the class time.

The Mathematical Tasks

All the mathematical tasks that were done in groups were investigated by the researcher to find commonalities between them. Some ideas such as their purpose, nature and the qualities of outputs are discussed in the sections that follow.

Purpose/role of the tasks   Collected copies of daily lesson plans revealed that providing practice exercises is always a part of the planned lessons. And everytime this part of the lesson plan is implemented, the teacher required the students to do it in groups. Hence, it can be said that these mathematical tasks were mainly intended for practice and consolidation of the lessons. On the next page is a sample of practice exercises taken from the Lesson 6 plan.

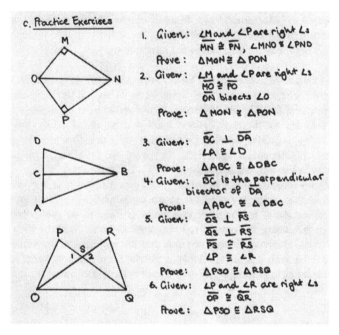

c. Practice Exercises

1. Given: $\angle M$ and $\angle P$ are right $\angle$s
$\overline{MN} \cong \overline{PN}$, $\angle MNO \cong \angle PNO$
Prove: $\triangle MON \cong \triangle PON$

2. Given: $\angle M$ and $\angle P$ are right $\angle$s
$\overline{MO} \cong \overline{PO}$
$\overline{ON}$ bisects $\angle O$
Prove: $\triangle MON \cong \triangle PON$

3. Given: $\overline{BC} \perp \overline{DA}$
$\angle A \cong \angle D$
Prove: $\triangle ABC \cong \triangle DBC$

4. Given: $\overline{BC}$ is the perpendicular bisector of $\overline{DA}$
Prove: $\triangle ABC \cong \triangle DBC$

5. Given: $\overline{OS} \perp \overline{PS}$
$\overline{QS} \perp \overline{RS}$
$\overline{PS} \cong \overline{RS}$
$\angle P \cong \angle R$
Prove: $\triangle PSO \cong \triangle RSQ$

6. Given: $\angle P$ and $\angle R$ are right $\angle$s
$\overline{OP} \cong \overline{QR}$
Prove: $\triangle PSO \cong \triangle RSQ$

Figure 3. Intended practice exercises in groups

In this particular practice exercise, the class was divided into six groups, each of them was assigned to work on a different item. This was quite different from the usual way for more often than not at least two groups were to work on the same item independently.

Of the eight lessons where group tasks were provided for practice, there were four that required the group to provide geometric proofs involving triangle congruence and properties of quadrilaterals (Lessons 6-8 and 15) while the other four were exercises on measures of angles and sides in quadrilaterals (Lessons 10-12 and 14). These tasks required students to apply what they learned from the lesson presentation, which were mainly through teacher exposition. In addition, despite not being mentioned by the teacher, these tasks were meant to encourage students to interact by their very nature of being a group activity.

There was one lesson though where students were given the task that was not meant as a practice exercise. This was in Lesson 8 where students were asked to work in groups at the beginning of the lesson to introduce the topic on relationships in triangles involving altitudes and medians. The class was asked to draw any triangle. Then half of them were asked to join the vertex to the midpoint of the opposite sides, while the remaining half were asked to draw a perpendicular by joining the vertex to the opposite side. The teacher, as shown in the following transcript, facilitated the processing of answers:

```
14:18 Teacher:  Okay, here…Triangle DMN.  How many [line] segments,
                ah, can you draw from the, ah, from the given
                triangle?  Oh, from the given triangle?
14:37 Teacher:  Yes, ah, Sher.
14:14 Sher:     Three.
14:40 Teacher:  There are three.  Okay?  Now, ahhh, in how many
                points, these three segments intersect?  In how many
                points?  Ariel.
14:54 Ariel     In one point.
14:55 Teacher:  At one point.  Now, this segment, [traces the
                segments] with which is the segment drawn from the
                vertex to the midpoint of the opposite ray [side] is
                called, ah, oh what do you call the segment drawn from
                the, ah, vertex to the opposite, oh from the midpoint
                to the opposite side?  Ah, Kay.
15:28 Kay:      Median.
15:29 Teacher:  That is what you call as median [writes]. Now the
                median of a triangle, remember the median of a
                triangle is the segment from the vertex to the
                midpoint of the opposite side.  Now what about this
                triangle? How many segment can you draw perpendicular
                to the opposite side?
```

It was apparent from the teacher's questions that this activity was meant to let the students see the number of points of intersections of medians in a triangle and also to let them recall what median is. The discussion of altitudes proceeded in the same manner. Since the discussion on the point of intersection was not pursued any further, it was obvious that the purpose of this activity is for students to recall medians and altitudes in preparation for discussions on formulating proofs involving medians and altitudes of triangles, which was the lesson for the day.

Nature of the tasks   The usual practice was to have two or three groups doing exactly the same task. The remaining groups would have a similar task, only the question but the illustration and some of the given information remained the same. Nevertheless, these tasks can generally be described as mostly exercises that are quite different from the given examples. Figure 4 at the next page are the two items taken from Lesson 8 where teacher discussed their solutions before a group task was given.

Item 1.

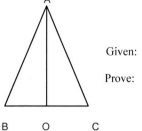

Given: Isosceles triangle with $\overline{AO}$ as
         the median
Prove: ΔBAO ≅ ΔCAO

Item 2.

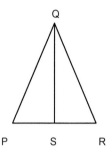

Given: Isosceles triangle, QS the bisector of ∠Q
Prove: $\overline{QS}$ is the altitude

Figure 4. Example items

At a glance, these two items, which were used during the teacher exposition, appeared to be similar to what was given to the students as their group task as shown in Figure 5 below.

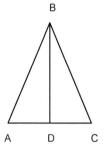

Given: $\overline{AB} \cong \overline{CB}$; $\overline{BD}$ bisects $\overline{AC}$

Prove: $\overline{BD} \perp \overline{AC}$

Figure 5. A task in Lesson 8

The drawing in the two examples and that in this task all looked like isosceles triangles. But when the given information was considered, it was clear that there were differences. In the first example, the task was to establish that line segment AO is a median based on the given corresponding lengths of sides. In the second example, corresponding lengths of sides and angles were given and it was establish that line segment QS is the altitude. But during the practice, the task for this group of students was to establish that $\overline{BD} \perp \overline{AC}$, which is actually establishing that line segment BD is the altitude or the perpendicular bisector. This was different from the second example because what were given there were all about the two congruent sides and congruent angles of the triangle. With this group task, the students arrived at an answer where they used the SSS Congruence to establish that $\overline{BD} \perp \overline{AC}$. Below was their answer:

Table 1. The students' proof for the task in Lesson 8

Statements	Reasons
1. $\overline{AB} \cong \overline{BC}$ $\overline{BD}$ bisects $\overline{AC}$	given
2. $\overline{AD} \cong \overline{DC}$	definition of segment bisector
3. $\overline{BD} \cong \overline{BD}$	reflexive property
4. $\triangle DBA \cong \triangle DBC$	SSS congruence
5. $\overline{BD} \perp \overline{AC}$	the median is a segment from the vertex angle $\perp$ to the base

Somehow this group showed a solution that could be different from the teacher's expected answer. This was implied when the teacher gave a suggested solution that did not happen in other lessons. This was what he said:

Teacher: Okay, now if you will try to analyse, ah…Number 1, you
            don't need to prove that the two triangles are
            congruent. Di ba? Tingnan nyo, kung kung ia-analyse
            lang natin mabuti. Kahit hindi na natin ito i-prove,
            pwede. (*Isn't it? Look here, if we try to analyse
            well. Even if we won't prove this, it can be*).
            [Covers the fourth statement with his stick]. Because
            what we need here is to prove that triangle ABC is
            isosceles. Is that correct?
Students: Yes.
Teacher: Is that correct?
Students: Yes.
Teacher: From this, AB is congruent to BC, so we can say that
            this two, ah, this triangle ABC is isosceles. Okay?
            So, well, anyway, ah, the statement and the reasons
            the proofs are, are correct. Okay, let's have letter
            B. Okay, group two.

From this last statement it was obvious that the teacher accepted the answer as correct. Further discussion regarding the proofs, such as the reason in item 5 was missed out. It could have been emphasised here the importance of establishing first that $\angle ADB$ and $\angle CDB$ are a linear pair and since of equal measures, each would be 90 degrees. And from here it can be claimed that $\overline{BD} \perp \overline{AC}$ or $\overline{BD}$ is a median. One thing that was apparent here is that this task could have multiple solutions. As well, the other given tasks on geometric proofs are also of this nature, only that there was no evidence that indicated encouragement to let students provide multiple solutions. If students had been required to show different ways of arriving at the answer, then this could entail much time and cooperative thought. This would partly explain why in the graph (refer to Figure 1) it was found that much time has been wasted off-task, which was close to a third of the time they were supposed to do group tasks on geometric proofs. Thus, in the section that follows, a more elaborate discussion on how students go about doing geometric proofs on their own is discussed.

Adidactical situations on doing geometric proofs The teacher was found to provide time for students to do tasks on their own, so in this section the discussion will focus on the types of adidactical situations the groups were involved in while doing geometric proofs. It was apparent that the action and communication patterns could be observed. But it appeared arguable to claim that there is an explicit validation pattern as well. As shown in the transcript below, the interactions of the group members when they worked on the task in Lesson 6 was limited to one member providing the answer.

30:38 Teacher: Close that book, exercise tayo ngayon eh. *(Close that book, we'll do an exercise now.)*

30:49 Ram: BC. Mabibilang mo ba yung seven? *(Can seven be counted?)*

30:53 Teacher: Write the given. Come on! Analyse first the given. Mark all the given parts.

31:17 Ram: Given eh. Given yan. ABC, yan. *(It's given. That's given. That's ABC).* ABC is congruent to.

31:25 Teacher: Sabi ko na nga ba sa inyo yan. Yung bisect, bisect na yan. *(I have told you that. That bisect, bisect.)*

31:31 Ram: ABC, parang ganon, o. *(ABC, something like that, see)* Yes. [21 sec] Angle ABC. B! B.

31:57 Mark: Right angle.

32:02 Ram: Angle BCD are right angles. Definition of perpendicular lines.

32:28 Mark: Nawalan ng tinta. *(Run out of ink.)*

32:30 Ram: Uy, bilisan mo! *(Hey, hurry up!)* Perpendicular lines.

32:48 Teacher: US. Where's US?

32:51 Ram: Angle. Angle ADB is congruent to angle A...CB.

32:53 Teacher Perpendicular to BS. So if those segments are perpendicular?

33:00 Kath: They are right angles. Then they form a right angle.

33:10 Ram: All right angles are congruent. Di kasya, number four hanggang seven. Pagkasyahin mo na lang. *(Not enough space, number four to seven. Just adjust to fit these in)*

33:38 Mark: Pagkakasyahin natin yan. *(We'll make these fit in)*

33:44 Ram: The triangles.

33:53 Mark: Of?

34:06 Ram: Are right angles, are right triangles. Right triangles. Oo *(yes)* right triangles. BC is congruent to AC. Segment AC. [21 sec] DC is congruent to AC. Definition, definition of. [3 sec] Definition of segment bisector.

35:01 Mark: Anong sunod? *(What's next?)*

35:08 Ram: Bale, CB is congruent to AD. Tama, Mark? *(Like, CB is congruent to AD. Right, Mark?)* [7 sec] Definition of segment, ah, reflexive property [3 sec] Lagyan mo 'to Mark, oh, ng ano. *(Write this there, Mark, oh, the what)* LL Congruence. Triagnle ABC. Kabit na! *(Post it!)*

In this transcript it was obvious indeed that not much discussion took place to arrive at the proof. There were only two out of the ten students in this group who did the task for only about five minutes, one providing the answer and the other writing what has been said. Hence, an action pattern is apparent here because no discussion took place to arrive at the answers. It was obvious that the ideas came mainly from Ram and that Mark was just writing these ideas on the manila paper. There was an attempt to start exchanging messages like when Ram asked "CB is congruent to AD. Right, Mark?" But there was no reply from Mark and so it was clear that in this task the action pattern dominates.

In Lesson 15, it was quite a different case (refer to Figure 2 and the accompanying transcript). Here, a few members of the group were exchanging messages. There were agreements and disagreements. However, going through the remaining transcripts it was noticeable that the exchange of messages was limited and so not enough to claim that there was an explicit validation pattern. Even when there was an instance for them to settle the confusion over the mathematical statement made, the exchange of ideas was inadequate to enable them to resolve this on their own. The transcript below would support this statement.

```
41:09 Mark:      SE congruent to OM.
41:11 Ail:       SE is congruent to OM [writes].  By what reason?
41:20 Mark:      Parallel lines are congruent.  Parallel ba? (Is it
                 parallel?)
41:25 Ail:       Sigurado ka? (Are you sure?) [Then writes]
41:30 Teacher:   All of you should draw SM, tama ba? [draws segment
                 SM]. Ginawa nyo ba yon? (All of you should draw SM,
                 right? Did you do it?)
41:37 Students:  Opo. (Yes)
41:38 Teacher:   Oh! [Teacher approaches this group]
41:42 Mark:      Ano, ang, ano! (What, the what!) Parallel.
41:52 Teacher:   Mark, may I see your work.
42:01 Ail:       SE…is congruent to OM.  Parallel.
42:01 Teacher:   Parallel?  Hindi ganyan yan ha (It's not like that,
                 okay).  SE, is parallel to, OM.  Parallel hindi
                 congruent, shhh! (Parallel not congruent, shhh!)
                 [This group made the correction]
```

It is clear here that Mark was also unsure of the mathematical reason he provided. But rather than getting agreements or disagreements from the group, another member, Ail just threw back the question asking him if he was sure. Even without the answer from Mark, Ail appeared to accept the wrong statement for she started to write this on their answer sheet. However, this statement was corrected when the teacher intervened, a behavior being discouraged in adidactical situations.

In all the geometric proofs tasks, it was found that there was neither initial discussion on how to go about arriving at the proofs nor much exchange of judgements while they were working on the proofs. To investigate further the interactions that went on among themselves, the part of the lesson where they were supposed to present the group's outputs to the whole class is also discussed here. The purpose was to see if there was a better exchange of ideas during this part of the lesson. Shown below is a Lesson 6 output of the group that was written on the manila paper and posted on the board. Figure 6 was the problem for this lesson.

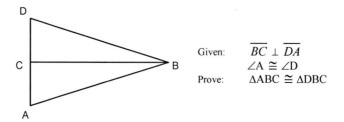

Given: $\overline{BC} \perp \overline{DA}$
∠A ≅ ∠D
Prove: △ABC ≅ △DBC

Figure 6. The assigned problem for the group

The table below shows their solution to the above problem.

Table 2. The geometric proof of the group to the given problem

Statements	Reasons
1. $\overline{AD} \perp \overline{BC}$	given
2. ∠DCB and ∠ACB are right angles	definition of ⊥ lines
3. ∠DCB ≅ ∠ACB	right angles are congruent
4. △DCB and △ACB are right triangles	definition of right triangles
5. $\overline{DC} ≅ \overline{AC}$	definition of line segment bisector
6. $\overline{AC} ≅ \overline{AC}$	reflexive property
7. △ABC ≅ △DBC	LL congruence

As shown, the proof was clearly laid in a two-column format and every statement made has its corresponding reason. When it was the turn of this group to explain their solution to the whole class, it was Mark who came in front and started to 'explain' their solution. But based on the transcript, he mainly read what was written on the manila paper, no elaborations made and so it took him about a minute to do it. No comments or questions about the solution were raised by anyone or suggestions for another way of arriving at the proof. The teacher just said "Okay. That is LL congruence. Next group." This appeared to signal an accepted answer. It was apparent that the class missed out to analyse the proof that was presented. A clarification to the proof in item 5 appeared to be needed for it was given that $\overline{BC}$ is perpendicular to $\overline{DA}$, but no mention that it is a line bisector as well. Although it could be established that it is indeed a bisector, based on the given information, the figure can be claimed as an isosceles triangle, or the corollary to the perpendicular bisector theorem could be used to support the claim. As revealed, this could have been a very good opportunity for students to really do mathematics by exchanging judgements through assertions and theorems, or opportunity for the teacher to clarify students' misconceptions. But these opportunities did not occur in the presentation and processing of this output.

The episode above was typical of what had happened in the other presentations of the group's outputs on geometric proofs. No arguments, clarifications and elaborations were made. Again, the action pattern dominated the presentations. Moreover, it was apparent that the purpose of these presentations was to exchange information and not on the exchange of judgements. It could be argued though that some students may have the skills and are not intimidated to exchange arguments with the class and could even suggest corrections to the teacher's work. This happened in Lesson 14, a student was captured arguing with the teacher and his classmates regarding the answer to their group's output, as presented to the whole class. But then this particular lesson this was not on geometric proofs. So it is can be said that students may not be at ease to exchange judgements when the topic is on geometric proofs.

It was clear that the teacher attempted to provide students with adidactical situations, an effort to engage students to do mathematical tasks in a large class especially during the practice and consolidation parts of the lessons. However, it was found that exchange of information dominated rather than exchange of judgements, probably due to the nature of tasks, which were mainly exercises, hence students finished these tasks earlier than expected.

Summary

In summary, this class appeared to have established some practices while engaging on mathematical tasks. They usually worked in large groups, although very few participated in the discussions. When they do the tasks they used mixed language to converse: Filipino and English. These tasks were usually allotted one-fifth of their class times, but not all this time was spent doing the tasks for there were off-task times recorded. Whether or not there was time wasted depended partly on the nature of the tasks. Tasks that required a definite answer and not multiple solutions, appeared to need less time.

When the tasks were on geometric proofs, some practices were also noticed while the students were doing these on their own. They did two-column proofs by making statements and its corresponding reasons in sequence. This was supplied by one or a few members of the group, with no initial discussions to generate ideas on how to proceed to making proofs. Hence, the action pattern dominated and to some degree there was a communication pattern. Outputs were written on a manila paper then posted on the board, after which a member of the group read what was written on the manila paper, then the teacher would comment, mainly to confirm that it was an accepted answer. Evidence on students asking questions and clarifications or discussions on other ways of solving the problem were not observed. It is also apparent that the adidactical situations here on geometric proofs involved less participation from most students and that the opportunity for them to develop new ideas and skills through group discussions for exchange of judgements rarely happened.

WHAT IDEAS CAN BE DERIVED FROM HERE?

Reflecting on these results could generate some ideas for those involved in the improvement of teaching and learning of mathematics, especially on geometric proofs. Also, these results could provide insights for teachers handling large classes where addressing every student's needs appears impractical. The discussions that follow summarise some findings and its corresponding implications.

About one-fifth of the class time was allotted to group work, the demand of the tasks appeared to require less time and not much collaboration and interaction. Nevertheless, students' preference to do the tasks in groups was documented and there were some students who were able to support teacher's discussions. In a large class as this, engaging all students to participate in doing mathematical tasks appeared to require further investigations. Probably, reducing the group size could be an aspect to look into, although this may mean a need for more resources. In a country where resources are limited, providing more materials such as manila paper and pentel pens could be a concern. Hence, a well-planned group task could be taken into consideration where every student's participation is maximised. These tasks could demand from them not only an exchange of information but also an exchange of judgements, thus enhancing their reasoning, problem solving and communication skills. This would imply the upgrading of teacher's skills on conducting group tasks that are appropriate for a large class and taking into consideration the time allotment as well.

Tasks that were given to students were mainly intended for practice and consolidation. These tasks, usually one item per group, appeared to be short exercises. There was no apparent encouragement for students to do the tasks in more than one method. This is opposed to what is being encouraged by NCTM (2000) for it was mentioned that tasks should be designed in a way that students are able to show more than one method of arriving at the answer. In this way, it could engage and challenge students to do mathematics and the results could be a good basis for discussing important mathematical ideas. Since in this study there was no apparent encouragement for students to do the tasks in more than one method, it was not surprising that the tasks required less collaborative thinking and hence most often they finished these in a shorter time. This appeared to be the true in other mathematics classes in the country for in the study of Bernardo, Prudente and Limjap (2005) they mentioned that questions the teachers used were not the kind that would have made the students think, and that these teachers may have an appreciation and some understanding of mathematical tasks that require students to think, but failed to practise and realise the approach in an effective way. This appeared to imply that the teachers were indeed at the stage of attempting to make changes in the mathematics classrooms to engage students to do more thinking. It is apparent that teachers could encourage more active participation from the students by providing more thought-provoking tasks.

Students did geometric proofs in sequence with no initial discussions on how to go about it. They wrote the proofs that were available to be viewed by the whole class, which Brousseau (1997) encouraged for easier discussions of answers. With this, it was easier to notice the gaps in the solutions. However, the teacher and students missed out on discussing these gaps. This tells us that both the students and the teacher have difficulty doing geometric proofs or, it could be that making justifications is not highly valued. What the teacher admitted though during the interview was just on the difficulty of teaching this topic for he said "ang hirap magturo ng proving" (it's difficult to teach proving). Although there was no probing question in that interview that would elaborate his statement, it was apparent that enhancement of the teacher's skills on teaching proof is implied here. There could be a need for the teacher to show to the students a way of proving/thinking where the process of arriving at the proof could be clearly modelled. Henningsen and Stein (1997) mentioned this modelling of high-level performance by the teacher as one of the factors of sustaining engagement of students to do the tasks.

In adidactical situations on geometric proofs, it was only the action and communication patterns that were noticed. There was no explicit validation pattern observed and that students tend to interact in smaller groups, leaving the other members doing nothing. This would imply a smaller group size would be beneficial, hence increasing the number of groups. In a large class, this would mean the teacher would be dealing with more groups to monitor their work and a need for more materials or other resources. Also, since their interactions were limited to exchange of information and not exchange of judgement, which should be desired being the nature of doing geometric proofs, a need to re-design the way geometric proofs is taught and learnt is in order. An aim to develop among students the attitude of proofs could be given importance. As mentioned by Brousseau (2006), doing proof is not innate but is developed and sustained by particular didactical situations. Again, a need to enhance teacher's competency in designing worthwhile mathematical tasks in a large class, especially on tasks that focus on problem solving, reasoning and communication skills, which are important skills in doing proofs is implied here.

In all these results, it is obvious that students preferred to be engaged in doing mathematical tasks in a large class. However, the number of students actively engaged in the tasks was only a few and the majority remains idle. Henningsen and Stein (1997) mentioned some of the factors that inhibit students to participate, but it was not related necessarily to doing geometric proofs. It would be an area to pursue for further studies on what really inhibits most students to be engaged in doing group tasks on proofs. Also, it would be good to look into the needs of teachers to address the needs of students, especially on their problem solving, reasoning and communication skills with considerations on situations like large class size and limited resources. Moreover, it could be worth considering the idea of Brousseau (2006) on didactical engineering. Here, teachers should be involved in a sort of didactical play to produce not just situations or problems or even curricula for entire sectors of mathematics, but also experimental designs in the teaching of mathematics. Also, teachers could try doing a lesson study (Stigler & Hiebert, 1999). This lesson study appeared to be workable in the Philippine classrooms for a few schools have been doing it (Ulep, 2007). Hence, while the practice at the moment is to do group mathematical tasks that do not demand much collaboration and cooperative thought, the teacher has the power to change this by being involved in other forms of professional development such as the lesson study. They themselves should have much to say about the design and use of worthwhile mathematics tasks in such situations.

At this point, it is arguable to claim that the minimal engagement of students to do mathematical tasks in a mathematics class in the country has to do much with large class size. In some countries that have large class sizes, although they may not be as large as this particular class under study, Pong and Pallas (2005) found that the practices of teachers and the amount of curriculum taught do not differ much as those with smaller class sizes. What was another interesting finding in their study is that Asian countries such as Singapore, Korea and Hong Kong (SAR, China) have relatively large class sizes and performed well in international tests. They found that these Asian countries have a centralised educational system. The Philippines has a similar system yet performed low in international tests (Mullis et al., 2005). So it would be interesting to do further studies in the country on more effective means of engaging students in the learning of mathematics considering constraints such as large class size and limited resources, the latter of which may be unique to the general education system of the country.

Overall, this study showed that in a large class, engaging students to do mathematical tasks has resulted in a few students actively participated in doing the tasks and that there was minimal exchange of mathematical judgements, especially on doing geometric proofs. However, this may not be unique to a large class for it was apparent that it has to do with the selection of tasks, time management and some other factors, and hence has also to do with teachers' preparedness to design and implement mathematical tasks suited to the class, and therefore implying a need for further studies in these areas.

REFERENCES

Asuncion, C. J. (1981). *Factors related to teachers' perceived difficulties in teaching geometry.* Unpublished master's thesis. University of the Philippines, Diliman, Quezon City.

Basic Education Assistance for Mindanao [BEAM] (2007). *Report on the results of the region-wide assessment in Mathematics, Science and English.* Department of Education, Davao City.

Bernardo, A., Prudente, M., & Limjap, A. (2005). *Exploring mathematics and science teaching in the Philippines.* Retrieved August 19, 2008 from:
http://project.jica.go.jp/philippines/0125062C0/english/project/02.html

Brousseau, G. (1997). *Theory of didactical situations in mathematics,* 1970-1990. (N. Balacheff, M. Cooper, R. Sutherland & V. Warfield, Eds. & Trans.) Dordrecht: Kluwer.

Brousseau, G. (2006). Mathematics, didactical engineering and observation. In J. Novotná, H. Moraová, M. Krátká, & N. Stehliková (Eds.), *Proceedings of the 30th Conference of the International Group for the Psychology in Mathematics Education, 30*(1), 3-18.

Burger, W. F., & Culpeper, B. (1993). Restructuring geometry. In P. Wilson (Ed.), *Research ideas for the classroom* (pp. 140-154). New York: Macmillan Publishing Company.

Campita, E. (1981). *Junior high school students' readiness for geometry.* Unpublished master's thesis, University of the Philippines, Diliman, Quezon City.

Carteciano, J. (2005). *NRCP/DOST addresses dire state of S&T education in the regions.* Retrieved February 3, 2009 from: http://www.gov.ph/news/default.asp?i=13481.

Clements, D. H., & Battista, M. T. (1992). Geometry and spatial reasoning. In D. A. Grouws (Ed.), *Handbook of research on mathematics teaching and learning* (pp. 420-464). New York: Macmillan.

Crowly, M. (1987). The van Hiele model of the development of geometric thought. In M. Linquist (Ed.), *Learning and teaching geometry, K-12,* 1987 Yearbook. Reston, VA: National Council of Teachers of Mathematics.

Cuevas, G. (1990). Increasing the achievement and participation of language minority students in mathematics education. In T. J. Cooney & C. R. Hirsch (Eds.), *Teaching and learning mathematics in the 1990s* (pp. 159-165). Reston, VA: National Council of Teachers of Mathematics.

Davidson, N. (1990). Introduction. In N. Davidson (Ed.), *Cooperative learning in mathematics.* Menlo Park, Calif.: Addison-Wesley.

Department of Education (DepED). (1998). *The Philippine secondary school learning competencies.* Pasig City: Author.

Department of Education (DepED). (2002). *Operations handbook in mathematics: 2002 basic education curriculum in the secondary level.* Pasig City: Author.

Ferido, M. B. (1999). Conceptual change in a cooperative learning environment. *The Asia-Pacific Education Researcher, 8,* 152-177.

Gordon, R. (2008). *RP needs P5.3 billion to hire 39,000 public school teachers.* Retrieved February 3, 2009 from http://www.senate.gove.ph/press_release/2008/1004_gordon1.asp

Henningsen, M. A., & Stein, M. K. (1997). Mathematical tasks and student cognition: Classroom based-factors that support and inhibit high-level mathematical thinking and reasoning. *Journal for Research in Mathematics Education, 28,* 524- 549.

Herbst, P. (2002). Engaging students in proving: A double bind on the teacher. *Journal for Research in Mathematics Education, 33,* 176-203.

Knipping, C. (2004). Challenges in mathematical reasoning and proof. *The International Journal on Mathematics Education, 36,* 127-128.

Leiken, R., & Zaslavsky, O. (1997). Facilitating student interactions in mathematics in a cooperative learning setting. *Journal for Research in Mathematics Education, 28,* 334-354.

Mullis, I. V. S., Martin, M. O., & Foy, P. (2005). IEA's TIMSS *International report on achievement in the mathematics cognitive domains.* Boston: TIMSS and PIRLS International Study Center.

National Council of Teachers of Mathematics [NCTM]. (2000). *Principles and standards for school mathematics,* Reston, VA: Author.

National Institute for Science and Mathematics Education Development [NISMED]. (1996). *A report on the Needs Assessment Survey.* Quezon City: Author.

National Institute for Science and Mathematics Education Development [NISMED]. (1998). *A report on the SMEMDP national training program.* Quezon City: Author.

National Statistics Coordination Board [NSCB]. (2007). *Students' scores in achievement tests deteriorating.* Retrieved February 3, 2009 from http://www.nscb.gov.ph/factsheet/pdf/FS-200705-SS2-01.asp

Pascua L. B. (1993). Secondary mathematics education in the Philippines today. In G. Bell (Ed.), *Asian perspectives on mathematics education* (pp. 160-181). Northern UK: Rivers Mathematical Assocciation, Lismore.

Philippine Council for Mathematics Teacher Educators [MathTEd]. (2007). *The proposed basic mathematics framework.* Quezon City: Author.

Philippines-Australia Science and Mathematics Education Project [PASMEP]. (1992). *Teaching Mathematics III.* Quezon City: Author.

Philippines-Australia Science and Mathematics Education Project [PASMEP]. (1993). *Teaching Mathematics IV.* Quezon City: Author.

Pong, S., & Pallas A. (2001). Class size and eighth-grade math achievement in the United States and abroad. *Educational Evaluation and Policy Analysis, 23,* 251-273.

Senk, L. (1989). Van Hiele levels and achievement in writing geometric proofs. *Journal for Research in Mathematics Education, 20*, 309-321.

Stigler, J. W., & Hiebert, J. (1999). *The teaching gap. Best ideas from the world's teachers for improving education in the classroom.* New York: The Free Press.

Ulep, S. (2007). *Developing mathematical thinking through problem-based lessons.* Progress report of the APEC project: Collaborative studies on innovations for teaching and learning mathematics in different cultures (II) – Lesson study focusing on mathematical thinking. Japan: University of Tsukuba, Center for Research on International Cooperation in Educational Studies.

Walmsley, A., & Muniz, J. (2003). Cooperative learning and its effects in high school geometry classroom. *The Mathematics Teacher, 96*, 265-274.

Webb, N. M. (1991). Task-related verbal interaction and mathematics learning in small groups. *Journal for Research in Mathematics Education, 22*, 366-389.

Florenda Gallos Cronberg
Formerly at the National Institute for Science and Mathematics Education
Development
University of the Philippines-Diliman
The Philippines

YOSHINORI SHIMIZU

CHAPTER FIVE

A Task-Specific Analysis of Explicit Linking in the Lesson Sequences in Three Japanese Mathematics Classrooms

INTRODUCTION

Mathematics textbooks in Japan, which are commercially available from publishing companies, usually include several chapters on different mathematical topics. Each chapter, which typically constitutes a teaching unit, is edited in such a way so that the teachers can use one or two pages within each class period, and spend roughly fifteen to twenty class periods to complete the full chapter. Also, each chapter is divided into several sections that constitute sub-units within the entire unit.

A mathematics lesson in Japan is usually planed and implemented as part of the sequence of several lessons within the teaching unit on a certain mathematical topic. Even when a teacher just follows the textbook page by page, being unaware of the instructional sequence for teaching mathematical topic, she after all follows the sequence in the teaching unit. Each lesson in a unit has a different purpose in order for attaining the goals of the entire unit. The lesson at the introductory phase of the entire unit, for example, may look like more problem-solving oriented, whereas the lesson at the final phase of the unit may have an emphasis on practising what the students have learned. The roles of mathematical tasks posed in classrooms in the sequence of lessons, thus, differ at least from the teacher's perspective.

In the classroom, teachers want students to understand mathematical ideas by explicitly mentioning the connections among ideas and students' experiences. For this purpose, each mathematical task in the classroom needs to be connected with another task in certain ways. It should be noted that both the entire unit and sub-units constitute a coherent body in terms of mathematical ideas and that teacher try to connect a series of problems posed in the sequence of lessons. This means that we cannot ignore the place of each lesson in the unit as well as the relationship between lessons, when we explore the role of mathematical tasks in classrooms.

The research design in the Learner's Perspective Study (LPS) includes collecting data of a sequence of at least ten consecutive lessons followed by video-stimulated recall interviews with the teacher and students on the same day of implementation of the lesson (Clarke, 2006). A significant distinguishing

Y. Shimizu, B. Kaur, R. Huang and D. J. Clarke (Eds.), Mathematical Tasks in Classrooms around the World, pp. 87–101.

characteristic of the study is its documentation of the teaching of sequences of lessons, rather than just a collection of single lessons. This research design provides researchers with the opportunity to explore a 'larger picture' of the structure of lessons in which each lesson is embedded.

The research reported in this chapter examines the contexts in which mathematical tasks are posed in classrooms through the analysis of the videotaped sequence of ten consecutive lessons in each of the three Japanese eighth grade classrooms that participated in the Learner's Perspective Study (LPS). Particular attention is given to explicit linking within a single lesson and across multiple lessons. As is discussed below we define explicit linking as an utterance by the teacher (or students) that refers to ideas or experiences that have appeared in other lessons or in the part of the same lesson.

EXPLICIT LINKING IN MATHEMATICS CLASSROOMS

One of the goals of LPS is to complement the findings of other international studies such as Third International Mathematics and Science video Studies (TIMSS) (Hiebert et al., 2003; Stigler, Gonzales, Kawanaka, Knoll, & Serrano, 1999), among others, of classroom practices in mathematics. The goal seems to be attained, in particular, when we re-examine the findings from the TIMSS Video Study, which analysed the videotapes from a collection of single lessons, by analysing the data from LPS, which documented the teaching of a lesson sequence in the same classroom.

In the TIMSS 1995 Video Study, explicit linking in mathematics lessons in Germany, Japan and the United States was analysed by using sub-sample of 90 lessons out of 231 sample lessons in three countries. Here, explicit linking was defined as a reference by the teacher to ideas or events from another lesson or part of the same lesson:

> We defined linking as an explicit verbal reference by the teacher to ideas and events from another lesson or part of the lesson. The reference had to be concrete (i.e., referring to a particular time, not to some general idea). And, the reference had to be related to the current activity. (Stigler et al., 1999, p. 117)

The ideas and events to which the teacher refers in a lesson can be either mathematical or non-mathematical. Linking can be made among mathematical concepts, skills, or procedures. Also, teachers may start the lesson by recalling or reviewing what was done in the previous lesson by linking to a particular student's experience in the classroom. Explicit linking as defined in the TIMSS 1995 Video Study covers functions of teachers' verbal efforts from both mathematical and pedagogical points of view.

The analysis showed that the highest incidence of linking, both across lessons and within lessons, was found in Japanese lessons. Teachers of Japanese lessons linked across lessons significantly more than did teachers of German lessons, and linked within lessons significantly more than teachers of both German and U.S

88

lessons (Stigler et al., 1999). The findings suggest that Japanese teachers intentionally link ideas and experiences in lessons so that such links are beneficial to students' learning.

TIMSS 1999 Video Study analysed mathematical processes suggested by problem statements (Hiebert et al., 2003). The mathematical processes used when solving problems appear to shape the kind of learning opportunities for students. The study found that the lessons from Japan contained a larger percentage problems with statements focused on making connections. These problem statements implied the problem would focus on constructing relationships among mathematical ideas, facts, or procedures.

> Although mathematics lessons in all the targeted countries included problem statements that focused on making connections, the lessons from Japan contained a [significantly] larger percentage of these problems (54 percent) than all the other countries except for the Netherlands (24 percent). (p. 98)

It seems natural for the researchers to explore characteristics of Japanese lessons further to examine occurrences of explicit linking both within and across lessons, for any lessons to be coherent the teacher needs to connect or link between students ideas and experiences. Sekiguchi (2006) proposed the framework for analysing coherence in lessons in which connections among lessons made by teachers seems to serve for maintaining coherence across lessons.

Also, examining explicit linking may enable us to understand more about the social processes in the classrooms. For example, the analysis of explicit linking may shed light on the function of the situation of *institutionalisation* (Brousseau, 1997) which reveals itself by the passage of a piece of knowledge from its role as a means of resolving a situation of action, formulation or proof to a new role, that of reference for future personal or collective uses.

The research reported in this chapter examines the contexts in which mathematical tasks are posed in the classrooms by analysing the videotaped sequence of ten consecutive lessons in each of three Japanese eighth grade classrooms participated in the Learner's Perspective Study. Particular attention was given to explicit linking within a single lesson and across lessons.

The following research questions were investigated in this chapter: (a) To what extent do the Japanese LPS teachers employ explicit linking in the course of teaching a lesson sequence? (b) What are the impacts of explicit linking on students' learning in terms of the role of mathematical tasks presented in the consecutive lessons?

DATA AND METHODOLOGY

Data Collection

The LPS, a classroom study of videotaped lessons, specified that the collection of data involved videotaping a considerable number of consecutive lessons in each school (Clarke, 2006). The technique for undertaking this research involved the development of complex "integrated data sets" that combined split-screen video records of teacher and students with transcripts of post-lesson interviews and copies of relevant printed or written material. The data of this study includes videotaped classroom data for ten consecutive mathematics lessons and post-lesson video-stimulated interviews with the teacher and students in each of three participating eighth grade classes.

Data collection for the current chapter included videotaping ten consecutive single lessons, each ranging in length from between 40 and 50 minutes, in three public junior high schools in Tokyo. The teachers, one female and two males, roughly represented the population balance of mathematics teachers of the school level. The topic taught in each school corresponded to the three different content areas prescribed in the National Curriculum Guidelines; linear functions from "Mathematical Relations", plane geometry from "Geometry", and simultaneous linear equations from "Number and Expressions".

The data from the LPS allowed for analysis of explicit linking of the single lesson as well as across a number of consecutive lessons. Indeed, design of the LPS, including the initial choice of participating countries, anticipated the comparison of the LPS analyses of videos of lesson sequences supplemented by the post-lesson reconstructive accounts of teachers and students with Stigler and Hiebert's analyses of the videotapes of single lessons.

Method for Analysis

First of all, we need to be specific on what constitutes links. As suggested by the finding of TIMSS Video Study, in Japanese mathematics classrooms the teacher may try to explicitly link together ideas and experiences that she wants her students to understand in relation to each other. The links can be made between current topics to the experience in previous lessons as well as those in the same lesson. The links may also be constituted by connections between different/similar mathematical ideas. For example, the teacher may refer to the concept of proportionality when she teaches concept and definition of a linear function, or to the concept of congruence when she teaches the concept of similarity. Thus, explicit linking may be made between mathematical concepts and ideas as well as from such concepts and ideas to the students' experiences in classrooms.

We define explicit linking as an utterance by the teacher (or students) to particular ideas or experiences from another lesson or part of the same lesson. Students' utterances were examined only when they could be identified as public talks, that is, utterances directed to all the classroom participants. Three coders coded a total of thirty transcriptions from videotaped lessons independently. When discrepancies in coding among coders appeared, they were resolved with discussions.

RESULTS

Explicit Linking in each Classroom

Table 1 shows the result of the coding of explicit linking within and across lessons in each school (J1, J2 and J3 stand for the schools that participated). As Table 1 shows, all the lessons were explicitly linked to other lessons in all schools and most lessons (28 lessons out of 30) were linked to some parts of the same lesson. These results seem to be consistent with the result of the TIMSS Video Study.

There was only one lesson without explicit linking out of ten lessons at school J2 and J3 respectively. As for school J2, for example, there was no explicit linking within the lesson J2-L06 in which students were learning how to apply the ratio of similarity to find the length of sides of a triangle. Most part of the lesson was spent for the calculation of some numbers for using and/or finding the ratios or length of the sides.

Table 1. Numbers of lessons that included explicit linking within and across lessons in each school

School	J1	J2	J3
Within lessons	10	9	9
Across the lessons	10	10	10

Explicit Linking within Lessons

Table 2 shows the result of coding of explicit linking within each lesson in each school (L01 to L10 stand for the videotaped lessons). The table simply tells that more links were found in some lessons (e.g. J2-L01 and J3-L02) than others and that there are differences among three classrooms in the frequencies of explicit linking.

Table 2. Numbers of explicit linking within each lesson

Lesson	L01	L02	L03	L04	L05	L06	L07	L08	L09	L10	Total
J1	4	5	1	1	5	6	2	2	1	2	29
J2	14	3	4	6	3	0	2	1	5	2	40
J3	2	8	3	4	1	1	2	0	2	1	24

The teachers often started the lesson by explicitly previewing what the class would be engaging in for the following part of the lesson. Also, they often summarised and highlighted what they had done at the end of the lesson. The following example (J3-L03) describes how the teacher at the end of the lesson emphasises the importance of what they had learned during the lesson.

Transcript 1: J3-L03

```
00:43:08:15 T:    Yes, um, today, we will end here but we did
                  something extremely important today. Um, it will
                  have to be next week, solving the equation from
                  KINO's question will have to be next week.
00:43:22:13 T:    But if we finish up to here, I think you'll be able
                  to solve tons of equation. Check the calculation
                  when you need to and I'll ask you sometimes. I'll
                  ask you to show me how much you can do but is that
                  ok?
00:43:35:18 T:    I think we were able to finish just about
                  everything, up to the important ways of thinking of
                  equations. You should be able to solve everything.
                  Ok? Now, I'll give you the rest of the time to jot
                  things down.
```

Key to symbols used in transcripts in this chapter
/	Indicates that one speaker cut in, interrupting another speaker before they had finished.
//	Marks the beginning of simultaneous/overlapping speech.
[text]	Comments and annotations, often descriptions of non-verbal action.
. . . .	Indicates that a portion of the transcript has been omitted.

In the excerpt of transcription from the J3-L03, in which the students were learning to solve simultaneous linear equations, the teacher summarised and highlighted what they had done in the form of general comments. The comments were made at the final minutes of the lesson. He noted that the class had done "something extremely important" (00:43:08:15), emphasising that the students "would be able to solve tons of equation" (00:43:22:13) and they "should be able to solve everything" (00:43:35:18). Also, he encouraged the students to "check the calculation when you need to."

At the end of the lesson, after some discussions on two alternative ways of checking the solution to the simultaneous linear equations, the teacher strongly emphasised that what they had done was extremely important. He then asked the students to jot things down on their notebook. In this case, the teacher appeared to promote students' reflection on what they had done and on the importance of checking the results. The teacher pointed out the part of blackboard on which an important idea was described.

Also, the teacher made explicit reference to what the class will do in the next week. The decision as made by the teacher that the question raised by a student in this lesson would be explored in the lesson in the next week. This is an example of explicit linking of 'looking forward'. Thus, the lesson did not exist as standing alone but interconnected to each other. We will see this aspect in the next section.

Explicit Linking across Lessons

Table 3 shows the result of coding of explicit linking across lessons in each school. Several lessons included links from ideas and experiences in the current lesson to those in the previous lessons, to those in the lesson outside the sequence, and even to those in the previous grade. It was similar to the case of linking within lessons that more linking were found in some particular lessons (e.g., J1-L02, L03 and L07; J2-L05, L06 and L07; J3-L02, L03 and L04) than others. There were more cases of explicit linking across lessons than those within a lesson.

Table 3. Numbers of explicit linking across lessons

Lesson	L01	L02	L03	L04	L05	L06	L07	L08	L09	L10	Total
J1	5	11	11	2	6	6	13	8	3	4	69
J2	4	2	4	9	14	11	19	5	3	6	77
J3	7	25	18	13	3	2	6	3	2	6	85

Lessons often started with teacher's comment on what they had done in the previous lesson. Typically, as the following excerpt from J1-L03 shows, the teacher tries to recall students' memories on the related topics they just finished and to remind them of their experiences.

Transcript 2: J1-L03

```
00:01:02:13 T    Yesterday,  //We had so much work to do in just one
                 class, and rushed through a bit fast.
00:01:09:03 T    So, let's take a look and try to remember what we
                 did last time, and go over it before we go on.
00:01:06:17 S    //I cannot find it.  Oh, here it is.
00:01:21:01 T    Um, do you all remember the equations, those we
                 talked about in class yesterday, um,/
```

In some cases, the teacher makes an explicit linking to the topics taught in the previous year. The teacher at J3, for example, mentioned the topic taught in the previous grade. The topic of lesson (J3-L03) was solving simultaneous linear equations by using the 'method of subtraction'. The teacher mentioned the students' experience of checking the solution of (a single) linear equation with one variable, which was taught in seventh grade.

Transcript 3: J3-L03

```
00:03:30:28 T    [While writing on the blackboard] What I'm going to
                 write now is the number two under the question two
                 that we did yesterday and we're only going to do
                 that now.
00:03:34:29 T    I'm only going to write number one, saying, solve
                 the following system of equations. We solved this
                 system of equations yesterday, right?
00:03:51:23 T    We were able to get the answer by subtracting from
                 both sides and continuing to solve.  And, the answer
                 to this was x is three and y is seven, right?  No
                 problems, right?
00:04:13:23 T    Compare this with what's written in your notebooks.
                 Ok?  And, today, uh, well, let's check to see if
                 these are correct.  How should we check these?
```

```
00:04:25:18 T    Well, the results of your knowledge of equations
                 from first year of junior high will be tested here,
                 the results of your hard studying.  I would like to
                 test your memories.
```

Here the teacher mentioned his intention to 'test' students' memories of checking the answer to the equation. The message would be a strong reminder and an alert.

Also, linking between two consecutive lessons was done in another particular way. Namely, the homework assigned at the end of previous lesson was used not only for practising and reviewing what the students learned, but also the topic to be discussed at the very beginning of the next lesson. The following example is an excerpt of transcription from J2-L02.

Transcript 4: J2-L02

```
00:00:31:04 T    You all had homework to do last night.
00:00:38:06 T    No one could finish it during class time.
00:00:44:02 T    So how did you go with that?
00:00:49:04 T    Is there anyone who came up with an answer that
                 would like to share it the class?  Any volunteers?
00:00:58:20 T    So did you give it a try?
00:01:00:17 T    Did you manage to figure out which triangle square
                 matches with triangle ABE?
00:01:10:22 T    Anyone?
00:01:16:00 T    Don't be shy!
00:01:21:10 T    I'm sure there is someone who got an idea.
00:01:30:04 T    [To KAWA] You have something written in your
                 notebook.  Can you share it with the class?
00:01:34:19 T    Come on!
```

As the example illustrates, homework was used as the 'connector' with which the students were supposed to link their experiences in two consecutive lessons.

The results of the analysis reveal that all the three Japanese LPS teachers employed explicit linking in the course of teaching a lesson sequence. Multiple lessons are interrelated by explicit linking in the way that mathematical ideas that appear in the current lesson are connected to students' experience in the previous or forthcoming lessons as well as part of the same lesson The transcripts cited above describe how each linking was made with the teacher's intention in each context. Explicit linking was made as a reminder for the students to go further on the related topic with the previous one. Also, the teachers explicitly linked between what was going on in the current lesson and forthcoming topics for the purpose of previewing.

Two types of linking: 'Looking back' and 'Looking forward'

There were two types of linking, looking back and looking forward. While 'looking back' linking means an explicit linking that links the current ideas or experiences to the previous ones, 'looking forward' linking means an explicit linking that links the current ideas or experiences to the forthcoming ones. As mentioned above, multiple lessons were interrelated in the way that mathematical ideas that appear in the current lesson were connected to students' experience in the previous or forthcoming lessons as well as part of the same lesson. Table 4 shows the result of coding of explicit linking within and across lessons in each school as classified into two types.

Table 4. Numbers of 'Looking back' and 'Looking forward'

School		J1	J2	J3
Within lessons	Looking back	18	19	11
	Looking forward	28	21	13
Across the lessons	Looking back	56	64	66
	Looking forward	13	13	19

As Table 4 shows, in all classrooms explicit linking of looking back across the lessons are found to be most frequent. The teachers tried to make connections between the current event to the previous experiences by referring to what has been learned in the classroom.

Explicit linking and mathematical tasks: The case of J1

In this section, the role of explicit linking is considered in relation to the tasks in the classrooms. We will take the case of J1 for this purpose. The main mathematical content taught in the videotaped classroom was 'linear function'. The teacher intended to achieve the goals of the entire unit by having the students examine the changes and variables in a few problem situations and think about them in terms of diagrams, graphs, and mathematical expressions. Then she intended to introduce the domain of change, independent variable against an dependent variable, the concept of the rate of change, and so on.

The videotaped lessons included four major parts that constitute sub-units. The teacher began the first lesson by presenting the following Stairs Problem (see Figure 1), the problem that was the topic of the lesson extended for three class periods. The students then explored the questions posed by the teacher as shown below.

The first three figures have been drawn for you. Draw the next two figures by stacking one cm sided squares on top of each other. What changes when the number of steps changes?

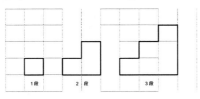

Figure 1. The Stairs Problem

The first lesson started with finding variables in the Stairs Problem. The teacher asked her students to find as many variables as possible in the situation with respect to change. The teacher's intention was to explore the relationship between the numbers of steps and the perimeters, and then the relationship between the numbers of steps and the numbers of right angles. In the second lesson she focused on the relationship between the number of steps and length of perimeter and asked the students to explore it. She further asked students to explore the relationship between the numbers of steps and the numbers of right angles in the third lesson.

Then, in the fourth lesson, the teacher posed the following Origami (paper folding) Problem in the classroom (see Figure 2). The class spent four class periods discussing and solving the problem.

Here is a yellow paper with length of 12 cm and width of 15 cm. What happens when we fold the paper like the following? Explore the relationship between two changing values.

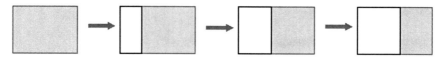

Figure 2. The Origami Problem

The teacher used the problem situation for four lessons. She started by asking students to find variables found in the action of paper folding and the resulting shapes. She then asked students to explore the relationship between length of perimeter and the area of rectangle, which is the next example of linear function.

The videotaped sequence of lessons corresponds to the planned lessons in the unit plan prepared by the teacher at J1. As Table 5 shows each lesson was embedded in the sub-unit within the entire teaching unit of linear function. There was slight difference between the planned lesson sequence and the implemented lessons. For example, although the teacher intended to spend two class periods for the Stairs Problem, the class spent three class periods in total exploring the relationships in that task.

Explicit linking seemed to play key roles in posing mathematical tasks within the lesson sequence. Firstly, explicit linking was used for connecting two consecutive lessons. The teacher often started the lesson by saying something like this: "Let's take a look and try to remember what we did last time, and go over it before we go on." The task for the first lesson in J1 was to explore the changes and variable in the Stairs Problem. In the second lesson, by reminding the changes and variable in the Stairs Problem explored in the first lesson, the class could focus on the relationship between the number of steps and length of perimeter. The relationship between numbers of steps and the perimeters was one of the findings in the classroom. By posing the tasks in this way and then by linking them explicitly, the teacher intended to maintain the continuity of students' learning and to capitalise on the students' experiences. This was also the case for the third lesson, in which

Table 5. The Unit Plan of Linear Function and Corresponding Lessons at J1

Teaching Unit	Sub Units	Planned lessons in sub-units	Lessons observed
Linear Function (16 class periods)	1. Changing variable and linear function—Part One	Lesson 1-1: Finding variables in the Stairs Problem	J1-L01
		Lesson 1-2: Exploring the relationship between the number of steps and length of perimeter	J1-L02 J1-L03
	2. Changing variable and linear function—Part Two	Lesson 2-1: Finding variables in the Origami Problem	J1-L04
		Lesson 2-2: Exploring the relationship between the length of perimeter and the area of rectangle	J1-L05 J1-L06
		Lesson 2-3: Reflecting on the exploration	J1-L07
	3. Change of Values of linear function and the Graph	Lesson 3-1: Drawing the graph of linear functions: slope and y-intercept	J1-L08
		Lesson 3-2: Drawing the graph of y $2x$ 4	J1-L09
			J1-L10
	4. Finding the expression of linear functions (Three class periods)		---
	5. Applying a linear function (Three class periods)		---
	6. Simultaneous linear equations and linear functions (Two class periods)		---
	7. Use of functions in daily life (One class period)		---

the relationship between the numbers of steps and the numbers of right angles was explored. Thus, with the explicit linking, the continuity between tasks in the consecutive lesson was maintained and strengthened.

Secondly, explicit linking within the same lesson can have impact on students' deeper understanding. In some cases, students' previous experiences of using important mathematical methods are referenced repeatedly. In J1, the teacher referred to the students' experiences in the previous year of using tables, graphs, and mathematical expressions to explore the change in the problem situations. The teacher asked the students to remind them of ways of examining 'change'.

Transcript 5: J1-L0

```
00:26:50:15 T    Ok, well, now, how should we examine this?
00:26:57:10 T    For example, I weigh myself on the scale everyday,
                 and when I record it, I write it like this.
00:27:08:10 T    Then well I can write it and examine the changes.
```

```
00:27:14:16 T     How did you arrange these in seventh grade?  Do you
                  remember?
00:27:20:09 Ss    Graphs.
00:27:22:01 T     Graphs.  Oh, sure.  We use graphs.  What else?
00:27:29:13 T     If you remember.  If you've forgotten, it's ok.
00:27:37:13 T     What else did you use?
00:27:43:28 T     Do you remember anything, OGA?
00:27:47:00 T     Like what kind of things you wrote down when you
                  were examining things in seventh grade, like graphs.
00:27:55:06 T     Forgot?  How about you, MAWA?
00:28:00:02 MAWA  (  )
00:28:05:03 T     Hmm?  Hmm?  What?
00:28:08:04 MAWA  (  )
00:28:09:00 T     Tables.  Oh, yes, tables.  You're right, we use
                  tables.  Ok.
```

Explicit linking between the different grade levels can also have impact on students' understanding. When the class was discussing mathematical expressions of linear functions, the teacher explicitly mentioned the concept of proportionality, which the students learned in seventh grade. The concept of linear function was linked to the related concept so that the students could build a broader conceptual network. Thus, by linking a mathematical idea or concept to the generalised one, or even to the specialised one, the students can have deeper understanding of the topic as embedded in the network of related concepts.

In sum, explicit linking plays key roles in posing mathematical tasks in the classroom in many ways. Mathematical tasks can be connected in a mathematical sense. Moreover, mathematical tasks in classroom are connected each other in terms of explicit linking in the way that mathematical ideas related to the tasks are connected to students' experience in the previous lessons, or to an expected experience in the forthcoming lessons, as well as part of the same lesson. The analysis suggests that the functions of mathematical tasks posed in classrooms need to be considered within the contexts that are consisted of multiple links among ideas and experiences of classroom participants.

DISCUSSION

Mathematical Tasks Posed in Multiple Links of Prior Ideas and Experiences

The analysis in the previous section of explicit linking in consecutive lessons reveals that multiple lessons are interrelated in the way that mathematical ideas that appear in the current lesson are connected to students' experience in the previous lesson as well as parts of the same lesson. In some cases, the connection can be extended to the expected experiences in forthcoming lessons even in the next grade. In the classroom, teachers intended to have their students understand mathematical ideas as connected to each other by explicitly mentioning the connections among ideas and students' experiences.

Mathematical tasks in classrooms, thus, appear differently when we locate them in the sequence of lessons as embedded within the multiple links of ideas and experiences. Each task is embedded in the contexts of mathematical structure and meanings as well as students' prior experiences around related ideas and concepts.

The functions of mathematical tasks posed in classrooms need to be considered within the contexts of such prior experiences in the classroom.

It should be noted that both the entire unit and sub-units constitute a coherent whole in terms of mathematical ideas and that the teacher tried to connect a series of problems posed in the sequence of lessons. This means that we cannot ignore the place of each lesson in the unit as well as the relationship between lessons, when we explore the nature and roles of mathematical tasks in the classroom.

Types of Linking and Their Impact on Students' Learning

In the TIMSS 1995 Videotape Classroom Study, certain recurring features that typified many of the lessons within a country, Germany, Japan, or the United States, and distinguished the lessons among three countries were identified as "lesson patterns" (Stigler & Hiebert, 1999). The following sequence of five activities was described as the Japanese pattern: reviewing the previous lesson; presenting the problems for the day; students working individually or in groups; discussing solution methods; and highlighting and summarising the main point.

The analysis of explicit linking serves for understanding the lesson events. For example, Shimizu (2006) identified 'Matome', which means "sum up one's main point in conclusion" or "pulling together", as the specific lesson event type for characterising classroom practices. Japanese teachers often organise an entire lesson around just a few problems with a focus on the students' various solutions to them and they think that "summing up" is indispensable to any successful lesson in which students' solutions are shared and pulled together in light of the goals of the lesson (Shimizu, 1999). Since the teachers place an emphasis on finding alternative ways to solve a problem, Japanese classes often consider several strategies. It would be natural for the classes to discuss the relationships among different strategies proposed from various viewpoints such as mathematical correctness, brevity, efficiency and so on. The teaching style with an emphasis on finding many ways to solve a problem naturally invites certain teacher's behavior for explicit linking for summarising purposes.

On the other hand, Stigler and Perry (1988) found *reflectivity* and *coherence* in Japanese mathematics classroom as its distinct characteristics. The meaning they attached to coherence is similar to that used in the literature on story comprehension. Explicit reference to the relations among events in lessons is expected to strengthen coherence of them. As for reflectivity, Japanese teachers stress the process by which a problem is worked and exhort students to carry out procedure patiently, with care and precision. The reflection of what has been going on in the classroom is promoted by explicit linking among experience in lessons.

Explicit linking also seems to correspond to the function of the situation of *institutionalisation* (Brousseau, 1997). In the classroom, the solution of a problem, if it is declared typical, can become a method or a theorem. Before institutionalisation, a student can't make reference to this problem that she knows how to solve. Faced with a similar problem, she must once again produce the proof. On the other hand, after institutionalisation she can use the theorem without giving its proof again or the method without justifying it. Institutionalisation thus consists of a change of convention among the actors, a recognition (justified or not) of the validity and utility of a piece of knowledge, a modification of this knowledge – which is "encapsulated" and designated – and a modification of its functioning. Thus to the institutionalisation there corresponds a certain transformation of the common repertoire accepted and explicitly referenced.

The Issue of Units for Data Collection and Data Analysis

As was the case in the TIMSS Videotape Classroom Study, a research design of the international comparative study of mathematics lessons may use 'lesson' as the unit of both data collection and analysis. It is natural to consider a lesson as a basic element of practice of teaching and learning. However, a single lesson as a administrative and organisational unit may not be a meaningful unit from the participants' perspectives. For the teacher who plans and controls the teaching unit, in particular, a single lesson may not be enough for teaching a particular topic from a mathematical point of view or for her educational intentions.

The analysis described in this chapter suggests that multiple lessons are related in each other in the way that mathematical ideas and students' experiences constitute a coherent body and that process of mathematics teaching and learning in the Japanese classroom cannot be adequately represented by an analysis of a collection of single lessons. Events in a lesson sequence can have different function and meanings to the teacher and learners. Needless to say, it is an important aspect of the teacher's work not only to implement a single lesson but also to weave multiple lessons that can stretch out over several days into a coherent body of the teaching unit. Then, if each lesson is analysed as 'standing alone', it is not possible to capture the dynamics of the teaching and learning process and to reconstruct the meanings of the evens to the participants.

CONCLUDING REMARKS

The analysis of explicit linking in consecutive lessons reveals that multiple lessons are interrelated by explicit linking in the way that mathematical ideas that appear in the current lesson are connected to students' experience in the previous or forthcoming lessons as well as part of the same lesson. The connections among mathematical tasks are analysed in the sequences of lessons to show that those tasks are connected to each other within the teaching unit by teachers' effort to link students' ideas and experiences explicitly. The analysis suggests that mathematical tasks in classrooms should be considered as posed in such contexts. Functions of mathematical tasks posed in classrooms need to be examined within the contexts of multiple links among ideas and experiences shared by classroom participants. They appear differently when we locate them in the sequence of lessons as embedded within these multiple links.

The analysis also suggests that mathematics teaching and learning in Japan can be understood better with not only a set of distinct lessons but also with a sequence of consecutive lessons. The result suggests that the units of data collection and data analysis for the study of lessons are crucial for the international comparisons. The analysis in this chapter also demonstrated the richness and potentials of the collected data as well as the strength of the methodology in the Learner's Perspective Study. A further study is needed which explains the influences of linking on students' understanding of mathematical concepts and procedures.

ACKNOWLEDGEMENTS

The author would like to express his thanks to Taeko Hirai, Yuki Masuda and Kaoru Matsuda for their work on the analyses reported in this chapter. The research reported in this paper was supported by the research grant (grant ID: 19330196) by the Japan Society for the Promotion of Science.

REFERENCES

Brousseau, G. (1997). *Theory of didactical situations in mathematics.* (N. Balacheff, M. Cooper, R. Sutherland, V. Warfield, Eds. & Trans). Dordrecht: Kluwer.

Clarke, D. J. (2006). The LPS research design. In D. J. Clarke, C. Keitel & Y. Shimizu (Eds.), *Mathematics classrooms in twelve countries: The insider's perspective* (pp. 15-36). Rotterdam: Sense Publishers.

Hiebert, J., Gallimore, R., Garnier, H., Givvin, K. B., Hollingsworth, H., Jacobs, J., Chui, A. M. Y., Wearne, D., Smith, M., Kersting, N., Manaster, A., Tseng, E., Etterbeek, W., Manaster, C., Gonzales, P., & Stigler, J. W. (2003). *Teaching mathematics in seven countries: Results from the TIMSS 1999 video study.* Washington, DC: NCES.

Sekiguchi, Y. (2006). Coherence of mathematics lessons in Japanese eighth-grade classrooms. In J. Novotná, H. Moraová, M. Krátká, & N. Stehliková (Eds.), *Proceedings of the 30th Conference of the International Group for the Psychology in Mathematics Education, 30*(5), 81-88.

Shimizu, Y. (1999). Aspects of mathematics teacher education in Japan: Focusing on teachers' roles. *Journal of Mathematics Teacher Education, 2*(1), 107-116.

Shimizu, Y. (2006). How do you conclude today's lesson? The form and functions of 'Matome' in mathematics lessons. In D. J. Clarke, J. Emanuelsson, E. Jablonka, & I. A. C. Mok (Eds.), *Making connections: Comparing mathematics classrooms around the world* (pp. 127-146). Rotterdam: Sense Publishers.

Stigler, J. W., Gonzales, P., Kawanaka, T., Knoll, S., & Serrano, A. (1999). *The TIMSS videotape classroom study: Methods and findings from an exploratory research project on eighth-grade mathematics instruction in Germany, Japan, and the United States.* Washington, DC: U.S. Government Printing Office.

Stigler, J. W., & Hiebert, J. (1999). *The teaching gap.* New York The Free Press.

Stigler, J. W., & Perry, M. (1988). Cross cultural studies of mathematics teaching and learning: Recent findings and new directions. In D. A. Grouws & T. J. Cooney (Eds.), *Perspectives on research on effective mathematics teaching* (pp. 194-223). Reston, VA: NCTM & Lawrence Erlbaum

Yoshinori Shimizu
Graduate School of Comprehensive Human Sciences
University of Tsukuba
Japan

JARMILA NOVOTNÁ AND ALENA HOŠPESOVÁ

CHAPTER SIX

Linking in Teaching Linear Equations – Forms and Purposes:
The Case of the Czech Republic

INTRODUCTION

Linking may be perceived as an elementary phenomenon which underlies the process of comprehension and construction of new concepts. We always compare any new experience with already existing experience; we look for similarities and differences. It is regarded as natural in the education process that we build on what the students are already familiar with. The teachers expect that the students will look for links to previously acquired knowledge and will construct knowledge nets (Berger & Luckmann, 1967). Experienced teachers look for ways to help their students in this process. Frequently, mathematical tasks provide the means by which teachers assist students in forming these links. Closer investigation reveals that the teachers' methods of drawing attention to the already acquired knowledge – linking – may take various forms. These forms mirror the teacher's intentions. The various forms of linking are facilitated through the use of different mathematical tasks and activities – for example, problem solving and proof. This chapter stems from an analysis of teaching linear equations (students aged 14-15) in two Czech schools. It proposes a classification of forms of linking with respect to the anticipated goal.

THEORETICAL FRAMEWORK

The essential part of 'doing' mathematics is solving problems. For each problem/task, there exists knowledge that enables solving it. But not always does the solver have it in his repertoire of knowledge. A student's learning can be characterised as widening his/her repertoire of knowledge:

> The teaching consists of triggering the creation of new elements to be added to the repertoire by means of messages formed exclusively from the repertoire of the receiver so that they are intelligible. It is clear that the rule for a teacher who adopts this model would be never to introduce a new piece of knowledge except by a known method of construction based on known concepts. (Brousseau, 1997, p. 54)

Y. Shimizu, B. Kaur, R. Huang and D. J. Clarke (Eds.), Mathematical Tasks in Classrooms around the World, pp. 103–118.

The teacher's main task is to create an environment suitable for such a widening.

In the *Theory of Didactical Situations in Mathematics* (TDSM) (Brousseau, 1997), learning is seen as a sequence of identifiable situations (natural or didactical) reproducible and leading regularly to the modification of a set of behaviours of the students, modifications which are characteristic of the acquisition of a particular collection of knowledge; teaching means the devolution of a learning situation from the teacher to the student (Brousseau, 1975).

In TDSM, one of the fundamental teacher's tasks in a didactical situation is institutionalisation. It refers to the passage of a piece of knowledge from its role as a means of resolving a problem or proof to a new role that of reference for future personal or collective uses. Institutionalisation consists of a recognition (justified or not) of the validity and utility of a piece of knowledge, a modification of this knowledge and a modification of its functioning. Institutionalisation can consist of an addition to the repertoire, but also of the rejection of a common belief suddenly recognised as false (Brousseau & Sarrazy, 2002). The institutionalisation can be understood as 'looking ahead', to solving new tasks or problems, to learning new theories, to proving or discovering new theorems and so on.

Shimizu (1999) mentions Stigler's study (Stigler et al., 1999, p. 117, in Shimizu 1999) of explicit linking of knowledge across lessons and within a single lesson. In the study, linking is defined as an explicit verbal reference by the teacher to ideas or events from another lesson or a part of the lesson. The reference is considered to constitute linking to the extent that it is concrete (that is, referring to a particular time, not to some general idea) and the reference must be related to the current activity. Later Shimizu (2007) elaborates the idea of such interrelations:

in the way that mathematical ideas in the current lesson are connected to students' experience in the previous or forthcoming lessons as well as part of the same lesson. (p. 177)

It covers both 'looking back' as well as 'looking ahead'.

In this chapter, we are focusing on one part of Shimizu's point of view, the connections to students' previous experience – 'looking back': What are the prerequisites that the teacher refers to when solving new problems, developing new domains of school mathematics? We restrict our considerations to the domain of linear equations in eighth grade mathematics classrooms in the Czech Republic. In agreement with Shimizu (2007), we call these teachers' actions 'linking'. We consider both linking within a single lesson and across lessons.

In this chapter, we focus on 'useful linking' in which the teacher coherently or intuitively (experience based) recalls previous students' knowledge or experience that is useful for their successful work on the piece of mathematics. The aim is to build nets of knowledge (Berger & Luckmann, 1967), consisting of structures and links. We believe that teachers have a certain repertoire of prerequisites ('pieces' of knowledge) that they see as essential for the new didactical situation and that they have a pattern for recalling them. We formulated our purposes in the following questions:

- What are the prerequisites that the teacher refers to when solving tasks from the domains of linear equations, their systems and algebraic word problems? Which type of tasks does the teacher use to make this relationship relevant for students?
- How can linking observed in Czech lessons be classified?
- What are the advantages and disadvantages of frequent linking?
- What is the role of the didactical contract (Brousseau, 1997) in developing links to students' previous knowledge?

DATA COLLECTION

In the research reported in this chapter we analysed linking in video recordings of ten consecutive lessons on the solution of linear equations and their systems in the 8th grade (students aged 14-15) classrooms of two lower secondary schools in the Czech Republic – in the following text, we will refer to them as classrooms CZ1 and CZ2. Both schools are located in a county town with approximately 100,000 inhabitants. The method of data collection was based on the Learner's Perspective Study (LPS) framework (Clarke, Keitel, & Shimizu, 2006). We compared our findings with our long-time experience from observations of lessons in different research projects.

The teachers are experienced (the CZ1 teacher was approaching the end of her professional career with more than 30 years of experience, and the CZ2 teacher has been teaching for more than 20 years) and respected by parents, colleagues and educators, although their teaching strategies differ: the CZ2 teacher mostly focuses on the question "How?" as she develops problem solving strategies in relation to each problem. The CZ1 teacher pays more attention to the question "Why?" and tries to plant the new knowledge on her students' previous knowledge. On the other hand, the CZ2 teacher trusts much more in her students' independent discovery.

FORMS OF LINKING AND THEIR PURPOSES

The research reported in this chapter examines the forms of linking in Czech schools. It does not claim to be exhaustive, to cover all forms used by mathematics teachers in all educational settings. Nevertheless, the experience from our observations of mathematics lessons in several countries leads us to believe that the main forms of linking are covered in the following text.

When presenting our classification of linking, we do not claim to give a hierarchy of their usefulness and influence on the level of students' understanding of mathematics. We distinguish two basic forms of linking:
- A priori linking (APL)
- Ad hoc linking (AHL)

A PRIORI LINKING

The teacher using his/her experience from teaching the topic plans to recall in advance the needed knowledge that should be already known to the students. Having in mind the prerequisites needed for successful learning of the piece of knowledge, he/she brings back the part of mathematics that the students have already come across.

APL may have the form of a theoretical discourse (CZ1-L02, 00:55) or can be presented as a solving procedure for a suitable problem (CZ1-L02, 15:35).

CZ2-L02, 00:55

```
T:          Where did you first meet equations? In the fourth?
Students:   In the fifth.
T:          In the fifth? (The teacher goes to the blackboard and
            turns it round - see Figure 1)
```

Figure 1. Teacher at blackboard: Introducing "equations"

```
T:          I would say it was already in the first [she points at
            the first row on the blackboard]. Johnny has 3 cars
            [points at number 3 in the record on the blackboard]. How
            many cars does he need [she points at x] to have 5 [she
            points at number 5]? Equation, isn't it? Recently I've
            taken a colleague's lesson in the second grade. They were
            solving the problem: 70 minus x equals 40 [she points at
            the corresponding places in the record on the blackboard]
            or x plus 20 ... It was recorded exactly like this. So
            this is also an equation. And here I've written down
            three problems that we solved in the sixth grade. [She
            points at the record of 3 equations.] So we came across
            them already a long time ago. We were able to solve so
            complicated equations already in the sixth grade. But we
            used diagrams to solve the equations. You will remember
            that we had there something like this. Remember? [She
```

```
goes to the other blackboard and she reconstructs the
procedure in cooperation with her students - see Figure
2]
```

Figure 2. Teacher at blackboard: Reconstructing the procedure

Key to symbols used in transcripts in this chapter
[text]   Comments and annotations, often descriptions of non-verbal action.
. . . .   Indicates that a portion of the transcript has been omitted.
...   A pause of one second or less

CZ1-L02, 15:35

```
T:          How can I see that the equation does not have any
            solution? Denisa.
Denisa:     The left hand side will not equal the right hand side.
T:          Yes, there will be a contradiction. For example ... what
            for example, Vasek?
Vasek:      For example 2 equals 12.
```

APL can have two forms, *linking across lessons (APL-Across)* or *linking within a single lesson (APL-Within)*. In both cases, APL might be used by the teacher *before* or *inside* a solving procedure of a problem or a proof (we will shortly speak about an 'activity'). If the reference occurs after the activity, we see it as a form of institutionalisation. As mentioned earlier, in our analyses we do not include institutionalisation in linking.

When the teacher uses the 'before activity' form of APL, the students often do not see the immediate use of the recalled piece(s) of knowledge. It is known to the teacher, not to the students (see also paradoxes of the didactical contract in the TDSM, Brousseau, 1997). They are supposed to apply it at the appropriate moment later on.

Examples of APL-Across

i) Before Activity

CZ1-L03, 06:22 (linking to the previous lesson)

```
T:          And now let's return to what we solved. We finished the
            last lesson also with a word problem, a word problem with
            velocity, time and distance, and we solved it using an
            equation. Now I will ask ...
```

CZ1-L02, 03:10 (linking to a more remote lesson)

```
T:          Today and also in the following lessons, we will also
            need this, we haven't revised it for quite a long time.
            How did we say it, how is it with the numbers mathematics
            calculates with? ...
```

The 'before activity' form of APL is often used by the teacher in anticipation of a student's common mistake. The teacher presents the linked knowledge related to a mistake before correcting it or before solving a similar problem. (For example CZ1-L04 starts with the correction of a common mistake in the students' homework.)

The CZ1 teacher often uses the 'inside activity' form of APL in the course of the work on a new piece of mathematics. Usually this occurs when the teacher expects the students not to remember an algorithmic step or to make a common mistake and plans to use it only as required.

ii) Inside Activity

CZ1-L02, 18:37 (linking to the previous lesson when solving the first equation with the unknown in the denominator, with infinitely many roots)

```
T:          And yesterday we said that we can do this step when,
            when ...
Student:    When I will not multiply by zero.
```

CZ1-L02, 03:10 (linking to a more remote lesson when solving a speed/distance word problem)

```
T:          So, what type of a problem is it? You will certainly
            recognize it. You must remember ...
```

The 'inside activity' form of APL can be successfully applied as motivation for a more complicated problem. For example in CZ1-L5 (10:40), the students' results when solving an equation with a parameter for various values of the parameter are used as motivation for solving the equation with the 'general' parameter.

A special case of APL is linking a priori to the previous lesson (usually during a series of lessons developing the same topic). The teacher reminds the students of what they were supposed to learn from the activities of the last lesson. The most frequent reason is the teacher's belief that students need more than one lesson to grasp the new piece of knowledge including the desired terminology.

CZ2 (postlesson interview L02)

T: Already I expect it to get running a bit from the following lesson; so in the next lesson we will probably revise the simple equations or equations with parentheses and then we will add those with fractions.

Examples of APL-Within

i) Before Activity

CZ1-L02, 43:10 (linked to CZ1-L02, 15:35, see above)

T: Let us come back to the equation where we had infinitely many solutions. If I meet a condition that I have to record, take care of it at the end. ... In the problem that we did together, it was important to include the condition in the conclusion.

ii) Inside Activity

CZ1-L02, 35:49 before solving the second equation with the unknown in the denominator, the root is 5, the domain of the equation contains all real numbers different from 3)

T: One more thing. Look here, you found that the root of this equation is 5, so what with it? We passed the condition and it's not necessary to take it into account any more. But in this case [she points on the first equation] that we did together, when we got ...

It is necessary to note that teacher CZ1 often starts a new procedure by a well-arranged recapitulation of previous knowledge. It can be seen as multiple linking.

AD HOC LINKING

By *ad hoc linking* we understand the linking integrated by the teacher as a reaction to what the students do or say when solving a new problem or when they are presented with a new mathematical topic. Mostly, it is a reaction to an incorrect answer or a step of the solving procedure requiring the use of a piece of knowledge that should have already been known to the students. It is the teacher's reaction to the immediate situation in the classroom. The success of AHL depends on the teacher's experience and pedagogical skills.

AHL can also occur as the teacher's reaction to student questions, for example, in the case of their individual solving of problems. Let's consider CZ1-L10 (13:30), the AHL-Across to the properties of a tetrahedron was provoked by the context of the word problem chosen for solving by one of the students.

AHL can have two forms, *linking across lessons (AHL-Across)* or *linking within a single lesson (AHL-Within)*. It is used by the teacher *inside* an activity. A special case of AHL-Within is the individual help provided by the teacher during individual work in the lesson. (AHL is often introduced in a similar manner to the 'inside activity' form of APL. The particular form can be recognised only when looking at it in the context of the students' reactions and actions or during the post-lesson interview with the teacher.)

Examples of AHL-Across

CZ2-L02, 27:25 (solving the equation $3(2-x) - 4 = 1 - 2(x-2)$)

T: We are starting the solution. Together, together, Lucka. If we have brackets in the equation, we try to get rid of them. As, apart from brackets, we have also other expressions there, we have to ditch them, by multiplying the brackets. And we already know how to multiply a binomial by a number. Attention when multiplying by minus! …

Examples of AHL-Within

CZ1-L02, 37:20 (creation of the equation for the "speed/distance" word problem, x = time)

Student: x + x + 1
T: How do we calculate the distance, Michal? We said it some minutes ago.
Michal: Speed times time.

TEACHERS' CHOICES OF PREREQUISITES FOR LINEAR EQUATIONS

The data from CZ1 and CZ2 were analysed from the perspective of topics of linking. Table 1 shows the list of prerequisites occurring in the individual linking forms separately for each school. It only concerns APL because it represents the linking considered by the teachers as a fundamental help for their students. The sign — in the table means that APL to this item did not explicitly occur.

Table 1. Topics of APL in each school

CZ1	CZ2
Number sets (types, relationships)	Number sets (focusing mainly on the hierarchy of arithmetic operations, elimination of parentheses, division and multiplication by 0)
Sets and operations with them	—
—	Equations at the elementary level (solution based on the "inverse" passage in diagrams)
Fractions, common denominator, complex fractions Mixed numbers	—
—	Absolute value, square, square root
Linear functions, direct and indirect proportionality Rational functions Functions, forms of definition, graphs, domain, range	—
Inequalities (esp. linear), truth values, methods of resolution	—
—	Process of mathematisation of word problems
Polynomials, esp. monomials, binomials	—
Algebraic expressions, their domains and simplification	Algebraic expressions, their domains and simplification
Percentages	Percentages
Formulas needed for solving typical school word problems (e.g. distance = speed × time, calorimetric equation)	Formulas needed for solving typical school word problems (e.g. distance = speed × time)
Conversion of physical units	Conversion of physical units

Table 1 clearly indicates important differences in APL linking in the two schools. Whereas the CZ1 teacher uses (in 7 topics from 10) the linking to theoretical issues, the CZ2 teacher does it in 3 topics out of 8. In the rest, the linked topics are practical, connected directly to the technique of the individual problem solving.

In a recent study (Binterová, Hošpesová, & Novotná, 2006), the didactical contract (Brousseau, 1987) was identified as one of the most important factors influencing classroom interaction. It was reported that

Students' expectations that the teacher keeps referring to their previous knowledge that is useful when solving the assigned problem(s) led sometimes to the mistakes. (p. 278)

It was evidenced there that linking is in the didactical contract in classroom CZ1 and that breaking this contract by the teacher leads to failures of the students. In CZ1, the students are accustomed to being reminded of the 'theory' while the students in CZ2 expect the teacher to remind them of the individual facts that they may or may not include in a structure related to their present work.

THE TEACHING STYLES IN CZ1 AND CZ2 AND LINKING

Let us start with comparison of the occurrences of linking in classrooms CZ1 and CZ2 (Table 2). It will serve as the basis for comparing the teaching styles of the two teachers. We do not include relationships towards 'real life situations'; the table is restricted to linking to school subjects' content.[i]

Table 2. Numbers of linking during the lessons[ii]

School	Form of linking	Lesson									
		1	*2*	*3*	*4*	*5*	*6*	*7*	*8*	*9*	*10*
CZ1	APL-Across before	2	5+3	3+*1*	0	1	0	2+*1*	4	0	1
	APL-Across inside	5	2+*1*	1	1+*1*	1	0	0	6+*1*	0	3
	APL-Within before	1	1	0	0	1	0	1	0	0	0
	APL-Within inside	0	1	0	0	0	1	*1*	0	1	0
	AHL-Across	2	1	4+*1*	5	3	2	2	0+*1*	2	3
	AHL-Within	0	3	1	3	0	2	0	1	0	0
CZ2	APL-Across before	2	2	*1*	2	1+*1*	0	4	1	1+*1*	0
	APL-Across inside	3	2+*1*	0	0	*1*	0	0	0	1	0
	APL-Within before	0	0	0	1	0	0	1	0	0	0
	APL-Within inside	0	0	0	0	0	0	1	0	1	0
	AHL-Across	3	2	1	6	1+*1*	0	0	0	1	3
	AHL-Within	0	0	0	1	1	0	0	0	0	0

It is apparent at the first sight that the table shows important differences not only between the two classes but also between individual lessons in each of them.

Differences between Lessons

In both classes, the differences can be explained as a consequence of the lesson aim. Table 3 indicates that in both classes, the number of APL decreases and AHL increases when the lesson is focused on practice. In each lesson, mathematical tasks are used as the strategic vehicles for the various forms of linking. Our analysis was concerned less with task types and more with task use to support linking.

Table 3. Lesson aims and number of APL

Lesson	CZ1	APL/AHL	CZ2	APL/AHL
1	Presentation of new subject matter	8/2	Solving introductory tasks for new subject matter	5/3
2	Presentation of new subject matter	13/4	Presentation of new subject matter through problems	5/2
3	Practice and application	5/6	Practice and application	1/1
4	Practice and application, students' individual work	2/8	Practising prerequisites, development of the new subject matter through problems	3/7
5	Correction of individual work, new subject matter	3/3	Development of the new subject matter through problems	3/3
6	Practice and application, new subject matter	1/2	Test, practice	0/0
7	Practice and application, students' individual work, new subject matter	5/2	Word problems presented through problem types	6/0
8	Correction of individual work, new subject matter	11/2	Special types of word problems presented through their solving	1/0
9	Check of understanding, written test	1/2	Special types of word problems presented through their solving	4/1
10	Correction of the test, summary of the learned subject matter	4/3	Special types of word problems presented through their solving	0/3

Differences between the Classes

There is a significant difference between the number and forms of linking (see Figure 3) used in the two classes.

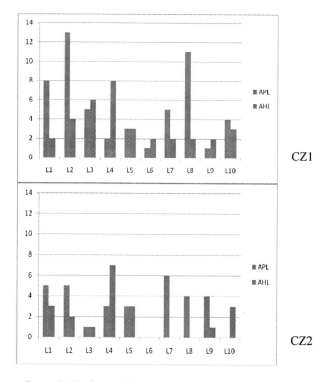

Figure 3. Number and forms of linking in CZ1 and CZ2

In order to construct a firm knowledge net, the CZ1 teacher roots the new subject matter in the theory that the students are supposed to be familiar with. In most cases, she inserts it before solving problems, sometimes even far before the activity for which it is really needed (for example, in L2, 3:20, number sets are recalled but not used until L2, 22:10 and further). The number of APL applied inside the solving procedure of a problem is considerably lower. In an earlier paper (Novotná & Hošpesová, 2007), we suggested that the reason for this teacher's behaviour might be based on her suspicion of students' abilities resulting in students' lack of self-confidence. Let us illustrate this by the comments of the CZ1 teacher and her students:

CZ1-L02 (post-lesson interview with the teacher commenting why they revised the formula for distance, velocity and time before solving the word problem)

```
T:          ... but my experience is that as soon as it is not used
            in physics any more, they now don't know - should I
            multiply or divide?
```

CZ1-L06 (post-lesson interview with the student)

```
Interviewer: And here, when solving the task, did you solve it with
             them, or on your own or …
```

114

```
Student:        Well, in the beginning, the multiplication on my own,
                and then I preferred to wait for the rest and continue
                with them.
Interviewer:    And now, if you were to solve the problem today, is it
                better? Or a similar one?
Student:        Well, may be a similar one, but if it were somehow
                different, I would probably not solve it.
```

The CZ2 teacher prefers the re-discovery of necessary facts and procedures through problem solving to linking across or within lessons. She believes that the students' success in mathematics can be reached by their successful completion of assigned tasks. AHL occurs much more often. It is not only the reaction to the students' mistake but often the teacher's immediate reaction to the students' performance and her attempt to prevent the occurrence of too many mistakes. The teacher's experience plays an important role in her decision to use a particular form of linking.

CZ2-L02 (post-lesson interview with the teacher)

```
T:              I really, if there exist one or two or three ways, I want
                to show them all... For example, one boy in the 9ᵗʰ grade,
                he always everything to the left and everything to the
                right and as if he was conducting a train; then he found
                the solution but it took him four times longer; he had to
                find himself if it was a good or a bad procedure.
```

DISCUSSION AND CONCLUDING REMARKS

Linking and TDSM

Linking is connected to the teacher's *a-priori analysis* of a didactical situation. The *a-priori analysis* is an important instrument enabling the teacher to manage the didactical situation in all its parts – devolution, a-didactical situation and institutionalisation (Brousseau, 1997). In the a priori analysis, the teacher tries to foreshadow the course of the lesson (Hrabáková, 2005):

– to reveal the steps of the lesson
– to predict the possible reactions and attitudes of students and his/her reactions (that is, about the obstacles and the errors that may occur, and about the ways to correct them)
– to discover the possible solving strategies (both the correct and incorrect ones)
– to determine what previous knowledge the students will need to apply their solving strategies successfully and what 'new' knowledge they may discover.

The teachers' decision to include APL seems to correspond to their a priori analysis of the didactical situation. Predicting the possible students' solving strategies, previous knowledge needed for a successful application of them and so on, results in preparation of the corresponding forms and places of linking in the classroom.

Linking, especially AHL, is susceptible to becoming a form of Topaze effect (Brousseau & Sarrazy, 2002; Brousseau, 1997). When used as a hint without checking the students' understanding of the relationship between the linked and the 'new' knowledge, we see it as the Topaze effect. Linking is used as a help to grasp the new knowledge and to place it into the existing knowledge net.

The analysis of linking just presented indicates that linking can have different roles in mathematical activities. It might be used, for example:

- as a means for recalling a needed piece of previous knowledge;
- as a demonstration of the need for the new knowledge due to lack of previous knowledge;
- as a tool for checking previous understanding;
- as a tool for clarifying something unclear from previous activities.

If we come back to the TDSM characterisation of the learning process, linking forms constitute not only a part of widening the repertoire of students' knowledge. They contribute to the structuring of this repertoire and to making the single pieces of knowledge available for further use. In a broader sense, they contribute to the development of mathematical literacy.

Our analysis, compared with Stigler's findings (in Shimizu, 1999), shows that linking could be an important feature of classroom culture and that it significantly influences the quality of knowledge grasped. The presented analysis of the forms of linking used by the CZ1 and CZ2 teachers indicates that linking has a positive effect on the students' learning. It also shows some unwanted effects, for example, students' expectation of being helped by CZ1 instead of trying to find useful linking independently. It was very rare that we would come across an appeal to look for linking in both the CZ1 and CZ2 data. One example of such an occurrence is CZ2-L01 where the teacher introduces the subject matter of equations with questions such as: *Have we learned anything like this? Have we done anything similar? What does this problem remind you of?* (see also the extract CZ2-L02, 00:55, in the discussion of a priori linking).

In post-lesson interviews with the CZ1 and CZ2 teachers, they both expressed their feeling several times that they are responsible for the "smooth progress of the solution of the task", using phrases such as: "I should mention ..." and "It could be recalled ....". Both teachers feel that their students' mistakes are a mark of their own failure. The teachers' feeling of responsibility for their students' results is a strong feature of Czech classroom culture (Hejný & Kuřina, 2001).

The authors of current educational reform in the Czech Republic (e.g. Novotná, 2006) are well aware of this fact. The very verbiage of the new curricular materials shows that the student is not an object of the teacher's action, but the architect of his/her own education – all the educational goals are formulated in the language of target student competencies. It is the task of the school to elaborate their own plan of how to create suitable conditions and atmosphere for development of the expected student competencies. However, it is our belief that it cannot be expected that the change in perspective and the shift of a part of the responsibility for results of one's own education to the student will occur quickly for the majority of the teaching public. Nevertheless, if we want Czech students to excel not only when solving routine mathematical tasks, but also to be able to solve mathematical problems and to cope in non-standard situations, it is essential to increase their responsibility in solving every single school mathematical task.

NOTES

[i] If APL is used for correcting the mistake in a solved problem, we include it in the 'inside activity' form of APL-Across. For example at the beginning of CZ1-L04, the APL-Across is done before other activities, but it is the correction of a mistake of the previous homework.

[ii] The number in italics denotes the corresponding form of linking to the previous lesson. If APL has the form of solving a sample problem we classify it as the 'before activity' form of APL.

ACKNOWLEDGEMENTS

The data analysed in this chapter were gathered by the team from the Pedagogical Faculty of the University of South Bohemia in České Budějovice chaired by Helena Binterová. The authors want to thank all the team members for providing us with the rich source of data. This research was partially supported by project GACR 406/08/0710.

REFERENCES

Berger, P. L., & Luckmann, T. (1967). *The social construction of reality: A treatise in sociology of knowing.* London: Penguin.

Binterová, H., Hošpesová, A., & Novotná, J. (2006). Constitution of the classroom environment: A case study. In D. J. Clarke, C. Keitel & Y. Shimizu (Eds.), *Mathematics classrooms in twelve countries: The insider's perspective* (pp. 275-288). Rotterdam: Sense Publishers.

Brousseau, G. (1975). A colloquium talk. See Warfield, V. (2006). *Invitation to didactique.* www.math.washington.edu/~warfield/Didactique.html (July 30, 2008).

Brousseau, G. (1997). *Theory of didactical situations in mathematics,* 1970-1990. (N. Balacheff, M. Cooper, R. Sutherland & V. Warfield, Eds. & Trans.) Dordrecht: Kluwer.

Brousseau, G., & Sarrazy, B. (2002). *Glossary of terms used in didactique* (V.Warfield, Trans.). Bordeaux: Université Bordeaux.

Clarke, D. J., Keitel, C., & Shimizu, Y. (Eds.) (2006). *Mathematics classrooms in twelve countries.* Rotterdam: Sense Publishers.

Hejný, M., & Kuřina, F. (2001). *Dítě, škola a matematika.* [Child, school and mathematics.] Praha: Portál.

Hrabáková, H. (2005). Analysis a priori of the "puzzle" activity. In J. Novotná (Ed.), *SEMT 05 Proceedings,* 349.

Novotná, J. (2006). *Czech Republic: Czech educational system.* In D. J. Clarke, C. Keitel, & Y. Shimizu (Eds.), *Mathematics classrooms in twelve countries* (pp. 335-338). Rotterdam: Sense Publishers.

Shimizu, Y. (1999). Studying sample lessons rather than one excellent lesson: A Japanese perspective on the TIMSS videotape classroom study. *ZDM,* 99 *(6),* 190-194.

Shimizu, Y. (2007). Explicit linking in the sequence of consecutive lessons in mathematics classrooms in Japan. In J. H. Woo, H. C. Lew, K. S. Park, & D. Y. Seo, (Eds.), *Proceedings of the 31st Conference of the International Group for the Psychology of Mathematics Education, 31*(4), 177-184.

Jarmila Novotná
Faculty of Education
Charles University Prague

JARMILA NOVOTNÁ AND ALENA HOŠPESOVÁ

Alena Hošpesová
Faculty of Education
University of South Bohemia České Budějovice

IDA AH CHEE MOK

CHAPTER SEVEN

Comparison of Learning Task Lesson Events between Australian and Shanghai Lessons

INTRODUCTION

Mathematical knowledge, in its fullest sense, includes significant, fundamental relationships between conceptual and procedural knowledge. (Hiebert & Lefevre, 1986, p. 9)

Meaningful learning of the subject should always contribute in one way or the other for building relationships between conceptual and procedural knowledge. To bring about such meaningful learning, appropriate tasks that students can engage in are essential. Tasks can range from simple drill-and-practice exercises to complex problem-solving tasks set in rich contexts. However, it is not the content of the tasks alone which determine the opportunity for learning. A challenging problem can be taught in such a way that students simply follow some routine procedures, whereas a simple task for some fundamental basic skills can be taught in a culture fostering mathematical understanding (Carpenter & Lehrer, 1999). The learning opportunity is thus determined by the learning environment which encompasses both the task and the interaction between the participants in the lessons. Therefore, the idea of 'learning task lesson event' (LT event) developed by Mok and Kaur (2006) which encompasses the task as well as what happens in the lesson makes a legitimate unit for analysis. A LT event is defined by both the content of task and how the task was taught in the lesson. In order to create an experience for students to learn such skills and concepts, teachers usually demonstrate and explain what they want their students to learn with examples or let their students explore some problems. Such examples or problems are called tasks or learning tasks in general. A LT event is characterised by its purpose for teaching something new or forming a part of a coherent sequence of the development of an object of learning. Therefore, following this definition, LT events in analysis do not include events working on items for the purposes of review, practice and repetition.

Via the comparison of the lessons between two different cultures (an Australian classroom and a Shanghai classroom), the author wants to investigate how the teaching in a LT event may contribute to the building of relationships between procedural and conceptual knowledge. There is no intention to claim that any

Y. Shimizu, B. Kaur, R. Huang and D. J. Clarke (Eds.), Mathematical Tasks in Classrooms around the World, pp. 119–146.
© *2010 Sense Publishers. All rights reserved.*

examples will represent the characteristics of a specific culture. However, it is assumed that teachers based on their own experience and understanding of pedagogy will develop a consistent style of pedagogy conducive to learning in their own classes, in their own schools and in the learning culture promoted by the curriculum. Such personalised style carries traits of the teacher's pedagogical belief and regional cultural aspects. An example as such will represent qualitatively a case study which can be lens for a better understanding of the nature of the learning and teaching for different topics in different cultures. Contrasting cases of different topics in different cultures can help to make similarities and differences more explicit. Therefore, the Learner's Perspective Study (LPS) lesson sequences from an Australian school (A1) and a Shanghai school (SH2) were compared with a focus on 'learning task lesson events' in this chapter.

A FRAMEWORK FOR PROCEDURAL AND CONCEPTUAL KNOWLEDGE

According to Hiebert and Lefevre (1986), conceptual and procedural knowledge of mathematics represents a distinction that has received a great deal of discussion and debate through the years. The distinction plays an important role in more general questions of knowledge acquisition. However, useful debates do not end at a differentiation between the two kinds of knowledge but the relationships between concepts and procedures and how either may benefit the learning of mathematics as a whole. In the analysis of the data, the ideas of *conceptual* and *procedural* are used. To illuminate the analysis in this chapter, the differentiation between conceptual and procedural knowledge by Hiebert and Lefevre are briefly quoted here:

> Conceptual knowledge is characterised most clearly as knowledge that is rich in relationships. It can be thought of as a connected web of knowledge, a network in which the linking relationships are as prominent as the discrete pieces of information.... The development of conceptual knowledge is achieved by the construction of relationships between pieces of information. ... A second way in which conceptual knowledge grows is through the creation of relationships between existing knowledge and new information this is just entering the system....The term abstract is used here to refer to the degree to which a unit of knowledge (or a relationship) is tied to specific contexts. Abstractness increases as knowledge becomes freed from specific contexts. (pp. 3-5)

> Procedural knowledge, as we define it here, is made up of two distinct parts. One part is composed of the formal language, or symbol representation system, of mathematics. The other part consists of the algorithms, or rules, for completing mathematical tasks .... It is useful to distinguish between two kinds of procedures by noticing the objects upon which they operate. ... A second kind of procedure is a problem-solving strategy or action that operates on concrete objects, visual diagrams, mental images, or other objects that are not standard symbols of our mathematical systems (pp. 6-7).

120

A THEORETICAL PERSPECTIVE FOR LEARNING

There are many theories contributing to an understanding of the nature of learning of teaching. The theoretical point of departure for learning in this chapter is taken from that of mediated learning. Teaching models developed from these cognitive and social cognitive theoretical backgrounds have been tried in different places and have reported promising teaching results, for example, the Cognitive Acceleration in Science Education (CASE) project for science teaching and the Cognitive Acceleration in Mathematics Education (CAME) project for mathematics teaching (for example, Adey & Shayer, 1994; Adhami, Johnson & Shayer, 1998; Mok & Johnson, 2000). The idea of mediated learning from Vygotsky (1978) is pertinent.

> The contribution of social constructivism is the notion of mediated learning which comes from Vygotsky (1978). Vygotsky's description of the Zone of Proximal Development is used both in psychological testing, where the learner's potential is to be estimated, and also to explain the dynamics of development. Each learner is assumed to have at any one time, in addition to sets of completed skills and strategies which enable him or her to succeed on conventional test items, a spectrum of half-formed or potential strategies which can be revealed by the technique of dynamic assessment and which may be turned into complete or successful skills either by chance, by spontaneous effort, or by the mediating influence of an adult or a peer. However, such cognitive development cannot be taught by any recognised instructional procedure. Therefore, a major skill of intervention teaching is managing the class so that the teacher's mediating activities maximise the opportunities each student has to make the next cognitive jump. A valuable part of such teaching is the small-group and ultimately whole-class discussion, where students share their incipient ideas and strategies in their own words and from which other students can take what they need. (Mok & Johnson, 2000, p. 289)

While these models apply key constructs in developing teaching intervention programs, these constructs also provide conceptual tools for analysis of how activities and interactions may support learning in lessons. The key constructs in these models are: concrete preparation, construction, cognitive conflict, metacognition and bridging. They are briefly explained below:

- *Concrete preparation* covers a range of activities which include the provision of relevant technical vocabulary which will be useful for students' subsequent activities.
- *Construction* is the process by which powerful strategies or concepts are generated to solve a problem.
- *Cognitive conflict* appears if children find a problem or task in which their methods and strategies appear not to work or to yield a contradiction, then the resulting mental conflict may challenge them to produce a higher-level strategy which does work.
- *Metacognition* means reflecting on one's own thinking.

121

– *Bridging* involves divergent thinking where a person uses their imagination to invent other uses in contexts quite different from those in which they have learnt an idea or skill

BACKGROUND OF THE TWO CLASSES

The data set in the study was taken from one Australian school A1 and one Shanghai school SH2 in the LPS. In total there were ten Australian lessons and 14 Shanghai lessons. The Australian lessons were on the topic of perimeter and area. The class size was 25 students and the average International Benchmark Test (IBT) (items taken from TIMSS Student Achievement Study, population 2) score is 27.2. The class level was Grade 8. The Shanghai lessons were on the topic of Simultaneous Equations. The class size was 46 students and the average International Benchmark Test IBT score was 33.1. The class level was Grade Seven. By comparing the content of the curriculum, the topic simultaneous equations was generally taught at year eight or nine in Australia. Besides, the IBT scores of the Shanghai students were slightly higher than the Australian students. Therefore, the matching of levels between the two classes was counted as suitable according to the matching of curriculum and the students' IBT scores although the Shanghai students were slightly younger.

THE METHOD OF ANALYSIS

There were two levels of analysis and the software StudioCode was used for coding. At the first level, a total of 24 lesson videos consisting of ten Australian lessons and 14 Shanghai lessons were viewed. The tasks and subtasks in each lesson were identified. The episode containing the task was coded as a continuous event in the StudioCode timeline. An event usually started from the teacher introducing the task and ended when all the related activities had finished. Therefore, the end of one task event was very soon followed by the beginning of the next event in the timeline. The events were then further classified as learning-task lesson events (LT events) and non-LT events based on the task and what happened during the event.

After the LT-events were labeled, activity codes were developed to code the nature of activities within the events. These codes were applied to both LT events and non-LT events. There are three types of coding. The first type consists of three codes: instruction, students carrying out their work and teacher's feedback to the whole class. These codes reflecting the major routine in an event are mostly non-overlapping and nearly cover the spectrum of all events. The second type identifies the nature of class organisation and they are individual seatwork, student discussion, student working on the board and teacher-led whole class interaction. The third type refers to some special features with respect to the content of the task events and they are subtasks, link to an earlier task and return to an earlier task.

In the second level, the transcripts and videos of the LT-events were studied in detail to understand the objectives and the nature of the LT-events, the styles of teacher-student discourses and how the interaction between the teacher and students may help to fulfill the objectives. Finally presented in this chapter, the LT events in selected lessons were analysed in order to elaborate the difference in pace and how the mediated learning may help students learn about the conceptual and procedural knowledge. The lessons by the Australian teacher were A1-L01 and A1-L02. The lessons by the Shanghai teacher were SH2-L04 and SH2-L05.

THE ANALYSIS AND RESULTS

What Counted as Learning Task Lesson Events: The Nature of LT and Non-LT Lesson Events

The nature of the LT-events is inevitably affected by the nature of the tasks. Therefore, a preliminary comparison was first made by counting the number of tasks and by the classification between LT events and non-LT events.

The main differentiation between a LT event and a non-LT event depends on whether there is the teaching of 'something new' or not. A LT event may be a demonstration of a new skill, an explanation of a new concept, an investigation or solving new problems. Following this guideline, task events serving the purposes of review, repetition and practice are not counted as LT events

Very different topics were covered in the two sequences of lessons. The A1 lessons were on geometry and the topics covered the ratio of circumference and diameter of a circle, the formula for the circumference, the area of a palm (the concept of area), areas of squares, rectangles and triangles. The SH2 lessons were on algebra and the topics were: linear inequalities, linear equations in two unknowns, methods for solving a system of linear equations in two unknowns (substitution and elimination), system of linear equations in three unknowns and application in word problems.

By a simple counting of the number of tasks per lesson, the average number of tasks per lesson is 2.9 for the Australian lessons (excluding two computer lessons), whereas in the Shanghai lessons the average number of tasks per lesson is 5.7. Both sequences of lessons contained task events for developing concepts and skills. In the preliminary comparison between the two sequences of lessons, there are four lessons containing tasks which needed manipulation of concrete materials or measurement activities, and two computer lessons one of which was on project work in the A1 lessons. The SH2 lessons mostly contained problems which could be worked out in paper and pencil and many of them contained subtasks. Therefore, the Australian lessons showed more variation in the nature of the tasks than the Shanghai lessons. The difference should be a result of the different contents, namely, mensuration and equations. Besides, it might also be a result of the teacher's choice of structuring the lessons.

Routine in the LT Events

After coding the lessons for LT and non-LT events, the respective video excerpts were also coded to trace the major routine in the LT events for both Australian and Shanghai lessons. It is very obvious that the pace in the Shanghai lessons was much faster than that in the Australian lessons. A Shanghai lesson always covered more tasks (including LT and non-LT) than an Australian lesson. Despite this difference, both teachers had a similar major routine of giving instruction about the task, followed by students carrying out the task and ending with the whole class paying attention to teacher-led interactive feedback. An iconic illustration of the pace difference can be easily shown by putting the timeline of the lessons in contrast (see Figure 1).

The timelines of A1-L01 and A1-L02

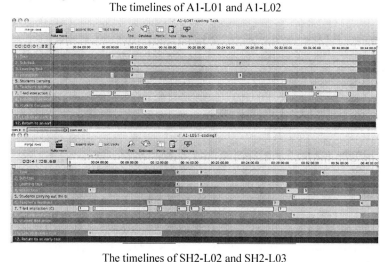

The timelines of SH2-L02 and SH2-L03

Figure 1. Examples of timelines of Australian lessons and Shanghai lessons

The routine in A1 Teacher A1 often began by giving instruction where she explained the task, followed by the students carrying out the task. In the period, a lot of between desks instruction or 'Kikan-Shido' (O'Keefe, Xu,& Clarke, 2006) took place. The event might have ended by the teacher giving feedback to the whole class but sometimes the teacher asked the students to finish the LT as homework. In the latter case, the next lesson began with a kind of review in which the teacher guided the class to go through in detail the LT in the last lesson. Although a review event is not readily counted as a LT event in the coding because it was not actually teaching something new, it plays an important role in the process of the students' learning. When this happened, the two lessons might appear to be a combined period with a strong link in terms of teaching contents.

The routine in SH2 Similar to teacher A1, teacher SH2 always began by his instruction, followed by the students carrying out the task and ended an event by giving feedback to the whole class. Besides the difference in the number of LT per lesson which affects the pace of the lesson, there are some other important differences between the lessons in A1 and SH2 which contributed to the difference in the pace and rhythm of the lessons. Like teacher A1, teacher SH2 always explained the task, yet the SH2 students were more ready to give answers whenever their teacher tried to elicit their ideas. Therefore, the SH2 pace appeared to be much in gear although the time spent on instruction might be roughly the same as those in A1.

The second contrast is that time taken by students in SH2 to complete tasks was much shorter than that in A1. There was Kikan-Shido while students engaged themselves in the tasks in both SH2 and A1 lessons. The contrast may partly a result of the different nature of the tasks and partly a result of the nature of the major activities during Kikan-Shido. Teacher A1 spent a lot of time in guiding student activities, which included giving information, eliciting response and scaffolding development. On the other hand, teacher SH2 did not spend as much time as teacher A1 with individual students, rather he often used this opportunity to select some students' work, which he might use in the later feedback to whole class. In other words, the Kikan-Shido of SH2 was often for the purpose of monitoring students' progress.

The third contrast is that teacher SH2 always finished all LT in one lesson while teacher A1 sometimes gave the unfinished LT as homework with a follow–up in the next lesson.

The Analysis of Two Australian Lessons A1-L01 and A1-L02: From the Concept of π to the Formula of C=2πR

The first Australian lesson A1-L01 had only one LT event which lasted for about 34 minutes, nearly the whole of the lesson. The event began with a brief teacher's instruction which lasted for about two minutes. The teacher explained orally the task to the students and below is the teacher's explanation:

T: Now, you've got the circles on page a hundred and seventy-
        four, I think. Four. A hundred and seventy-four. You've
        got circles labeled from 'a' to 'f', and you're going to
        use that piece of string to find the diameter, radius and
        circumference…In addition to the circles in the book, I'm
        going to put some on the board, so you'll need to come out
        and measure some of those as well. But I think some of you,
        so we don't all come to the board at the same time, um,
        some of you may want to do the ones at the board first, or
        after you've done a couple from the book. So we're using
        the string to measure the circumference of the circle as
        accurately as possible. I need you to be very, very
        accurate, as well as, I think, the table that requires you
        to fill in the radius and diameter. And I guess you don't
        really need to use the string to, to do that. You need to
        use a ruler. But when you come to the board you might want
        to use some string. Questions?

Key to symbols used in transcripts in this chapter

...   A pause of one second or less
( )   Empty single parentheses represent untranscribed talk. The talk may be untranscribed because
         the transcriber could not hear what was said
. . . . Omitted text
//   Marks the beginning of simultaneous speech.
[text]   Comments and annotations, often descriptions of non-verbal action
text   Italicised text indicates emphatic speech

The task was adopted from the textbook about measuring the radius and diameter of some circles to prepare a table for further work. It was straightforward and demanded mostly procedural and manipulative skills. While the teacher invited a few students to work on the board at the front of the class, the remaining of the class worked on the task as individual seatwork. The Kikan-Shido during this period was essential because the teacher moved between desks to give support, for example, to give individual encouragement, suggestions for making accurate measurement. To a student who worked faster than the others, the teacher gave him extra instruction for the next segment of the task so that he could continue at his own pace. Although the class was working on the same task, analysis showed that the students were in fact making different paces of progress through the task.

After about 15 minutes, the teacher gave the instruction of the second segment of the task, adding a column (Circumference over Diameter, C/D) to the table. To some, the teacher asked the students to observe the patterns of the numbers in the table. Then the students continued to work at their own pace. This lasted for another twelve minutes. Then the teacher resumed the whole class attention. The teacher-led interaction for the next four minutes was mostly soliciting answers from the students to prepare the table on the board. Then, the teacher led the students to inspect the table of data, and whole class teacher-led discussion truly began.

T: So let's have a look at his table, any comments?

This was a very open question. The first couple of answers showed that the students put their focus on accuracy of the measurement. Next, the teacher guided them to observe that the ratio C/D was close to three.

```
T:        Hands up if you were finding that your, the value for the
          circumference being divided by the diameter was around
          three?  Who noticed that?  When I, when I had a look at
          your tables it certainly seemed that way.  Now if, if I
          were to tell you that, that, that's in fact true, that that
          value should be around three, it seems to me you're doing
          the right thing what does this tell you about circles then?
```

Even pointing out this, the numbers in the table did not really convince the students of the results. A student commented that it was not always three. One commented that it was around three. Embedded in the feedback given by the teacher, the teacher was fully aware of the fact that the students had made different progress in the investigation of the table. In addition, a student, Levi, made a remark about calculating the circumference and the teacher picked up this point which was obviously one of the objectives of the task. The teacher immediately asked two brief questions about finding circumference (a circle with diameter of 20cm and a tree with diameter of 50m.) These examples to a certain extent confirmed the student's suggestion and also illustrated positively the predicting power of the property of the fixed ratio of C/D. The teacher's response was obviously spontaneous as a result of the student's observation and suggestions. It is a kind of diversion or bridging but it also indirectly helped to provide a background to the subsequent LT events, which were about using the formula of $C = \pi D$

```
T:        It's around three.  Yeah, so, so for, for any circle that
          you measure, for any circle that we draw Levi says that if
          you know the diameter if you multiply that by three you
          will get a figure that is very, very close to the
          circumference.  That's a very powerful statement to make.
          A very powerful statement to make.  Any circle that I draw,
          if I know the distance from here to here I can pretty much,
          I can pretty much work out what the circumference is by
          multiplying by three.
T:        So, if the diameter of my circle is twenty centimetres,
          what would the circumference of this circle be…around?
. . . .
T:        It would be around sixty centimetres.  If the circumference
          of my circle is one of those huge trees. Fifty metres. One
          of those, I've forgotten the name of those trees actually.
          Fifty metres. If I've got one of those huge trees and I
          want to know what, what, what the distance is around that
          tree trunk but I happen to know that it's fifty metres from
          one side to the other?  Frith?
Frith:    […]
T:        It might, the circumference  will be around a hundred and
          fifty metres.  There is something I need to tell you about
          this, this value though.  It's not three.  It's around
          three.  Amit, what were you going to say earlier?
Amit:     Three point one four.
T:        Is it three point one four?
Amit:     […]
T:        Ooh, three point one four one five.  Now Amit has had
          something to do with, with this particular value.
```

After the two examples, the teacher returned to talking about the value of π. By this moment, it was very near the end of the lesson. The teacher gave a relatively long teacher-talk about interesting information about π from the internet, which included the irrational number property, the computer calculation of huge number of digits for the value of π and recent achievement of a mathematician with respect to π.

A1-L05: The different ways of representing the formula

In order to understand more about the possible effect and purpose of this LT-event in A1-L01, the analysis of A1-L02 continues here. A1-L02 began with a review of the measurement task in the last lesson. The teacher started by asking the students to give two rows of the results for yesterday table which the students readily answered. From the two rows, the teacher guided the students to recall the formula (C~3*D), then the ratio π, that π is irrational and the different approximate values for π in calculation. The teacher used a lot of recall questions and the students were more ready to answer the teachers' question when comparing with their responses in yesterday's LT event. Although this was not a LT event but a review, it was important for the concrete preparation of the learning activities in the next LT.

After the review, the teacher led the class to the first LT event in A1-L02 to find the circumference of a circle and the rule (3.14*D) was in fact suggested by a student (Michael). Then, the teacher commented on the approximate value of π and confirmed the rule "C is equal to pi multiplied by D". This confirmation concluded the discussion with a mathematical formalisation, that is, a representation of the results in symbolic formula. In the second LT event, the teacher demonstrated how to calculate the circumference if the radius was 19cm. By the nature of the task, the task seemed to be a practice item. However, when a student Olivia suggested the rule "2πr". The teacher built upon the student's comment and worked out this as an equivalent rule to "πD". The teacher was aware that the students might have diverse background and some might not know the new rule. The development of the class discourse was to elicit several alternative forms of the formula and see the equivalence by algebra. As a result, there was a jump from the practice of procedural knowledge (applying the formula) to a discussion at a conceptual level (seeking the alternative forms of an algebra formula).

```
T:        [to Olivia]   Now, Olivia, I'm interested in what you said
          earlier.  You gave me a different rule.  You didn't give me
          'C equals pi D.
Olivia:   [...]
T:        Olivia, Olivia.  You know about that, as well, do you?
          [to Olivia]   Would you like to repeat what you were saying?
Olivia:   [...]
T:        [to all]  O.K.  [Writes C = • D]  Now, we've got this rule,
          that will help us find the circumference of a circle...[to
          Olivia] ...and your're suggesting that there's another rule,
          two • r.  Go on, how'd you get it, where does that come
          from?

. . . .
```

T:	Yeah. So, how can you show me that they're exactly the same?
Liz:	Two Pi R is exactly the same as Pi D
T:	Why?
Liz:	[…]
T	Good. Good girl. [to all] Does everyone see that? That we can rewrite that pronumeral as 'D' as 'two R'. So if I take that first rule, which says that c is equal to • multiplied by the diameter…

. . . .

T:[to all]	Um, Instead of 'D', what's another way of referring to 'D'? The diameter is equal to? [to Liz] Liz?
Liz:	Two R.
T:	Two R.
T:[to all]	So I'm just going to substitute, instead of 'D', I'm just going to write 'Two R'. So that now says the circumference is equal to two pi two R. How does that match up with what I wrote just above? Are they the same?
Ben:	[…]
T	Who said 'No'?
Ben:	[…]
T:[to Ben]	Ben, why not?
Ben:	[…]
T:	So they don't look identical, do they? Um, what does two pi R mean in expanded form?
Ben	Two times Pi times R
T:	Good. What does, um, O.K… [Writes '• X 2 X R' on the board] So what, what's the difference now? So you were saying to me before the difference is in the order that, that…
Ben:	[…]
T:	pi by two, then by R? Two by pi, then by R. So if I were to substitute a radius of five centimetres into this one, and into that one, what would I get? Would I get… You don't know? [to Stephen] Stephen?
Stephen:	The first one is bigger than the top one.
T:	This one would be bigger than the top one? Why don't we try it, then? [to Michael] Michael, I'm going to need your help with the calculator, O.K. [to all] We're substituting…
S12:	[…] Wouldn't it be 'two r Pi'?
T:	[to S17] Two r Pi. Does it matter? Why don't we try that one as well? [to all] We've got all the, all the different combinations here. 'two R pi', two times r times pi. So we've got three different ways of writing this rule. I want to, I want to check what happens, what we get when we substitute r equal to five. So let met take those three, let me clean some board space here. If you've got a calculator, I want you to, to check our calculations as well while I do this. We've got c is equal to two times pi times R, we're comparing that when C is equal to pi times two times R, and we're comparing that to two times R times pi.

. . . .

T:	O.K., doesn't seem to make a difference. Why won't it make a difference? Liz?
Liz:	[…]
T:	Yep…Michael? Why would it, why won't it make a difference?
Michael:	[…]
T:	Amit?
Amit:	[…]
T:	Yep, which…And what do we know about multiplication? Monica?
Monica:	[…]
T:	O.K. so give me an example…So when you learnt your tables in primary school what did you notice? What's seven times

129

	eight? Fifty-six. What's eight times seven? Fifty-six. What's two times three times four? Anthony?
Anthony:	Twenty-four.
T:	Good. Anthony, what's *three* times two times four?
Anthony:	Twenty-four.
T:	You don't, you don't even have to calculate it do you? and what's four times…
Anthony:	[…]
T:	Wait, I don't think I've got all of that…there we go.
Anthony:	Twenty-four.
T:	Twenty-four…and I could go on for a little more…so…um…so…getting back to this…this is just a matter of…we could write the rule as two pi R, we could write the rule as pi two R, we could write the rule as two R pi , it doesn't matter because we've got three numbers being multiplied to each other and what we know about multiplication is that it doesn't matter which order the numbers come in. This is just a matter of usage now and you will find that …um…the agreed written rule around the world is to put the pronumeral first followed…sorry the coefficient first followed by pronumeral. So that's why our two comes first. This is what you would generally find. So now, because Olivia mentioned that before, you have a choice of two rules. So if you're looking for the circumference of a circle you may wish to use pi D or you may which to use two pi R. What situation might that happen in? You're so quiet today. Levi?
Levi:	If you only know the radius.
T:	If you only know the radius which one are you going to use?
Levi:	Um.
T:	A or B?
Levi:	B.
T:	B. Does it matter? No. Because all of you were telling me what the radius *and* the diameter were. When you wrote down the information before you told me both things so if you do that all the time it really won't matter it's whichever one you find more comfortable using. They give the exact, exactly the same answer.

Immediately after learning the formula C= πD, it is natural to expect students to practise and apply the formula to a similar task. There can also be a freedom of choice of formula between C= πD and C= 2πR to arrive at the answer. However, students do not come into lesson with an empty mind. Besides, mathematical phenomena and properties are subject to objective observation. To someone who is competent in algebra, the equivalence of the two formulae needs no explanation. However, to many students who may see this for the first time, this may be a kind of cognitive conflict which provides an opportunity of learning something important, namely in this case, a flexibility in the procedure to find the circumferences of circles and the nature of algebraic formula. It was very important that the teacher had picked up what the students had in their mind, let them have opportunity to reflect upon the situation and to say what they thought. In this episode, the teacher invited 11 students to express what they thought. Consequently the class discussion put focus on how the students saw the equivalence between different formulae instead of the numerical value of the circumference. This demonstrated how cognitive conflict could be explored and developed into a learning situation at a conceptual level. This was in fact promoted by the teacher's mediation. The teacher's why-questions, which were of metacognitive nature, provided a lot of guidance. In reality, the discussion of equivalent formulae was indeed at a more abstract level than finding circumference by applying a formula. Hence, there was a scaffolding of levels in the events. It also illustrated that a LT event needs to be categorised according to what happened in the event and not only by the task itself.

The Analysis of a LT Event in SH2-L02: From the Concept of the Solution for a Linear Equation to the Method of Substitute Equation

SH2-L02 consisted of 6 task events. The first one was a task for reviewing the meaning of a linear equation of one unknown. The second one was a LT event that lasted for about 17 minutes and was the only task event, which was labeled as a LT event in the lesson. The teacher taught the following concepts in this LT event:

– The meaning of a solution for a linear equation in two unknowns
– The concept of infinitely many solutions for an equation
– Substitute equation (using an expression in x to represent y)

The learning task in the LT event was about the problem of chickens and rabbits kept in the same cage. The teacher first gave two straightforward questions asking students to represent the given context in terms of linear equations in two unknowns. The students answered these two questions readily showing that they fulfilled the prerequisite of writing an equation. What happened demonstrated an example how the chicken and rabbit problem created a realistic context for the students. A realistic context here refers to a context which the students can handle and perform their mathematical skills (Van den Heuvel-Panhuizen, 2003). It may not refer to what happens in real life. The context can be either in symbolic or word problem format. The two questions are translated below:

– In a cage, there are chickens and rabbits as a sum of twelve, if we assume there are x rabbits, y chickens, so what will the equation be?
– In a cage there are chickens and rabbits, there are forty legs, if there are x rabbits and y chickens, so what will the equation be?

These questions and the review at the beginning of the lessons may well be seen as the concrete preparation for subsequent learning activities. After this brief introduction had set up the background for the learning task, the teacher asked the students to solve only question (1) above and this set off a search for the number of chickens and rabbits in the context of chickens and rabbits. At this stage, the teacher asked:

```
T:        Please think about, think about the first question. The
          first question, … in the cage, there are chickens, and
          rabbits as a sum of twelve, we have the equation x plus y
          equals to twelve, think about how many chickens are there,
          how many rabbits are there?
```

The students were asked to discuss in groups. Immediately, nearly all students in the class started talking while the teacher moved from one group to another to listen to the answers found in the groups. This discussion only lasted for about one minute. This is a kind of free exploration though brief and limited in content.

Then the teacher drew the class attention to him again and began a teacher-led interaction about 6 minutes long. The discourse for this segment of the lesson was dense and shifted from one focus to another under the teacher's directive questions.

The interaction began with the teacher inviting the class to give the different pairs of answers. After several students' suggestions, they came up with five pairs (11, 1), (4, 8), (8, 4), (6, 6) and (2, 10). The teacher asked the next question to shift the focus to the number of pairs of possible answers.

```
T:        Okay, stop now, in the discussion, some students say there
          for the first question, find out on your own, how many
          chickens are there, how many rabbits are there?
Cape:     If there is one chicken, so there are eleven rabbits.
T:        Oh, he says that if there is one chicken, how many rabbits
          are there? Eleven, any other suggestion!
Crystal:  If there are four rabbits, so there are chickens
T:        Oh, how many rabbits are there?
Crystal:  Four.
T:        If there are four rabbits, there are eight chickens, any
          other suggestions?
Charles:  If there are eight rabbits, there are four chickens.
T:        Oh, if there are eight rabbits, how many chickens are
          there? Four, okay this one.
Chen:     If there are six chickens, there are six rabbits too.
T:        There are six rabbits too, oh, …any other suggestions?
Clare:    If there are ten chickens, there are two rabbits.
T:        Chicken? How many chickens? Ten, how many rabbits? Two,
          okay, for the next question, for such pairs of numbers, how
          many pairs are there? How many pairs? …Cake.
```

In the discourse, the teacher asked some questions inviting the students to think about the problem or to review earlier answers, for example, the question "for such pairs of numbers, how many pairs are there?" Such questions are of metacognitive nature, which led the students to think and reflect upon the mathematical objects, their own work and thinking (in this case, the nature and number of the number pairs they had produced). After the search of possible pairs of answer, this question became easy and straightforward. A student suggested eleven pairs and the class readily followed. Confirming the number of pairs, the teacher asked another key question which brought the class into a new focus, "Let's think about, what is a solution of a linear equation in two unknowns, what does that mean?"

```
Cake:     Five and seven, six and six, eleven.
T:        Eleven, oh, so how many pairs are there?
E:        Eleven pairs.
T:        Eleven pairs so students think about that, substitute x
          equals to eleven, y equals to one into the equation, what
          is the sum of that at the left hand side?
E:        Twelve.
T:        Twelve, the right hand side is also twelve, so x equals to
          eleven, y equals to one is a pair of solution of the
          equation…, so students let's think about, what is a
```

```
           solution of a linear equation in two unknowns, what does
           that mean?
["E" represents the whole class answered in chorus.]
```

This again is a request for reviewing what has been done as a whole and brings the focus from examples to the meaning of a solution of a linear equation. The new shift made the class move onto a discourse with a focus on the meaning of a solution of an equation. There is a demand for generalisation and mathematical formalisation. The question asked how in general a pair of numbers might be qualified to be called a solution of an equation. The class responses immediately reflected the difficulty of this question. Only three students raised their hands. The teacher was fully aware of this. After a student (Carry) had suggested, "That can make the two sides of the linear equation in two unknowns equal to each other", the probing did not end. In order to fulfill the teacher's question, the class under the teacher's guidance came to conclude with a definition in formal mathematics language which the teacher confirmed by writing the answer on the board.

```
T:         Tell me, what does the solution of linear equation in two
           unknowns mean? There are only three students willing to put
           up their hands! Okay, this student, tell us?
Catty:     Among the numbers of solutions of the linear equation in
           two unknowns, each of the solution is the solution of the
           equation.
T:         Among the solutions, that is about solutions, so I don't
           have to ask you what the solution means. For now I am
           asking about the meaning of solution of linear equation in
           two unknowns, right? Sit down, okay, this one.
Carry:     That can make the two sides of the linear equation in two
           unknowns equal to each other.
T:         A pair…
Carry:     A pair…
T:         A pair…
Carry:     A pair of values
T:         A pair of what, //values of unknowns
E:         //Values of unknowns.
T:         Good! Very good, what did she say as suits or satisfies the
           linear equation in two unknowns? A pair of values of the
           unknowns, that is called a solution of the linear equation.
T:         Sit down, for that is a pair of numbers, so we use a pair
           of big brackets to include them, indicating that they are
           related. Eleven can't be separated with one, if x is
           eleven, what is y? //One.
E:         //One.
T:         Because they are related, we use a pair of big brackets to
           indicate that…it suits…or [Teacher writing on the board]
           [Student putting up hand] say…satisfies…the linear
           equations in two unknowns…the pair of values…of the
           unknowns, we call that…a solution of the equation.
```

In this segment of the lesson, the object of discussion moves away from the context of chickens and rabbits to the action of reviewing the possibility of answers, next to the reflection upon the nature of the solution for an equation. In these shifts, there is an obvious demand of *moving up the levels of abstractness* collectively in the class discussion. While making this progress, the teacher at the same time corrected the usage of language of the students' answers. On the one hand, the teacher was teaching a more formal use of mathematical terminology. On the other hand, this may also be seen as a kind of preparation for later work.

The teacher-led interaction continued and again the teacher made a turning point by asking another key question, "If x and y indicates not real situation, that doesn't stand for rabbits, or chickens, so how many solutions are there for such an equation?" This question brought the class to a higher level of abstractness for working on an equation in a completely different context. That is, the variables x and y no longer represent the numbers of chickens and rabbits in a realistic context but any real numbers. This moving up in the level of abstractness would not be possible if the students still working on the results of specific number pairs for the twelve rabbits and chickens, and did not learn the general meaning of a solution. Therefore, this shift is a kind of bridging which is an interjection requiring the students to use what they have learned about other types of equations. This was obviously planned in advance by the teacher. This shift also brought the students to the next knowledge point for the lesson of the day, i.e., there are infinitely many solutions for such an equation.

```
T:      Okay, for this question, it is said that there are eleven
        pairs of solutions, if x and y indicates not real
        situation, that doesn't stand for rabbits, or chickens, so
        how many solutions are there for such an equation?
E:      Infinite.
T:      Infinite solutions, I want to know, is that possible to
        assume x as a negative number?
E:      Yes.
T:      Yes right? How about fractions?
T:      So we've got the number of solutions of linear equation in
        two unknowns, how many solutions are there?
E:      Infinite solutions.
T:      Infinite solutions…we call that the system of solutions of
        the equation. There are a lot of solutions, right! A lot,
        so let's discuss how should we solve the forth question.
```

The above six-minute teacher-led interaction showed a discourse of Socratic style, that is, the whole class filling in the answers, which the teacher wanted them to give. The discussion shows a number of critical shifts: from examples of numerical answers to a reflection on the answers (counting the number of possible answers), then to formalisation for the concept of "a solution of an equation"; from a word problem context to a symbolic context. There is a demand for *transcendence between the levels of abstractness* and this was done in a very short time.

While the analysis to this point shows how the teacher introduced the concept of solution, the analysis of the next episode shows how the teacher taught the class a procedure how to solve the equation by creating a substitute equation.

```
T:      For that, how can we solve four x plus two y equals to
        forty, and now can four x plus two y equals to forty be
        simplified Okay, this one.?
Cable:  Both of the sides to be divided by two…
T:      Um good, both of the sides of the equation, //to be divided
        by two.
E:      //To be divided by two.
T:      What should two x plus y be? //Twenty.
```

E: //Twenty.
T: This equation is simpler, so I want to know how can we
        solve the equation. Discuss now, that doesn't stand for
        chickens and rabbits, no actual meaning, what should the
        values of x and y be?

The teacher asked the students to solve in an abstract sense the equation
$4x + 2y = 40$ derived from the second question of rabbits and chickens. What
happened after this was very similar to what happened for the first question.
Because the teacher had asked the students to solve the equation, this might have
become a repetition. Unsurprisingly, the students were likely to repeat what they
did for the last equation. After the group discussion, the teacher again invited many
students to suggest answers. More students had the chance to speak and there were
8 pairs of answers including a negative number: (5,10), (6,8), (16,2), (8,4), (0,20),
(2,16), (40,0), (-4,28). The teacher then reaffirmed with the class that there were
infinitely many solutions. If the episode ended at this point, it would not be
counted as a part of the LT event because repetition would be the main purpose of
the activity. However, following this brief episode, we see that the objective of the
repetition is to provide a rationale for the demonstration of a procedure for solving
the equation. Therefore, this segment was still counted as a part of the LT event.
Based on what the students had experienced, the teacher raised a reflective
question, "It is very difficult to find the solutions one by one. So, is there a better
method?" This in fact is not a true question but a diversion/bridging leading to
what the teacher wanted to *demonstrate*, that is, rewriting a substitute equation
$y = 20 - 2x$, in other words, "to use an expression of x to represent y". The
students surely did not have a clue to comment on this novel abstract method. The
teacher immediately guided the students to find more values for x and y by using
this substitute equation till they were confirmed that the substitute equation was a
better method. After this, the teacher told the class that there was another substitute
equation, "to use an expression of y to represent x" and that they could use either
method. In this segment of teacher-student discourse, although there were
continuous interaction between the teacher and student, the style changed. It is
essentially the fill-in-the-blank type. The questions were straight forward and
leading to an obvious answer which the class readily gave in chorus.

T: For that, it is very difficult to find the solutions one by
        one. So, is there better method? …Look at the blackboard,
        the first step, we rewrite into y equals to twenty minus
        x…that is to use expression of x to represent y, alright?
T: See, after having such an equation, if x equals to zero,
        then we'll immediately know what the result of y is!
E: //Twenty.
        Twenty.
T: A solution is got. x equals to negative five, what does
        what equal to…?
E: Ten / Thirty.
T: Substitute five into the equation!
E: Ten / Thirty.
T: How should five be substituted into the equation! What does
        y equal to? What does y equal to?
E: Ten / Thirty.
T: How many?

135

E:	Thirty.
T:	What does twenty minus two, x equals to negative five, equal to!
E:	Thirty.
T:	So we have got its solution, that is x equals to negative five, y equals to thirty, so, I chose simpler steps, firstly…use substitute equation of x to represent y, having x, then find out y, by having one solution.
T:	As well, we can use expression of y to represent x, so let's see, two x equals to twenty minus y, x equals to twenty minus y over two, let's answer it, to use expression of x to represent y, …what is the name of it? …Charles.
Charles:	Use substitute equation of y to represent x.
T:	Right, what is to be represented by expression of y? x, that is possible, so, compare the two methods, which is more convenient?
E:	The first one.
T:	The first one is more convenient, what is used? Expression of x to represent y.
E:	Expression of x to represent y.
T:	When you work on the questions, use the one which is more suitable.

The teacher ended the LT event with a clear articulation of what the class had learned for the day, supplemented with writing on the board. Compared with the earlier episodes, this episode comprised of entirely of teacher-talk only with the exception of a chorus response to one teacher question. In this episode the teacher gave a very clear list of the mathematical content of the LT event as well as the lesson of the day. This episode showed a typical 'Matome' by the SH teacher, that is, how he made conclusions in a lesson (Shimizu, 2006).

T:	okay, today, we've talked about, nine point one, linear equations in two unknowns. [T writing on the board]
T:	To answer these questions, think about that! The first one is about linear equations in two unknowns, its characteristics are very clear, there are two unknowns.
T:	And, the power of the unknowns is one, so this kind of equation is called linear equation in two unknowns.
T:	The second one, the solution of the linear equation in two unknowns, it has to suit or satisfy a pair of values of the unknowns of the linear equation in two unknowns, that is called one of the solutions of the equation.
T:	So how many solutions are there for linear equations in two unknowns?
E:	Infinite solutions.
T:	We call the infinite solutions the set of solutions of a linear equation in two unknowns, finally we talked about the method to solve the equation, the first step, use expression of x to represent y, finding x as well as y, what if we find out y?
T:	There is an x, they are the pair of solutions of the equation. Because they are related, so a pair of big brackets is used to represent, that is the way to represent the solutions.

The Complementary Role of Non-LT Events in SH2-L02

Following this LT event, there were four non-LT events. The events were not direct repetitive practice but they helped to consolidate the concepts learnt in the last LT event. The content of the four non-LT events (non-LT1 to 4) are described in table 1. Being very different from the learning task, the non-LTs are all abstract and symbolic in form and description. Each task has a very clear objective which asks the students to apply the knowledge they have just learned in the LT event. They may require the students to apply their conceptual or procedural knowledge but the instructions in the task are mostly procedural. For example, non-LT1 is purely procedural. It asks the students first write the substitute equation ($y = ...$), find the values of y for some given x and then write down the solutions of the equation. Non-LT2 asks the students to identify a linear equation in two unknowns from some given pairs. Non-LT3 and non-LT4 ask the students to determine whether a given pair of numbers is a solution for a given equation or not. It is important to note that although the non-LT events are not classified as LT events, it does not mean that the students did not learn anything in these events. In the analysis, with respect to the content of the tasks, subtle variations pertinent to the understanding of the object of learning are built in the design of the practice items (Huang, Mok & Leung, 2006). With respect to the nature of interaction, it is observed that these events are essential in helping students master the new knowledge. With respect to teaching activities and class organisation, they are very similar to the LT events. There were episodes of instruction, individual or group work, feedback to whole class by the teacher. There were a lot of opportunities for the teacher to give further supports, corrections and explanations to the students either individually or collectively in whole class setting. Therefore, these non-LT events play a significant complementary role to the LT events.

Table 1. The non-LT for consolidating LT events in SH2-L02

Non-LT1	3. Try it Given the equation $3x - 2y = 5$ Rewrite the equation to represent y by the expression of x. Find out the corresponding values of y when $x = -1$, $-\dfrac{2}{3}, \dfrac{3}{2}, 0$. Write down the solutions of the equations.
Non-LT2	4. Which of the following equations are linear equations in two unknowns? (1) $xy + 5x - y = 0$ (2) $2x^2 - 3x = 5$ (3) $x - 4y + 5 = 0$ (4) $\dfrac{x}{6} + \dfrac{2y}{3} = 1$ (5) $x + 1 = 6z$ (6) $\dfrac{6}{x} - 2y = 3$

Non-LT3	5. Justify the given values of x and y and see whether they are the solutions of the equation, put a tick if it is, put a cross if it is not. $2x - 3y = 6, (x = 0, y = 4)$ $x - 5y = -2, (x = 7, y = 1)$ $5x + 2y = 8, (x = 2, y = -1)$ $2x - y = 4, (x = 2, y = 2)$
Non-LT4	6. For the following pair of values $\begin{cases} x = 0 \\ y = 3 \end{cases}, \begin{cases} x = 0 \\ y = \dfrac{1}{2} \end{cases}, \begin{cases} x = -2 \\ y = 2 \end{cases}, \begin{cases} x = \dfrac{1}{2} \\ y = 2 \end{cases}, \begin{cases} x = 2 \\ y = -1 \end{cases}$ Which are the solutions of the equation $2x + y = 3$? Which are the solutions of the equation $3x + 4y = 2$?

Repetition of an Activity Pattern but Still Considered as New Knowledge: The Chicken and Rabbit Problem Revisited in SH2-L03

Lesson SH2-L03 began with two tasks which reviewed what were learnt in SH2-L03. The reviews helped the teacher to ensure that the students could master what was learned in the last lesson and the knowledge would prepare them to learn what was followed in this lesson. Then the lessons continued with two LT events. The events show a strong reminiscence of the lesson the previous day (SH2-L02). The chicken and rabbit problem was revisited with a slight modification and the context was used to teach the concept of a system of linear equations. The second LT event was a procedural task showing how to solve a system of linear equations. The chicken and rabbit problem was translated below:

> Guess it: How many chickens and rabbits are there? There are x rabbits and y chickens in a cage. There are altogether twelve heads, and forty legs. How many rabbits and chickens are there in the cage?

The question presented as a coherent problem was in fact the two questions the class had worked through in detail yesterday. The context was familiar to the class but the question was no longer the same problem because the students had to consider both constraints together. A student (Cobot) immediately suggested to write down two equations: $x + y = 12$ and $4x + 2y = 40$. Next, the teacher asked the class to simplify $4x + 2y = 40$ to $2x + y = 20$. Till this point, what had happened was simply a repetition of yesterday's work although the problem was rephrased. The activity was obviously concrete preparation. Then, the teacher gave a few pairs of numbers to start off the discussion and he asked the students to look for the answers in group.

```
T:         Good, so how many chickens and rabbits are there? …Let me
           give you some pairs of numbers. [Speaking while writing on
           the board] The first pair: x equals two, y equals four; the
           second pair: [CASH, CATHY making corrections] x equals
           four, y equals twelve; the third pair: x equals eight, y
           equals four, there are many pairs like that, …for now,
           discuss with your classmates how many chickens and rabbits
           there are? [Students discussing] [Teacher walking around]
```

The discussion time allowed by the teacher was very brief. The teacher resumed the attention of whole class very soon. In the discourse, it was clearly shown that the objective of the problem was not the solution of the problem but the concept of a system of linear equations in two unknowns. At the same time, the teacher used a student's answer (Capella, "eight rabbits and four chickens") to show that an answer needed to satisfy both equation and why the two equations then formed one system. A student (Carry) suggested the name "a system of linear equations in two unknowns". This answer received the teacher's affirmative welcome both in oral and written form.

```
T:         Okay, stop now. How many chickens and rabbits are there in
           the question? … Why?
Capella:   There are eight rabbits, four chickens.
T:         Why not ten and two, ten plus two is twelve!
Capella:   Because when you substitute x equals two, y equals ten into
           two x plus y equals twenty (…)
T:         Oh, it may not be suitable to substitute two and ten into
           the second equation, so is it suitable to substitute four
           and twelve into the second equation?
E:         No.
T:         Oh, no suitable, how about eight and four?
E:         Suitable.
T:         For they can satisfy both the first and second equations,
           in this question, the values of the pair of numbers have to
           satisfy the first equation and also the second equation. In
           mathematics, we use a pair of big brackets to join them
           together. [Writing on the board while speaking] For that,
           we can have a [showing a slide]…in mathematics, we call
           this a system of linear equations [Writing on the board]…a
           set of equations formed by the combination of linear
           equations is called a system of linear equations. So,
           according to the characteristics of the system of linear
           equations, what kind of system is it?... The second girl in
           the row.
Carry:     A system of linear equations in two unknowns.
T:         A system of linear equations in two unknowns. She said that
           it is a system of linear equations in two unknowns [Writing
           on the board].
```

Immediately after this, the teacher brought the new mathematical object into focus and asked the class to inspect its characteristics, "What is a system of linear equations in two unknown?" The class led by the teacher then discussed the appropriateness of the name according to the power of the unknowns, the number of unknowns and the number of equations. While the learning objective was to obtain a process of generalisation for a mathematical definition, the answers were apparently negotiable and based on observation of facts.

T:	What is a system of linear equations in two unknown? Can you tell me? Try, that's alright even if you get it wrong, okay, this student is good today, you.
Clean:	There are two unknowns, and the power of the unknown (…) is one…we call this linear equations in two unknowns…
T:	A system of linear equations, um.
Clean:	A system of linear equations in two unknowns.
T:	He said that equations that have two unknowns, and the power of the unknowns is one is called a system of linear equations in two unknowns. You seem to have very different opinions.
Cell:	Two or above (…)
T:	Two or above, um.
Cell:	Equation of linear equations in two unknowns (…).
T:	A system formed by linear equations in two unknowns, good, let me write it down [Writing on the board], that is a pair of linear equations in two unknowns, right? That is also linear equation in two unknowns, he says there should be two or above, so let me write one more [Writing on the board]
T:	So, two or above, is this system of equations still called a system of linear equations in two unknowns?
E:	No.
T:	Why?
E:	Because there are three unknowns.
T:	Ai, there are three unknowns right? Right or not? Okay, does anyone have anything to add? … Cake.
Cake:	Two, um, in the coefficients …[CATHY raising her hand][CASH shaking his head]
T:	In the system of linear equations.
Cake:	In the system of linear equations, there are two unknowns, and the power of the unknown is …
T:	The power…
Cake:	Combination of equations having power of one is called a system of linear equations in two unknowns.
T:	Good, please sit down. He said that in the system of linear equations, his basic definition is correct, in a system of linear equations, there are two unknowns, [Writing on the board]…there are two unknowns [Writing on the board], and the power of the unknowns is one [writing on the board] is called a system of linear equations in two unknowns

The next part of the discussion, the teacher brought the class back to the solution of the equations. He revived the attention to a student's early answer of (8, 4). Then, the teacher showed his prepared tables of answers for each individual equation as supporting evidence. After he had made sure that the whole class saw that (8, 4) satisfied both equation, he concluded by giving the formal meaning of a solution, "the solution that satisfies all equations in the system is called the solution of the system" and ended this LT event.

Comparing carefully this pair of twin events, the LT event (SH2-L03) and the last LT event (SH2-L04), there were a lot of repeated features. The first similarity was the repeated context of chickens and rabbits, the same equations and familiar numerical answers. The second similarity was the repetition of activities for moving up the levels of abstraction. In both cases, the students were asked to think about the chicken and rabbit problems. Then they were guided to think about the mathematics equations and solutions at an abstract level. Next, they concluded with a summary of mathematical definitions.

Comparing the two twin events, two kinds of mathematical knowledge are taught or experienced. The first kind is content specific which concerns specific concepts and procedures such as a type of equations, the properties and names of the concepts, some basic skills or strategy for solving equations. The second kind is generic in nature and process oriented. It is the reflection upon mathematical facts to move up the level of abstractness, generalisation and use of mathematical formal language. These are important mathematical capacities which need to be cultivated in the process of learning. The twin events show how the teacher made these capacities become replicable and be practised by the students in a relative familiar context by introducing small variation in the tasks and the key questions in the class discourse.

CONCLUSION AND DISCUSSION

The LT events from an Australian and a Shanghai lesson sequences have been compared. The findings discussed are specific to the lesson sequences compared and are by no means generalisations of lessons in Australia or Shanghai. For the lessons studied, the first level of comparison shows that the pace of a Shanghai lesson is faster than that of an Australian lesson. The time spent on Kikan-Shido is more significant in the Australian lessons, whereas the Shanghai lessons have more time spent in whole class discussion. So was the difference in the nature of the functional activities during Kikan-Shido. Therefore, the teacher's mediation in the Shanghai lesson has more chance to be shared collectively in public. The students also due to greater availability of the whole class discussion in terms of time and the teacher's guidance have more opportunity to articulate mathematics in public. In contrast, the Australian students had greater freedom and more time to complete tasks by exploring their own way and in their own pace. There were likely to be more scaffolding activities while the teacher was helping the students as an individual. Consequently, there is apparently less time devoted for acquiring a uniform understanding of the mathematical object in the lesson.

The Shanghai lessons are characterised by the greater number of tasks, the complexity in the nature of the task, the nature of the teacher-student interaction in the class discourse, and the very short individual/group student work between periods of teacher-led whole class. The LT-lessons events are not the only events which contributed to the learning. Learning as a whole is supported in an essential way by lesson events of other nature such as review (Mesiti & Clarke, 2006), Kikan-Shido (O'Keefe et al., 2006), Matome (Shimizu, 2006) and lesson events of a practice nature (Huang et al., 2006). All these different tasks and events cluster in one SH lesson and produce a lesson of rapid pace and dense content. In contrast, the Australian lessons are characterised by fewer tasks and students working at a more leisurely pace. Likewise, both teacher-led whole class discussion and Kikan-Shido support the learning in an essential way. In both cases, the class activities may contain repetitions for different purposes in learning.

For a better understanding of how the mathematics subject matter may be brought about by the teaching an LT event, in the next level of analysis, the LT

141

events in two Australian lessons and two Shanghai lessons were scrutinised within the framework of conceptual-procedural knowledge and a model of mediated learning. Despite the difference in contents, the analysis shows how conceptual and procedural knowledge might be taught. What happened in the LT events is obviously a blended result of the tasks, the teacher's teaching style and the capacity of the students. Via the conceptual tools of concrete preparation, cognitive conflict, metacognition, bridging, the analysis shows that how the knowledge can be possibly taught in an atmosphere conducive to learning. In both cases, conceptual and procedural knowledge are shown not to be taught in isolation. The teaching of concepts always starts by building a realistic context which students can imagine and handle (Van den Heuvel-Panhuizen, 2003), for example, data obtained by the students' actual measurement of circles, the chicken and rabbit problem and familiar form of equations. The building up of such context usually involved the students' demonstration of their proficiency of their procedural knowledge. This process by some means provides a kind of concrete preparation which equips the students with a ground of manageable ideas and data. Concepts are built upon observable mathematical facts such as patterns in numbers, relationships between variables, generalisation of the characteristics of equations and solutions. Nevertheless, concepts do not emerge by themselves, the teacher's guidance in the process of mediation is thus crucial in the development. In an effective discourse, examples of cognitive conflict, metacognition and bridging could be observed. They may be brought in spontaneously or according to the teachers' plans either by the teachers or by the students.

This chapter has attempted to make a contribution in two ways. Firstly, it shows how analysis can utilise an event-coding technique in combination with the constructs in a learning model for a legitimate unit of LT events. In this way, the analysis brings about an understanding of the teaching and learning in two different cultures. The method will be worthy to apply in the exploration of the other LPS data sets.

Secondly, it gives support to the feasibility of the model of mediated learning. The analysis of the LT events within the model of mediated learning provides an understanding of how the pedagogical model of mediated learning can be implemented in different mathematical topics and teaching pace. This is made possible by the teacher's skilful mediation and planning of tasks. The mathematical complexity in the object of discussion depends a lot on the topic and the teacher's style of leading the class discourse. For example, in the Shanghai LT events, the teacher helps the students to see a strong networking between different mathematical objects such as a single linear equation of one unknown, two unknowns, and a system of linear equations of two unknowns, the meaning of solution in a word problem context and an abstract context. The observation of the relationships between these mathematical objects is often achieved by deliberate partial variation of the context and constraints between problems and questions (Huang et al., 2006). The juxtaposition of the mathematical objects in a closely packed way within a LT event or between LT events may also help the students to observe some relationships by contrast. This pedagogical arrangement is one factor for the apparent efficiency in completing a lot of content in a lesson. On the other hand, the Australian example (A1-L02) also shows how the teacher's mediation can empower the transcendence of learning from a procedural practice item to a conceptual level but maintaining a leisurely pace, which give more room for accreditation of the students' contribution in developing a lesson.

A final point to make, the twin LT events in the Shanghai lessons show an interesting example of how some generic mathematical processes in an abstract level may be repeated. On the one hand, one may argue that the repetition of activity pattern has the advantage of relative easy management and students may find it easily to learn the new concepts such linear equations in one unknowns and solutions, a system of linear equations in two unknowns and solutions. On the other hand, one may ask whether the repetitive nature may make the contents look too familiar to arouse sufficient motivation. Therefore, it is important to see what is repeated and what may possibly be achieved in the repetition. Besides easy management, the analysis of the two twin events shows a demonstration of a kind of generic mathematical process as well as how the process could be repeated. The teacher planned and carried out a generalisation and shifts from a word problem to a higher level of mathematical abstractness. He used the same technique in the LT event the next day. In the second day, the students became familiar with how to employ the mathematical terms and properties; thus, they participated more actively in the negotiation in the processes of making generalisation and mathematical formalisation. In other words, the mathematical terminology and properties became more manageable to the students. Underlying the apparent repetition, some capacities of generalisation and abstraction may become new mathematical tools for the students to practise. Such a mathematical process is obviously important and difficult to achieve in a few learning episodes. The analysis shows with evidence that the strategy worked well with this class in these LT events. The feasibility and effectiveness of such teaching strategies in other context and cultures may be worthy to explore in future studies.

ACKNOWLEDGEMENTS

The author would like to thank the Research Grants Council of Hong Kong, the Seed Funding Programme for Basic Research of the University of Hong Kong, and the Small Project Funding Programme also of the University of Hong Kong, for funding the project.

REFERENCES

Adey, P., & Shayer, M. (1994). *Really raising standards.* London: Routledge.
Adhami, M., Johnson, D. C., & Shayer, M. (1998). Cognitive development and classroom interaction: A theoretical foundation for teaching and learning. In J. D. Tinsley, & D. C. Johnson (Eds.), *Secondary school mathematics in the world of communication technologies* (pp. 205-213). London: Chapman & Hall.

Carpenter, T. P., & Lehrer, R. (1999). Teaching and learning mathematics with understanding. In E. Fennema, & T. A. Romberg (Eds.), *Mathematics classrooms that promote understanding* (pp. 19-32). Mahwah, NJ: Lawrence Erlbaum Associates.

Hiebert, J., & Lefevre, P. (1986). Conceptual and procedural knowledge in mathematics: An introductory analysis. In J. Hiebert (Ed.). *Conceptual and procedural knowledge: The case of mathematics*. Hillsdale, NJ: Lawrence Erlbaum Associates.

Huang, R., Mok, I. A. C., & Leung, F. K. S. (2006) Repetition or variation – 'Practice' in the mathematics classrooms in China. In D. J. Clarke, C. Keitel, & Y. Shimizu (Eds.), *Mathematics classrooms in twelve countries: The insider's perspective* (pp. 263-274). Rotterdam: Sense Publishers.

Mesiti, C., & Clarke, D. J. (2006). Beginning the lesson: The first ten minutes. In D. J. Clarke, J. Emanuelsson, E. Jablonka, & I. A. C. Mok (Eds.), *Making connections: Comparing mathematics classrooms around the world* (pp. 47-72). Rotterdam: Sense Publishers.

Mok, I. A. C., & Johnson, D. C. (2000). Reasoning algebraically with IT: A cognitive perspective. *Mathematics Education Research Journal, 12*(3), 286-302.

Mok, I. A. C., & Kaur, B. (2006). Learning tasks. In D. J. Clarke, J. Emanuelsson, E. Jablonka, & I. A. C. Mok (Eds.), *Making connections: Comparing mathematics classrooms around the world* (pp. 147-164). Rotterdam, Netherlands: Sense Publishers.

O'Keefe, C., Xu, L. H., & Clarke, D. J. (2006). Kikan-Shido: Between desks instruction. In D. J. Clarke, J. Emanuelsson, E. Jablonka, & I. A. C. Mok (Eds.), *Making connections: Comparing mathematics classrooms around the world* (pp. 73-106). Rotterdam: Sense Publishers.

Shimizu, Y. (2006). How do you conclude today's lesson? The form and functions of 'Matome' in mathematics lessons. In D. J. Clarke, J. Emanuelsson, E. Jablonka, & I. A. C. Mok (Eds.), *Making connections: Comparing mathematics classrooms around the world* (pp. 127-146). Rotterdam: Sense Publishers.

Van den Heuvel-Panhuizen, M. (2003). The didactical use of models in realistic mathematics education: An example from a longitudinal trajectory on percentage. *Educational Studies in Mathematics, 54,* 9-35.

Vygotsky, L. S. (1978). *Mind and society*. Cambridge: Harvard University Press.

Ida Ah Chee Mok
Faculty of Education
University of Hong Kong
Hong Kong SAR, China

CHAPTER EIGHT

Implementing Mathematical Tasks in US and Chinese Classrooms

INTRODUCTION

The efforts to pursue high quality classroom instruction in the United States have led to an increased interest in exploring instructional practices in high achieving educational systems in East Asia, including China. It has often been observed that classroom instruction in China is exam oriented, lecture dominated and strictly controlled by the teachers, all of which seem to be associated with a passive learning environment (Biggs & Watkins, 2001). However, some studies found that there was some active and student-centred learning taken place in Chinese classrooms (Huang & Leung, 2004; Mok, 2006; Stevenson & Lee, 1995). While educators and researchers have been putting forward an argument for student-centred teaching for years, comparative studies indicated that the teaching observed in US eighth-grade mathematics classes did not reflect the innovative pedagogical practices advocated in reform documents and recent research (Jacobs et al., 2006; Wood, Shin, & Doan, 2006). Based on a detailed analysis of three US classrooms taught by competent teachers, Wood, Shin and Doan (2006) were struck by the finding that "the presentations are divested not only of reasons, but are also completely devoid of any richness of thought that allows the learner to reason and gain insight into what one is doing mathematically when using the procedure" (p. 83).

These disappointing descriptions of mathematics classroom instruction in the United States and China led us to compare the classrooms in the two countries to get a deeper understanding and possibly shed light on ways to improve classroom instruction in both countries. Huang and Cai (2007) conducted an analysis of pedagogy associated with using representations in US and Chinese classrooms in which linear equations were extensively explored. They found that the US teachers tried to develop multiple representations simultaneously over a sequence of lessons through different activities, while the Chinese teachers tried to develop symbolic representations and graphic representations through the use of tabular and numerical representations to solve problems. These findings contribute to our understanding about the reasons that US students choose concrete strategies and drawing representations both for fostering understanding of a concept and also for solving problems (Cai, 2004; Cai & Lester, 2005).

Y. Shimizu, B. Kaur, R. Huang and D. J. Clarke (Eds.), Mathematical Tasks in Classrooms around the World, pp. 145–164.

Researchers have long tried to characterise the nature of the classroom instruction that maximises students' learning opportunities (Brophy & Good, 1986; National Academy of Education, 1999). Since classroom instruction is a complex enterprise (Leinhardt, 1993), researchers have attempted to identify important features of classroom instruction in order to improve teaching. A mathematical task is one of the important constructs in research about classroom instruction (Doyle, 1983; Hiebert & Wearne, 1993; Stein et al., 1996). Mathematical tasks provide intellectual environments for students' learning and the development of mathematical thinking. Doyle (1988) argues that tasks with different cognitive demands are likely to induce different kinds of learning. Tasks govern not only students' attention to particular aspects of content, but also their ways of processing information. Understanding the nature of mathematical tasks, in particular, how they are set up and implemented in classrooms is crucial to achieving high quality classroom instruction (Henningsen & Stein, 1997; Martin, 2007). In this paper, we investigate the cognitive demands of mathematical tasks and the strategies for implementing the tasks in US and Chinese classrooms in order to get a better understanding of the nature of classroom instruction.

THEORETICAL CONSIDERATIONS

Mathematical Tasks and Quality of Student Learning

The role of mathematical tasks in engaging students in thinking and reasoning about important mathematical ideas has been recognised and explored by many researchers (Cai & Lester, 2005; Doyle, 1983, 1988; Hilbert & Wearne, 1993; Stein & Lane, 1996; Stein et al., 2000). Although mathematical tasks are given different terms such as "instructional tasks" (Hiebert & Wearne, 1993) and "academic tasks" (Doyle, 1983), generally mathematical tasks refer to projects, questions, constructions, applications, and exercises that students engage (Cai & Lester, 2005). Mathematical tasks are central to students' learning because "tasks convey messages about what mathematics is and what doing mathematics entails" (National Council of Teachers of Mathematics [NCTM], 1991, p. 24). Mathematical tasks can provide an intellectual environment in which students learn and develop mathematical thinking. The nature of mathematical tasks can potentially influence and structure the way students think and serve to limit or to broaden their views of the subject matter (Henningsen & Stein, 1997). A number of studies have shown that teachers play important roles in implementing cognitively demanding tasks in classrooms (Henningsen & Stein, 1997; Stein & Lane, 1996). For example, Henningsen and Stein found that engaging students with cognitively high demanding tasks not only requires the teacher to select and appropriately set up worthwhile mathematical tasks, but also to proactively and consistently support students' cognitive activity without reducing the complexity and cognitive demands of the task.

Factors Associated with the Maintenance and Decline of Tasks' Cognitive Demand

Mathematical tasks often lend themselves to certain types of conversations that may stimulate rich discourse, which, in turn, fosters higher order thinking (Silver & Smith, 1996). According to Stein, Smith, Henningsen and Silver (2000), mathematical tasks can be examined in terms of their cognitive demands as set up by the teacher and implemented by the students in classroom. Further, mathematical tasks are categorised into two levels of cognitive demand with four categories: the lower level includes *memorisation, procedure without connection, and* the higher levels includes *procedure with connection* and *doing mathematics.* Tasks classified as memorisation consist of memorising the equivalent forms or facts. Tasks classified as a procedure without a connection consist of performing standard procedures without connections to understanding, meaning, or concepts. Tasks classified as procedures with connections involve either thinking about relationships among different concepts or using procedures and doing so in a way that builds connections to underlying concepts and meaning. Tasks classified as doing mathematics entail asking students to explore the relationships among the various representations of concepts without providing conventional procedures. The difficulties of maintaining higher order mathematical thinking and reasoning throughout task implementation were noted by researchers (Doyle, 1988; Stein, Grover, & Henningsen, 1996). In fact, Stein et al. (1996) found that only about 50% of the tasks that were set up to require students to apply procedures with meaningful connections were implemented effectively. Henningsen and Stein (1997) identified and illustrated several classroom-based factors that support or inhibit high level mathematical thinking and reasoning. The following factors were associated with assisting students to engage at high levels: the appropriateness of the task for the students as well as supportive actions by teachers such as scaffolding and consistently pressing students to provide meaningful explanations or make meaningful connections. In addition, several factors were identified as contributing to the decline in the cognitive demands of tasks. These factors included unsystematic exploration and an inappropriate amount of time (either too little or too much) allotted for the tasks.

The mathematical tasks that the students engage in this study are questions, problems, applications, and exercises. This study intends to examine the distribution of mathematical tasks at different levels and the factors that maintain or reduce cognitive demand of mathematical tasks in US and Chinese classrooms.

METHOD

Data Resource

The schools and teachers. In this study, we selected data from the Learner's Perspective Study (LPS) (Clarke, Keitel, & Shimizu, 2006), one school in China and one school in the United States. We selected these schools because of the similarity of the content and comparability of the mathematical backgrounds of the students in these schools. In the Chinese classrooms (Hong Kong, Macau, and

Shanghai) all the teachers in each city taught the same content: *a system of linear equations with two unknowns.* However, there was only one classroom in the United States (US2 in the LPS) that explored linear relations. With regard to Chinese classroom selection, we considered two features: cultural background and school reputation. Due to the long history of British cultural influence on Hong Kong (more than one century of occupation by the U.K.) and the European cultural influence on Macau (more than four centuries of occupation by Portugal), we selected a school in Shanghai to contrast with the school from the United States because Shanghai schools were expected to be less influenced by Western culture. Three schools participated in the LPS in Shanghai. The first is a highly regarded school at the city level; the second is a highly regarded school at the district level (above average at the city level), and the third was a normal school at the district level. The US school was ranked in the top 20 percent of schools in the state of California. We selected the key school at district level as the Chinese representative school because we considered this would be the most similar to the US school.

In the US classroom, US2, ten consecutive videotaped lessons and relevant data were selected for the study. However, the Shanghai classroom, SH3, had fifteen consecutive videotaped lessons. Because the last five lessons were related to a system of equations in three unknowns, which is not relevant to our research topic of linear relations, we used the first ten lessons and relevant documents as the Chinese data for this study.

In the Chinese classroom, the teacher, Mr. Zhang, with a bachelor's degree in mathematics from the Teacher Education Institute, had 24 years of teaching experience. There were 55 seventh-grade students in the classroom, and the textbook was the unified official textbook in Shanghai. Each lesson lasted around 45 minutes. In the US classroom, the teacher, Ms. Nancy, with a bachelor's degree in mathematics and additional teacher education training (for example, participating in summer programs for in-service professional development), had more than 15 year of teaching experience. There were 36 eighth-grade students in the classroom. The textbook was *Integrated Mathematics: Algebra*, published by McDougal Little Inc. The lessons lasted 50 minutes each. However, all lessons were doubles, so Lesson One and Two were in fact taught consecutively as a 100 minute lesson. Both teachers were mathematics majors in college and quite experienced in mathematics teaching. The main differences were the classroom size and the lesson duration.

The contents and lessons. The main topics taught over ten consecutive lessons in the Chinese and US classrooms are shown in Table 1. Column one shows the phase of the topic development, and Columns two and three show descriptions of the topics and the lessons covering that topic for the Chinese classroom and the US classroom, respectively.

The table shows that the Chinese teacher started first with an introduction to the concept of linear equations and the solutions, then introduced the meaning of rectangle coordinate planes to graph linear equations, and the definition of the

148

system of linear equations with two unknowns and its solution. After that, several methods of solving a system of linear equations with two unknowns were introduced and consolidated.

The US teacher started by introducing the meaning of linear and non-linear relations in general and then discussed extensively the features of linear relations (different types of linear function). After that, she focused on the transformation of multiple representations (graphic, tabulated, symbolic and verbal) of linear and non-linear relations through group activities. Finally she applied this knowledge to solving word problems (i.e. application of linear equation). The teacher intended to develop the concepts (linear and non-linear relations) and foster understanding of the features of linear and non-linear relations, through multiple representations and students' group work.

Table 1. Topics covered in the Chinese and US lessons

Phase	Chinese lessons (Classroom – SH3)	US Lessons (Classroom – US2)
1	Meaning of linear equations with two unknowns and its solution (L01)	Meaning of linear and non-linear relations (L01-L02)
2	Concepts of coordinate plane and the coordinates; graph of linear equations with two unknowns (L02-L04)	General features of linear relations and multiple representations for linear and non-linear relations (L03-L04)
3	Definition and solution of system of linear equations with two unknowns and their solutions (L05)	Comparison and contrast of different representations (Tabulate, Graph and Symbol) (L05-L08)
4	Methods of solving linear equations with two unknowns such as the elimination method and the graph method (L06-L10)	Comparison and contrast of different representations; application of linear and non-linear relations (L09-L10)

When comparing the Chinese and US lessons, a number of differences were evident. In terms of lesson structure, the Chinese lessons were dominated by whole-class instruction, while group activity dominated the US lessons. In the US classroom, the students were divided into several groups, and different tasks were assigned to different groups; after group activities, there was some sharing with the whole class. While in the Chinese classroom, the lessons were delivered through whole-class teaching although there was frequent peer discussion of the tasks set by the teacher. Each US lesson included 'warm ups', which were related to the new topic to be learned in the lesson, but the warm ups were not related to the topics in the previous lessons. However, in the Chinese lessons, every lesson started with a review of knowledge learned in the previous lessons and developed new topics as a result of explanation and interaction between the teacher and students. Then, the students did some exercises and their solutions were shared in the class. In the US lessons, the teacher usually did not provide a summary for each lesson, while the Chinese teacher regularly summarised the key points of each lesson. This suggests that the Chinese teacher paid much more attention to building connections among ideas in the lessons than the US teacher did.

Data Analysis

The data were analysed in two dimensions. First, we analysed the cognitive demand of mathematical tasks in the first four Chinese lessons (SH3-L01 to SH3-L04) and the middle six US lessons (US2-L03 to US2-L08), because they included extensive coverage of linear relations. After that, we undertook discourse analysis of classroom interactions to identify factors that maintained or lowered the cognitive demand of mathematical tasks through their implementation.

Coding of mathematical task Using Stein et al.'s (2000) classification of cognitive demand of mathematical tasks (*memorisation, procedure without connection, procedure with connection,* and *doing mathematics*), the categories were illustrated by the topic taught in Table 2.

Table 2. Examples of cognitive demand of higher and lower level

Lower-Level Demand	Higher-Level Demand
Memorisation	*Procedures with connections*
How many points do you need to plot in order to draw a figure for a linear equation with two unknowns? (SH3–L04)	What are the similarities and differences between two graphs—a horizontal line and a vertical line? (US2–L07/L08)
Procedure without connection	*Doing mathematics*
Express y in terms of x or vice versa for the following two equations: (1) $2x - 3y = 5$; (2) $\frac{2}{5}x + \frac{1}{3}y - 1 = 0$ (SH3-L01)	Compare and contrast the following pairs of equations: (1) $y = 3x + 2$ and $y = -3x - 2$ (2) $0x + 3y = 6$ and $2x + 0y = 6$ (3) $y = x^2$ and $y = \frac{1}{x}$ (4) $y = 1 - 2x$ and $y = 1 - x^2$ (5) $2y = x$ and $y = 2x$ in terms of the T-charts of these equations, graphs of these equations, similarities of these equations, and differences of these equations. (US2–L05/L06)

Regarding the coding of cognitive demand levels of mathematical tasks, all the mathematical tasks (Appendix A) were put into the four levels by one research assistant and the first author independently. The rate of agreement was 70%, and the final agreement about initially disparate judgements was achieved through extensive discussion.

Sustaining or lowering mathematical demand of mathematical tasks as implemented As studies showed (Stein et al., 2000), cognitive demand levels are usually lowered when implementing a new mathematical task. We analysed the implemented cognitive demand level through classroom interaction. Maintaining or decreasing cognitive demand when implementing the tasks is now illustrated in the following excerpt. In the third Chinese lesson SH3-L03, the following problem was categorised as *doing mathematics*.

> If given only the coordinates of points A and B for a square, how can you find the other two vertexes so that the four points are the vertexes of one square?

Based on the following discourse during the process of solving the problem, it was judged that the students maintained the cognitive level as intended by the task.

1	T:	Let's exchange our ideas together. . .
2	T:	First we ask. . . Erica, please explain a bit, how did you draw it?
3	Erica:	The distance between A and B is four units.
4	T:	The distance between A and B is four units.
5	Erica:	The four sides of a square are equal, so the distance between the four sides are all four units, the coordinate of point C is (1, -4).
6	T:	So point C should pass point B, by drawing a perpendicular line through it. Where does the line end?
7	Erica:	After four units.
8	T:	Four units. [Teacher showing slides]
9	T:	Okay, let's think, oh, drawing outward four units, should it be used in this way?
10	T:	We've drawn up to the y-axis, how many units are there?
11	Erica:	Five units.
12	T:	So, that is not a square, at this time, the coordinates of point C and D should be. . .
13	Ss:	The coordinate of point C is (1, 4), the coordinates of point D is (1, 0) [Student in chorus]
14	T:	So we've got the coordinates of points C and D, right? Good, please sit down. Are there any other methods to draw the square?
15	T:	Eliza.
16	Eliza:	Our method of drawing is the same as that one; however, its square is pointing to the right, while ours is pointing to the left.
17	T:	The square is pointing to the right.
18	Eliza:	Another side of the square, [The side AB, is draw on the right hand side, CD is to the left hand side.]
19	T:	Would you explain more about how to draw it.
20	Eliza:	We use four as unit, then from point B, four units…that is (9, 0) (…)

Key to symbols used in transcripts in this chapter

...   A pause of one second or less

( )   Empty single parentheses represent untranscribed talk. The talk may be untranscribed because the transcriber could not hear what was said

....   Omitted text

[text]   Comments and annotations, often descriptions of non-verbal action

According to the above episode, the teacher asked one student to explain what she did ((1) ~ (11)); however, the explanation was not correct, so under the guidance of the teacher and with the help of other students, the correct answer was attained ((12) ~ (13)). At that moment, the teacher encouraged different methods or solutions to the problem, and another student explained a different solution (14~20). Thus, we judged that the students eventually solved these problems flexibly.

However, sometimes, the level of cognitive demand may decline as explained in the following example. In US lesson 7, the teacher gave the students two equations to graph on their whiteboards: $0x+3y=6$ and $2x+0y=6$. Later on, there was the following interaction between the teacher and students:

1 T:	All right folks, now, um, I'd just like to talk about getting you started with these two equations and making sure that everybody can follow through. And then in a moment we'll do the graph.
2 T:	Uh, I believe. Um, tell me um, Daniel. If I multiply zero times X, what's that product?
3 Daniel:	Zero.
4 T:	Zero. If it's zero, folks, it disappears. I don't need to write it down. I might write it down, but I don't need to.
5 T:	So we're gonna make the assumption here that this product was zero, obviously. So, we're thinking about it, but we don't have to write it down.
6 T:	But the equation can be rewritten in a- a- a more comfortable way, as just saying what, An- Andrew?
7 Andrew:	Three Y equals
8 T:	Three Y equals?
9 Andrew:	Six.
10 T:	Good, okay.
11 Manuel:	All right, All right.
12 T:	All right, solve for Y folks.
13 Victoria:	Two, Two.
14 T:	Two.

Based on above discourse, the students were guided to arrive at a predetermined expression $y = 2$ step by step, without any explanation. It seemed that the teacher was mainly concerned with the procedures but not the underlying conceptual understanding ((2) ~ (3), (7) ~ (14)). For example, students were not asked to explain why $0x = 0$ and how to solve $3y = 6$. Seemingly, the actual task was in the concept with connection category, but the task as experienced by the students was a procedurally operational process.

Factors associated with maintaining or reducing cognitive demands Stein et al. (2000) identified several factors associated with maintaining and reducing high-level demands. Based on their framework and using some trials and revisions, we developed a coding system, shown in Table 3.

Table 3. Factors associated with implementing mathematical tasks

Code	Decline Factors	Maintenance factors
Student thinking and reasoning (SR)	The teacher takes over the thinking and reasoning and tells students how to do the task (SRD)	Scaffolding of student thinking and reasoning (SRM) (see illustration below)
Demonstrating problem-solving behaviour (DM)	The teacher emphasises correctness or completeness of the answer (DMD)	Teacher or capable students model high-level performance (DMM)
Questioning style (QS)	Closed or yes or no questions (QSD)	Open, probing questions and agreement and drawing attention to pathways that could help (QSM)
Feedback of student answer (FB)	Students are not held accountable for high-order product or process (FBD)	Emphasising justifications, explanation through comments, or feedback (FBM)
Concepts connection (CC)	Teachers or students demonstrate answer without emphasising relevant conceptual connection (CCD)	Teacher draws frequent connections among concepts (CCM)
Exploratory activity (EX)	Inappropriate task or inappropriate exploratory time (EXD)	Appropriate task and sufficient exploratory time (EXM)

Some of the above codes are illustrated in the following excerpts. For example, with regard to the questioning style, the teacher in US2-L07 raised open questions to maintain implementing mathematical tasks at the high cognitive demands (QSM) as follows:

```
T:        Every group.  Either look back at your work if you were
          able to do these or if you had difficulty with these
          pairs in your homework.
T:        Get an idea now.  And I want every group ready to
          report a similarity.  One minute.  Find a similarity, a
          similarity between these two equations.
```

With regard to teacher feedback, the teacher in SH3-L03 commented on and built on the students' answers (FBM) as follows:

```
T:        Okay, let's exchange our ideas for this point on the x-
          axis. What are the characteristics of the coordinate?
          On the y-axis, what are the characteristics for such a
          coordinate? Fino.
Fino:     That is. . . the numbers on the x-axis, the former, um,
          the latter one must  be zero.
T:        The latter one. . . must be zero, so what coordinate is
          the latter one called?
Fino:     Vertical coordinates.
T:        Right, vertical coordinate is zero, on the x-axis.
Fino:     The coordinate on the y-axis is zero.
T:        The coordinate on the y-axis is zero. Are your
          discussion results the same as his?
Ss:       The same [Student in chorus]
```

153

However, after coding several lessons, it was found that sometimes teacher did not organise the students to focus on mathematical tasks as demonstrated below:

(US2-L08)

```
T:          Okay, so, um. . . the next time you come, we're going
            to be going back-- a preview of coming attractions
            here.
T:          We're going to be going back to waterworks just a
            little.  Waterworks, you remember waterworks.
T:          Um, you were working on some equations back then,
            graphing some functions and we had some, um, really
            good ones about the opening of the- of the waterworks
            park.
```

Then, we added one more code: unrelated mathematical task.

Finally, the first author and one research assistant developed a code system, and the research assistant used *Studiocode*, specific software for video analysis, to make codes of all the relevant episodes of implementing mathematical tasks in selected lessons.

RESULTS

The findings of this study are organised into two parts. First, the distribution of mathematics tasks is described; then, the time used in different events which contribute to maintaining or lowering cognitive demand of mathematical tasks when implementing, is presented and explained.

Cognitive Demand of Mathematical Tasks

Mathematical tasks set up. The number and types of mathematical tasks set up in the US classroom and Chinese classroom are listed in Table 4. The first column names the class with the total number of tasks, and the remaining columns present the number of tasks for different categories.

Table 4. Cognitive demand levels of mathematical tasks in the US and China

Classroom	Memorisation	Procedure without connection	Procedure with connection	Doing mathematics
US2 (10)	0 (0%)	1 (10%)	6 (60%)	3 (30%)
SH3 (23)	1 (4%)	2 (8%)	15 (65%)	5 (21%)

The table shows that the total number of mathematical tasks (10) in the selected US lessons is quite small when compared to the number of tasks (23) in the selected Chinese lessons. However, about one-third of the tasks in the US classroom involve doing mathematics while about one-fifth of the tasks in China are at the same level. The US and Chinese classrooms have 60% and 65% of the tasks at the procedure with connection level, respectively. In addition, the percentage of tasks in line with a procedure without the connection level is about 10% in both countries.

In addition, when looking at the percentages in lower level demands and higher level demands, it is clear that the percentage of higher-level demand tasks in both places is quite high and similar (90% in US vs. 86% in China). This finding suggests that both teachers emphasised mathematics instruction as advocated in the reform documents.

Mathematical tasks implemented. After carefully watching the videos, we found a few examples of declining of cognitive demand in the Chinese lessons, but we found more cases in the US lessons. Moreover, in some situations in the US lessons, it was difficult to judge whether a high cognitive demand was achieved because there was a lack of public sharing.

Factors Associated with Maintenance and Decline of Cognitive Demand

The percentage of time spent in different activities when implementing mathematical tasks is shown in Table 5.

Table 5. Percent of time spent in different activities in the US lessons

Category	L03/L04	L05/L06	L07/L08	Total
		(% values)		
SRM	4.2	0.0	3.0	2.6
SRD	5.7	10.5	7.5	7.7
DMM	1.5	0.0	0.0	0.6
DMD	3.7	3.2	8.3	5.0
QSM	2.7	0.0	1.1	1.4
QSD	8.8	0.4	0.0	3.5
FBM	8.5	0.0	0.0	3.3
FBD	6.2	0.0	18.2	8.3
CCM	9.3	12.7	4.8	8.8
CCD	0.0	0.0	0.0	0.0
EXM	13.4	23.4	22.4	19.2
EXD	26.9	0.0	0.0	10.3
Unrelated	6.4	0.0	16.4	7.8
Length (min)	104.6	78.5	89.5	272.6

Note: the abbreviated label in the first column represent the factors contributing maintaining and declining cognitive demands of mathematics tasks when they were implemented. The first two letters represent the type of factor, and last letter, M or D, refers to maintenance and decline. For example, SR-Student thinking and reasoning; DM-Demonstrating problem solving behaviour; FB-Feedback of student answer; CC- Concepts connection; EX- Exploratory activity.

The cells in the last row in the table represent the length (in minutes) of relevant lessons and the other cells in the table present the percentage of total lesson duration spent in each event (for example, 4.2 % of time in the US double lesson 3/4 was spent on events involving student thinking and reasoning).

The above table indicates that the US teacher was apt to emphasise the connection of concepts (CCM, 8.8%), and organise exploratory activities (EXM, 19.2%). However, sometimes, the task demands and exploring time were inappropriate when organising exploratory activities (EXD, 10.2%). In addition, the students were not sufficiently encouraged to justify and explain (SRD, 7.7%). Moreover, insufficient modeling of high level behaviors (DMD, 5%), more closed questioning, and occasional 'taking over' students' answers (QSD, 3.5%), or inappropriate feedback to students' answers (FBD, 8.3%) was found to cause a decline in the level of cognitive demands. The teacher also wasted time (7.8%) on unrelated activities. The time distribution in the Chinese classroom in the first four lessons is depicted in Table 6.

Table 6. Percentage of time spent in different activities in the Chinese lessons

Category	L01	L02	L03	L04	Total
			(% values)		
SRM	4.9	0.0	0.0	4.4	2.4
SRD	0.9	0.0	0.0	0.0	0.2
DMM	12.1	23.2	5.2	11.0	12.8
DMD	0.0	0.0	13.0	0.0	3.1
QSM	0.0	0.0	6.4	2.2	2.1
QSD	0.0	0.0	0.0	0.0	0.0
FBM	9.8	27.0	20.6	15.3	17.9
FBD	0.0	1.1	0.0	0.0	0.3
CCM	3.1	10.0	0.0	2.8	3.9
CCD	0.0	0.0	0.0	0.0	0.0
EXM	23.0	28.5	27.1	50	32.5
EXD	0.0	0.0	0.0	0.0	0.0
Unrelated	0.0	0.0	0.0	0.0	0.0
Length (min)	44.0	40.3	40.5	45.5	170.3

Table 6 shows that the most common activities in the Chinese lessons were the effective organisation of exploratory activity (EXM, 32.5%) and appropriate responses to students' answers such as praise. Using students' answers for further development of new ideas (FBM, 17.9%) was also a common strategy that maintained high levels of thinking. In addition, effectively demonstrating high levels of performance by the teacher or students (DMM, 12.8%) was used frequently to achieve a high cognitive level during the implementation of mathematical tasks. It was found that sometimes the teacher did not succeed in demonstrating a high level of cognitive demand (DMD, 3.1%).

Comparing the time distributions in different activities in the US and Chinese classrooms, we found that (a) the Chinese teacher used all of the classroom time to focus on mathematical task implementation while the US teacher spent some time focusing on other things; (b) the Chinese teacher maintained higher cognitive demands than the US teacher did. In addition, the Chinese teacher was more apt to organise exploratory activities than the US teacher was.

DISCUSSION

The US and Chinese teachers both presented their students with cognitively demanding tasks. This may reflect the positive influence of mathematics curriculum reforms in the two countries in the past decade.

The difficulties in implementing and maintaining high level cognitive demands in mathematical tasks has been recognised by many researchers (Doyle, 1988; Stein, Grover, & Henningsen, 1996). The challenges faced by the US teacher and Chinese teacher support previous findings about the factors associated with a decline of the cognitive level during the implementation phase. For example, the appropriateness of the mathematical task, the time for exploring, and the nature of the teacher support all influence whether the cognitive level is maintained. The findings of this study suggest that the Chinese teacher is more able to maintain a higher level compared with the US teacher. Given the fact that these two teachers are competent in terms of educational background and teaching experience by local standards, it will be interesting to explore the underlying reasons.

In conclusion, the sampled teachers in both countries are willing to provide mathematical tasks with the potential for high cognitive demand for their students to explore. The common strategies used for implementing mathematical tasks by the US and the Chinese teachers were to demonstrate high level performance, appropriately solicit and use students' answers, and appropriately organise exploratory activities. However, compared with the US teacher, the Chinese teacher was more frequently able to sustain the cognitive demand of mathematics tasks when implementing them.

It should be indicated that consecutive lessons from only one US classroom and one Chinese classroom were examined, researchers should be cautious in interpreting the findings of this study. However, they are useful for identifying a potentially fruitful topic for further study.

APPENDIX A

Table 1. Mathematical tasks in the US classroom

Lesson	Tasks code	Task content	Level
US2-L03/04	L03-T1	Copy, complete pattern. Explain your thinking. $2, 4, 8, \_, \_, \_$ $1, 3, 7, \_, \_, \_$ $\dfrac{1}{2}, \dfrac{3}{4}, \dfrac{7}{8}, \_, \_, \_$	4
	L03-T2	Each group got an equation. One student in each group was responsible for 1 expression. The goals are to match sets of graphs, equations, verbal descriptions of functions and tables. Students discuss topics both related to the equations and not related to the equations. The algebraic equations are: (a) $x = 2$ (b) $y = 2$ (c) $xy = 2$ (d) $x + y = 2$ (e) $y = x - 2$ (f) $y = x + 2$ (g) $y = x^2$ (h) $y = 2x$ (i) $y^2 = x$ (j) $2y = x$	4
	L03T3	The teacher gave the students the following 5 questions to answer in groups on their boards: What do these graphs have in common? (Teacher drew 5 straight lines at different angles.) Are they linear or non-linear? Is $x = 2$ vertical or horizontal? $y = 2x$ is a model of direct variation because it a) crosses through the origin b) passes through quad I. Is the slope of a graph with the angle positive or negative? Is the point (0,2) the x intercept or the y intercept?	3
	L04T4	The teacher had the students exchange white boards and gave them the following 5 new questions to answer: Rename $x + y = 2$ in terms of y. What is the slope of $y = -x + 2$? Are the symbols linear or non-linear? What does non-linear mean? Squaring results in what kind of shape?	3
US2-L05/06	L05T1	What is the slope of $y = 2x$, and feature of the graph. What is direct variation, the equation for which is $y = mx + b$, or $y = mx$ since b is 0 for direct variation? What are the slopes of the vertical line and horizontal line?	3

	L05T2	What is a function?	2
	L06T3	Compare and contrast the following pairs of equations: (a) $y = 3x + 2$ and $y = -3x - 2$ (b) $0x + 3y = 6$ and $2x + 0y = 6$ (c) $y = x^2$ and $y = \dfrac{1}{x}$ (d) $y = 1 - 2x$ and $y = 1 - x^2$ (e) $2y = x$ and $y = 2x$ in terms of the T-charts of these equations, graphs of these equations, similarities of these equations, and differences of these equations.	4
US2-L07/08	L07T1	The teacher gave the students two equations to graph on their whiteboards: $0x + 3y = 6$ and $2x + 0y = 6$	3
	L07T2	What are the similarities and differences between two graphs—a horizontal line and a vertical line.	3

	L08T3	Discussing the following pairs of equations
		(a) $y = 3x + 2$ and $y = -3x - 2$
		(b) $y = x^2$ and $y = \dfrac{1}{x}$
		(c) $y = 1 - 2x$ and $y = 1 - x^2$
		(d) $2y = x$ and $y = 2x$
		with regard to the following aspects:
		    1. Equation, T-charts
		    2. Graphs
		    3. Similarities (of different equations)
		    4. Differences (between different equations)
			4

Table 2. Mathematical tasks in the Chinese classroom

Lesson	Tasks code	Task content	Level
SH3-L01	L01T1	Wong Junior goes to the post office to buy several two-dollar and one-dollar stamps, at least one of each kind, costing a total of ten dollars. How many of each kind of stamps should he get?	4
	L01T2	Which of the following equations are linear equations with two unknowns and why? (a) $2x + 3 = 0$ (b) $x + 2y - 1 = 0$ (c) $\dfrac{1}{2}x = \dfrac{2}{3}y + 1$ (d) $2x + 5y = z$ (e) $x^2 + 2y = 1$ (f) $2xy = 5$	3
	L01T3	Exercise Question #1 Which of the following are the solutions of the equation $2x + 3y = 2$? Which of the following are the solutions of the equation $3x + 4y = 2$. $\begin{cases} x = 0 \\ y = \dfrac{1}{2} \end{cases}$; $\begin{cases} x = -2 \\ y = 2 \end{cases}$; $\begin{cases} x = \dfrac{1}{2} \\ y = 2 \end{cases}$; $\begin{cases} x = 1 \\ y = -\dfrac{1}{2} \end{cases}$; $\begin{cases} x = 2 \\ y = -1 \end{cases}$	2
	L01T4	Exercise Question #2 Substitute the equation of y to represent x and then substitute the equation of x to represent y for the following two sub-questions: (1) $2x - 3y = 5$ (2) $\dfrac{2}{5}x + \dfrac{1}{3}y - 1 = 0$	2
	L01T5	Question #3 In the equation $2x - 3y = 5$, when $x = 0, y = \underline{\quad}$; when $y = 0$, $x = \underline{\quad}$; when $x = -1\dfrac{1}{4}, y = \underline{\quad}$; when $y = 3, x = \underline{\quad}$.	3
SH3-L02	L02T1	How do you express the locations of points A and B? (1) Point A denotes the second dot and point B denotes the fifth dot in the following line: ● ●A ● ● ●B ● 1　2　3　4　5　6 (2) Point A denotes the dot at row 5 and column 2, while point B denotes the dot at row 2 and column 5 in the	*4*

		following 5×5 grid figure	
	L02T2	Draw a rectangular coordinate plane on your own worksheet.	3
SH3-L02	L02T3	Represent the pair of ordered numbers of the points A, B, C, D, E and F on the rectangular coordinate plane.	3
	L02T4	Work on the exercise in the textbook: Represent the coordinates of points A to N in a rectangular coordinate plane.	3
	L02T5	Before the carpenter drills the hole, he has to decide the location of the center of the hole. Show the coordinates of points A and B on the rectangular coordinate plane.	3
SH3-L03	L03T1	Here is a figure, there are three points A, B and C on the plane, please find out the coordinates of points A, B, C and the origin.	3
	L03T2	Given the coordinate of the point D (three, four), please find out the location of point D.	3
	L03T3	Given that the coordinates of the vertexes of the triangle are A (negative five, zero), B (negative one, four), C (five, zero), how do you draw such a triangle on the plane?	3
	L03T4	What are the characteristics of the coordinate of the points on the x-axis or y-axis?	4
	L03T5	Given a square in rectangle coordinate plane ABCD, find out the coordinates of A,B,C,D; [A(0,0),B(4,0),C(4,4),D(0,4)] Moving the square ABCD three units lower towards y-axis, find out the coordinates of points of A, B, C, D? [showing animated slides] Moving the square ABCD two units left towards the x-axis, find the coordinates of the points of A, B, C, D?	3
	L03T6	If given only the coordinates of points A (0,0) and B (4,0), for a square, how can you find the other two vertexes so that the four points are the vertexes of one square?	4
	L03T7	Write down the coordinates of the vertexes of the different figures, and answer them verbally.	3

SH3-L04	L04T1	How many solutions are there for the equation two x minus y equals three? Can you give us some examples?	2
	L04T2	Students please first write down part of the solutions of the equations at the bottom of the graph paper, and use pairs of ordered numbers x and y to represent, then plot them onto the plane.	4
	L04T3	Given several pairs of ordered numbers the class is to find out which pairs could satisfy the equation 2x-y+3=0 by substituting into the equation to calculate it.	3
	L04T4	Question 1: Can the points, which satisfy the equation and represented by the ordered pairs of numbers, be put on this straight line? Question 2: Are the points represented by the ordered pairs of numbers, but not satisfying the equation, also on the straight line?	3
	L04T5	Do you have to plot the points one by one when you want to draw the figure for a linear equation with two unknowns?	1
	L04T6	Draw the figures for the following equations on the same rectangular coordinate plane: (1) $x - 2y = 0$ (2) $2x - 3y = 5$	3

Note: Levels of Cognitive Demand of Mathematical Tasks:
1 Memorisational
2 Procedure without connections
3 Procedure with connections
4 Doing mathematics

REFERENCES

Biggs, J. B., & Watkins, D. A. (2001). *Teaching the Chinese learner: Psychological and pedagogical perspectives.* Hong Kong/Melbourne: Comparative Education Research Centre, the University of Hong Kong/ Australian Council for Education Research.

Brophy, J. E., & Good, T. L. (1986). Teacher behavior and student achievement. In M. C. Wittrock (Ed.), *Handbook of research on teaching* (pp. 328-376). New York: Macmillan.

Cai, J. (2004). Why do U.S. and Chinese students think differently in mathematical problem solving? Exploring the impact of early algebra learning and teachers' beliefs. *Journal of Mathematical Behavior, 23*, 135-167.

Cai, J., & Lester, F. K. (2005). Solution and pedagogical representations in Chinese and U.S. mathematics classroom. *Journal of Mathematical Behavior, 24* (3-4), 221-237.

Clarke, D. J., Keitel, C., & Shimizu, Y. (Eds.). (2006). *Mathematics classrooms in twelve countries: The insider's perspective.* Rotterdam: Sense Publishers.

Doyle, W. (1983). Academic work. *Review of Educational Research, 53*, 159-199.

Doyle, W. (1988). Work in mathematical classes: The context of students' thinking during instruction. *Educational Psychologist, 23*, 167-180.

Henningsen, M. A., & Stein, M. K. (1997). Mathematical tasks and student cognition: Classroom-based factors that support and inhibit high level mathematical thinking and reasoning. *Journal for Research in Mathematics Education, 8*, 524-549.

Hiebert, J., & Wearne, D. (1993). Instructional tasks, classroom discourse, and students' learning in second-grade arithmetic. *American Educational Research Journal, 30*, 393-425.

Huang, R., & Cai, J. (2007). Constructing pedagogical representations to teach linear relations in Chinese and U.S. classrooms. In J. H. Woo, H. C. Lew, K. S. Park, & D. Y. Seo (Eds.), *Proceedings of the 31st Conference of the International Group for the Psychology of Mathematics Education, 31*(3), 65-72.

Huang, R., & Leung, F. K. S. (2004). Cracking the paradox of the Chinese learners: Looking into the mathematics classrooms in Hong Kong and Shanghai. In L. Fan, N. Y. Wong, J. Cai & S. Li (Eds.), *How Chinese learn mathematics: Perspectives from insiders* (pp. 348-381). Singapore: World Scientific.

Jacobs, J., Hiebert, J., Givvin, K. B., Hollingsworth, H., Garnier, H., & Wearne, D. (2006). Does eighth-grade mathematics teaching in the United States align with the NCTM standards? Results from the TIMSS 1995 and 1999 video studies. *Journal for Research in Mathematics Education, 36*, 5-32.

Leinhardt, G. (1993). On teaching. In R. Glaser (Ed.), *Advances in instructional psychology* (Vol. 4, pp. 1-54). Hillsdale, NJ: Lawrence Erlbaum Associates.

Martin, T. S. (2007). *Mathematics teaching today: Improving practice, improving student learning* (2nd). Reston, VA: National Council of Teachers of Mathematics.

Mok, I. A. C. (2006). Teacher-dominating lessons in Shanghai: The insiders' story. In D. J. Clarke, C. Keitel, & Y. Shimizu (Eds.), *Mathematics classrooms in twelve countries: The insider's perspective* (pp. 87-98). Rotterdam: Sense Publishers.

National Academy of Education. (1999, March). *Recommendations regarding research priorities: An advisory report to the National Educational Research Policy and Priorities Board*. Washington, DC: National Academy of Education.

National Council of Teachers of Mathematics [NCTM] (1991). *Professional standards for teaching mathematics*. Reston, VA: The Author.

Silver, E. A., & Smith, M. S. (1996). Building discourse communication in mathematics classroom from the QUASAR Project concerning some challenges and possibilities of communication in mathematics classroom. In L. Schauble, & R. Glaser (Eds.), *Innovations in learning: New environments for education* (pp. 127-159). Hillsdale, NJ: Erlbaum.

Stein, M. K., & Lane, S. (1996). Instructional tasks and the development of student capacity to think and reason: An analysis of the relationship between teaching and learning in a reform mathematics project. *Educational Research and Evaluation, 2*, 50-80.

Stein, M. K., Smith, M. S., Henningsen, M. A., & Silver, E. A. (2000). *Implementing standard-based mathematics instruction*. New York: Teacher College Press, Columbia University.

Stein, M. K., Grover, B. W., & Henningsen, M. A. (1996). Enhanced instruction as a means of building capacity for mathematical thinking and reasoning. *American Educational Research Journal, 33*, 455-488.

Stevenson, H. W., & Lee, S. (1995). The East Asian version of whole-class teaching. In W. K. Cummings & P. G. Altbach (Eds.), *The challenge of Eastern Asian education* (pp. 33-49). Albany, NY: State University of New York.

Wood, T., Shin, S. Y., & Doan, P. (2006). Mathematics education reform in three US classrooms. In D. J. Clarke, C. Keitel, & Y. Shimizu (Eds.), *Mathematics classrooms in twelve countries: The insider's perspective* (pp. 75-86). Rotterdam: Sense Publishers.

Rongjin Huang
Department of Teaching, Learning and Culture
Texas A&M University
USA

RONGJIN HUANG AND JINFA CAI

Jinfa Cai
Department of Mathematical Sciences
University of Delaware
USA

GAYE WILLIAMS

CHAPTER NINE

Student-Created Tasks Inform Conceptual Task Design

INTRODUCTION

Over fifteen years as a teacher of secondary mathematics, I progressively developed a teaching approach that involved students beginning a topic in groups, and working on 'complex tasks' after a five to ten-minute introduction. By complex tasks, I mean, tasks that can be approached in many different ways, that value mathematical exploration more than moving in a linear direction towards a single solution, and that require students to explain and generalise. I developed this approach to make mathematics accessible to a greater number of students, and to decrease their anxiety about it. I was very surprised when I found able students reported that they understood mathematics much better, and enjoyed this process of learning.

As a teacher, I found I could design tasks that achieved these outcomes and that I could articulate some of the features these tasks possessed (Williams, 1996) but, I did not know why they 'worked'. Later, as a teacher-researcher, I studied student responses to my senior secondary calculus tasks and found that students were not so focussed on my task, as on questions they asked themselves as they worked with these tasks (Williams, 2000a). They were creating and exploring their own tasks!

In this chapter, I explore the types of questions students ask themselves to achieve such deep understanding. I use data from my research within the Learner's Perspective Study (LPS) to explore these ideas. I joined the Learner's Perspective Study (LPS) because I considered that classrooms of teachers who displayed 'good teaching practice' should be a rich source of data about student-created tasks. I was fascinated to find that when students did create their own tasks within the LPS (in Australia and the USA), and develop new understandings as a result, their teachers had not explicitly intended such activity, and were frequently not aware it had happened.

In my study within the LPS (Williams, 2005), the thinking of eighty-six students was studied in detail. These students came from six different classrooms in Australia (4) and the USA (2). Only eight student-created tasks were identified in total and these tasks were created by five of the eighty-six students, and seven of these tasks were created and solved individually. These five students varied in their mathematical performances in class. Kerri was in a class for students identified as

Y. Shimizu, B. Kaur, R. Huang and D. J. Clarke (Eds.), Mathematical Tasks in Classrooms around the World, pp. 165–184.

gifted, Leon, Pepe, and Eden were identified (by their teachers) as above average performance, and Dean stated that he struggled to pass mathematics which fitted with his teacher's description.

These five students created their own 'conceptual tasks' (Williams, 2005) where the term 'conceptual tasks' has previously been used to describe tasks designed by teachers and/or researchers to support student development of new mathematical understandings (see Lampert, 2001).

Student-created tasks from Kerri (USA) and Leon (Australia) were selected for the focus of this chapter. More detail about these cases can be found in Williams (2006; 2007a) respectively. Other students in my LPS study (Williams, 2005) who created their own tasks undertook the same types of thinking as they explored their self-created tasks. Dean differed to the other students in that his exploration was interrupted because he did not possess sufficient background knowledge to complete his 'constructing' process. Constructing is an 'observable cognitive element' of the process of abstracting (Dreyfus, Hershkowitz, & Schwarz, 2001b) where abstracting is the process of "vertically reorganising previously constructed mathematical knowledge into a new structure" (p. 377), and "vertical" refers to the forming a new mathematical structure as opposed to strengthening connections between a mathematical structure and a context ("horizontal", Treffers & Goffree, 1985). Thus, Dean was able to commence the developing of a new mathematical structure and progress a considerable way towards this, but a gap in his background knowledge meant he was unable to complete the process.

As these student-created tasks led to deep understanding, and the ways in which these students worked with these tasks included a progressive structuring of questions that elicited more and more complex processes of thinking, there is the potential to learn from these students. The following inquiry is the focus of this chapter: "How can conceptual tasks formulated by students, and their activity associated with them, inform the design of conceptual tasks more generally?"

PREVIOUS RESEARCH ON CONCEPTUAL TASKS

Over the past thirty years, research focused around tasks that provide opportunities for students to develop conceptual knowledge has increased (e.g., Cobb, Wood, Yackel, & McNeal, 1992; Krutetskii, 1976; Lampert, 2001; Tabach, Hershkowitz, & Schwarz, 2005; Williams, 2002b).

Conceptual tasks designed by Krutetskii (1976) included the following characteristics:

– They could not be solved using known procedures; and
– They could be solved in more than one way.

His findings about student thinking in responses to these tasks included:

– The 'mental activities' students employed in processing information during problem solving could be categorised
– Some students solved these tasks without the assistance of an 'expert other' (they 'spontaneously' created their own ZPD, Vygotsky, 1933/1966)

- These students posed questions that structured their future exploratory activity within the task
- Some students needed to be asked more explicit questions to focus them on relevant task features (they required an expert other, Vygotsky, 1978)
- Highly-capable students employed some mental activities not employed by others
- Highly-capable students curtailed solution processes and remembered in generalities
- Other students retained specific values and procedures not general principles.

In summary, Krutetskii found that students presented with unfamiliar problems in interview situations and asked to think 'out loud' about them, employed 'mental activities' that led to the development of new knowledge that was sometimes conceptual and sometimes procedural in nature. Students who developed conceptual knowledge structured their exploration with spontaneous questions. 'Spontaneity' (e.g., Thornton, 1999; Steffe & Thompson, 2000) involves student activity, that is not directly caused by an expert other but that can result from situations set up by expert others. Spontaneous questions that progressively structure exploration have been identified during individual written responses to unfamiliar tasks (Cifarelli, 1999), individual student responses to technology-supported games (Kieran & Guzmàn, 2003), and group work (Williams, 2000a, 2002a).

LINKS BETWEEN STUDENT THINKING AND CONCEPTUAL TASKS

We know some task features can provide opportunities for students to engage in thinking that leads to new conceptual knowledge (e.g., Hershkowitz, Schwarz, & Dreyfus, 2001; Lampert, 2001; Williams, 2002b; Wood, Williams, & McNeal, 2006). For example, the student studied by Hershkowitz, Schwarz and Dreyfus (2001) used multiple representations in a technological environment (including graphs and tables) to develop an understanding of how the curve of the graph represented the rate of change. It is time to focus in more detail on the questions students ask themselves during these exploratory processes, and how new understandings develop as a result.

To study student thinking during the development of insight, I integrated the observable cognitive elements of the process of 'abstracting' (Hershkowitz, Schwarz, & Dreyfus, 2001) with Krutetskii's (1976) 'mental activities' (cognitive activities). Hershkowitz, Schwarz and Dreyfus (2001) found the genesis of an abstraction passes through (a) a need for a new structure; (b) the construction of a new abstract entity; and (c) the consolidation of the abstract entity in using it in further activities with increasing ease (Hershkowitz, Schwarz, & Dreyfus, 2001). Dreyfus, Hershkowitz and Schwarz (2001b) found three observable cognitive elements within the process of abstracting: 'recognising' (seeing what mathematics could be used to assist the exploration), 'building-with' (using this mathematics in unfamiliar ways to progress the exploration), and constructing (the integrating of mathematical ideas during the developing of insight). These processes are 'nested'

167

within each other. For example, when constructing new knowledge, 'recognising' the mathematics needed and 'building-with' this mathematics are both nested within the constructing process.

The cognitive activities associated with information processing during the problem solving activity of high ability students were student initiated and student controlled (Krutetskii, 1976) and fitted as sub-categories of the observable cognitive elements identified by Hershkowitz, Schwarz and Dreyfus (2001). From least complex to most complex, these cognitive activities have been described as 'analysis', 'synthetic-analysis', 'evaluative-analysis', 'synthesis', and 'evaluation'. The hierarchical nature of these thought processes are implicit in Krutetskii's descriptions of them and supported by his empirical data (Williams, 2000b, p. 18).

Krutetskii (1976) described analysis as a process of examining a problem element by element, commenting that "to generalise mathematical relations one must first dismember them" (p. 228). Analysis can involve recognising or both recognising and building-with (Williams, 2005). Simultaneous analysis of several diagrams, graphs, representations, procedures, or areas of mathematics for the purpose of making connections between them (synthetic-analysis), and making judgements as a result (evaluative-analysis) are subcategories of building-with. Krutetskii described synthesising as identifying "generality hidden behind various particular details" or "'grasp[ing]' what was main, basic, and general in the externally different and distinctive [and finding] elements of the familiar in the new" (p. 240). In other words, synthesising involves integrating what is known to form something new. He described evaluating as considering the mathematics generated in terms of its consistency with what is already known and also how these new ideas can be used for other purposes. Both synthesising and evaluating occur as part of the constructing process and recognising is nested within this constructing in various ways including recognising a new purpose for the mathematical structure just constructed. These thought processes are illustrated through the cases described in this chapter.

This chapter examines the activity of Kerri and Leon for the purpose of identifying the questions they formulated to structure their explorations, the progressive complexifying of thinking that resulted, the new mathematical structures developed, and how the types of thought processes supported this development. By examining these processes, we should learn more about how to design tasks to promote such activity.

RESEARCH DESIGN

Context

Of the eighty-six students whose thinking was studied in detail (Williams, 2005), only five students spontaneously created their own tasks. The two students whose self-created tasks were selected as illustrative cases for this chapter are Kerri and Leon who each created their own tasks on more than one occasion. These five students who created their own tasks (Williams, 2005) were the only students identified developing new conceptual understandings rather than just learning new mathematical procedures. They came from schools that differed in perceived educational status, mathematical performances, cultural mix of the students, socio-economic status of school community members, and also in the teaching approaches used in their classes.

The other eighty-one students were not identified undertaking activity more complex than analysis. In other words, they did not simultaneously consider two or more pathways, representations, diagrams, mathematical topics (or some combination of these) for the purpose of making connections between them. Instead, they used mathematics that their teachers identified as relevant (recognised externally rather than spontaneously) to undertake procedures that the teacher had taught them to use (building-with but not spontaneous building-with).

The features common to the lessons in which students created tasks are:

– Mathematical topic commenced with exploration involving hands on activity
– Time to think without interruption
– Class members had the behavioural autonomy to think alone or with others.

Further descriptions of the activities that were common to these students, and personal factors that contributed to these activities can be found in Williams (2007a, 2006). It should be noted that the personal characteristic 'optimism' was found crucial to spontaneous thinking but is not a focus of this chapter.

The cases selected contained rich data to illuminate Kerri's and Leon's questions, thought processes, and insights, because both students were particularly reflective and articulate. These types of thought processes and structuring questioning were evident for the other three students (Eden, Dean, Pepe) but Dean did not progress beyond evaluative-analysis because he did not possess the cognitive artefacts needed to proceed further. Even so, Dean displayed thought processes more complex than analysis which was the most complex thinking identified in the activity of the other eighty-one students; most of whom were higher performers than Dean on their class tests.

Data Collection

The Learner's Perspective Study (LPS) (Clarke, 2006) research design was ideal for identifying students who created their own tasks, the questions they asked themselves, the thinking they undertook as they pursued their explorations, and the insights they developed. There were features of the LPS interview probes in the Australian interviews and some of the interviews in the USA that fitted with Ericsson and Simon's (1980) findings about how to generate high quality verbal data to study cognitive activity. These interviews: (a) stimulated student reconstruction of their lesson activity using salient stimuli (mixed image lesson video of the student [centre screen] and the teacher [in the corner]); (b) allowed the student to focus the content of the interview; (c) provided a sketch pad so that students who preferred to do so, could communicate using images and symbols to assist them; and (d) encouraged students to focus on lesson activity rather than on general questions that were not related to their specific activity. This guarded against researchers asking specific questions that included constructs the subject had not previously reported and "generat[ing] answers without consulting memory traces" (Ericsson & Simon, 1980, p. 217).

In their video stimulated interviews, the students identified when new learning occurred during the lesson and reconstructed their thinking during that time. The interview was my primary data source; video analysis was informed by these students' reconstructing their classroom activity and what they had attended to in the classroom. Teacher interviews, interviews with other students, and photocopies of student work added detail where insufficient detail was available from the student interview and lesson video. The conceptual understandings of other students in the class (who had not created their own tasks but rather had focused on the task as set by the teacher) were studied using lesson video, student interviews, teacher interviews, and student worksheets. This was used to demonstrate the learning advantages of the student-created tasks.

Identifying Spontaneous Activity

Spontaneous thinking was considered to occur when the social elements of the process of abstracting (Dreyfus, Hershkowitz, & Schwarz, 2001a) were internal (Williams, 2004). In other words, when the student:

– *Controlled* the recognising process
– *Controlled* the mathematical directions they took
– *Explained* and *elaborated* mathematical ideas for themselves
– Made their own decisions about whether they *agreed* with or *queried* mathematics they had generated.

Thus, where social elements of the process of abstracting arose from an internal rather than external source, student thinking was taken to be spontaneous. The sixth social element of the process of abstraction (attention) was crucial to the spontaneous questions students formulated to structure their future explorations. Students attended to complexities that became evident during their work with the task and spontaneous questions arose from these foci (Williams, 2000a).

ILLUSTRATIVE CASES: STUDENT-CREATED TASKS

This section describes Kerri's self-created task about linear functions, and Leon's self-created task about areas of triangles, and the subsequent activity of each student through:

– A narrative of student activity as they formulated and solved their task
– The types of questions they asked to structure their exploratory activity
– How these questions complexified their thinking and how this thinking contributed to developing new mathematical structures.

Narrative of Kerri's Linear Functions Task

Before the research period, Kerri's class was taught to find equations of linear graphs when two points were given by:

- Plotting two points
- Ruling a line through them
- Drawing a right-angled triangle with the line segment between points as hypotenuse
- Measuring the lengths of the other two sides of this triangle ('rise' and 'run')
- Finding the gradient of the line (ratio of rise to run)
- Finding the y-intercept of the graph by inspection
- Substituting the gradient and y-intercept into $y = mx + b$ to find the equation of the line.

When the students were tested on this procedure just prior to the research period, Kerri forgot her graph paper so she found another way to proceed. The following night while doing her homework, her understandings crystallised. The next day in class, the teacher taught procedures that were associated with Kerri's new understandings: finding the linear equation when given two points 'without using graph paper'.

In her interview after Lesson1, US School 3, Kerri reconstructed what she had done in the test and the insights she had developed during her subsequent homework. In her test, Kerri had:

- Made a sketch of the line between the two points
- 'Seen' a slope triangle "cuz you can picture a line in a little right triangle on it"
- Subtracted y values and subtracted x values of co-ordinates of the points to find lengths
- Calculated the gradient as the ratio of these lengths
- Substituted the gradient and a set of co-ordinates into the equation to find the y-intercept
- Found the equation by substituting the gradient and y-intercept into $y = mx + b$.

The method Kerri developed in her test involved steps she had previously been taught and new mathematical ideas she developed. Work she had undertaken previously included: a) calculating the gradient as a ratio, and b) substituting the gradient and the y-intercept into the general equation. New mathematical ideas she developed included:

- Recognised a right-angled triangle could be drawn on sketch of a line between the points
- Used her understanding of the Cartesian Coordinate System to find lengths a new way
- Combined previous knowledge of substituting constants *or* values of variables to find an unknown by substituting a constant *and* values of variables.

Kerri was pleased with what she achieved:

```
Kerri        If you find the slope  ....  [using the] difference of the
             points and .... then we can substitute, oh perfect. So I
             just wrote the equation.
```

Key to symbols used in transcripts in this chapter
....   Omitted text that does not alter the meaning of the quote
[text]   Comments and annotations, often descriptions of non-verbal action

By creating new ways of working mathematically, Kerri developed a procedure that enabled her to answer the test question. At this stage, she had not fully realised the implications: that the horizontal and vertical lengths could be found without the need for a diagram. When doing homework after the test, she gained insight. This homework involved plotting graphs and measuring lengths to find equations to lines when two points were given, and in addition, measuring the length of the line segment between the points given. Whilst doing her homework, Kerri measured the rise and the run on the graph paper for each question as required by the teacher, and simultaneously calculated the lengths using her own method. This thinking is an example of synthetic-analysis because there was simultaneously focusing on two methods; she measured and calculated at the same time, and thought about both methods as she did so. As a result, she made a judgement (evaluative-analysis) that each method always gave the same answer:

```
Kerri        I was doing my graph, and then I like realised like- really
             solidly, … I got the same answer, … [by measuring as] if
             you do the subtraction.
```

Kerri's understanding crystallised (synthesis): she realised that she did not need a diagram because her operations on the numerical values of the coordinates of two points always gave the measure of the lengths of horizontal and vertical lines separating them. She 'saw' the equivalence of attributes (line length) in the numerical and graphical methods and integrated the representations as a result.

Once, she realised that the Cartesian Axes System could be used as a tool to find vertical and horizontal lengths, she used this new insight along with Pythagoras' Theorem to extend the usefulness of this tool: the Cartesian Axes System could be used as a tool to find lengths of any segments where the coordinates of the endpoints were known. Kerri completed her homework:

```
Kerri        And then also … we had to find the distance between the two
             plots, and it was supposed to graph them too-… I was using
             Pythagoras' Theorem.
```

What Kerri knew 'really solidly' about finding lengths using coordinates was evident in class the next day when she queried whether the teacher was 'Finding the Equation of a Line without a Graph' as stated in the heading on the board. The teacher had demonstrated her procedure by making a sketch and using it to find the lengths by subtracting x values and y. Kerri queried the teacher's procedure: "You still graphed it". Kerri explained that it could be done without the sketch because the gradient could be found by operating on elements of the ordered pairs representing the points on the line:

```
Kerri        It would just be like the difference in y is two, and the
             difference in x is one.  So that's [what you need to
             calculate] your slope.
```

172

Towards the end of this lesson, the other members of Kerri's group plotted graphs and measured line segments and queried the validity of Kerri's approach to finding the distance between the two points on the line using Pythagoras. In her interview, Kerri described difference between what she was doing and what other students were doing thus demonstrating her deep understanding:

Kerri   [The questions] said graph and find the distance- and most people would graph the line, and then do the little thing [right-angled slope triangle]. But I would find what- see that'd be two and then one [subtracting *y* values, and then *x* values in co-ordinates], so you do um, *a* squared plus *b* squared equals *c* squared. ... if you make it a right triangle- it's the hypotenuse- not just the distance

Kerri's comments showed her generalised understanding: she could find rise and the run by operating on the *x* and *y* values in the co-ordinates, and saw the equivalence of the algebraic expressions for the hypotenuse (from Pythagoras' Theorem), and the length of the line segment between the two points. In other words, she had subsumed the line segment length into the algebraic expression for the hypotenuse thus extending how the Cartesian Axes System could be used as a tool for finding lengths by operating with *x* and *y* values of co-ordinates. The other students in this class had not developed such understandings. They still needed to plot and measure.

Types of Questions Kerri Asked

During her spontaneous explorations prior to the lesson described above, Kerri progressively asked questions to structure her future activity. I use 'future' as used by Cifarelli (1999) to capture the need for these questions to structure the way forward within an exploration that had already commenced.

In the test, when she found she did not have graph paper and so could not measure to find lengths, she asked herself "What can I do instead?" Once she had sketched the two points and the line between them, she analysed her sketch to find mathematics relevant to the situation: "What maths can I use to help?" She recognised she could use her knowledge of the Cartesian Axes System to find the vertical and horizontal lengths and proceeded to do so (recognising, and building-with).

Table 1. Types of questions Kerri posed and how they contributed to her developing understanding

Questions in Order Posed	What Was Involved in Answering the Question?	Complexity of Thinking Involved in Answering this Question
"What can I do instead?"	Drew a sketch and marked given information on it. Recognised lengths could not be measured.	Analysis: recognised the same diagram could be drawn as in the graphing method.
"What maths can I use to help?"	Recognising the difference between what was known in this instance and what was able to be found previously. This time the lengths were not known.	Analysis: Considered what was known in the previous situation that was not known here and looking for mathematics that could help find what was unknown this time.
"Can it help me find those lengths that I cannot find the other way?"	Recognised the properties of the Coordinate Axes System could be useful and used a numerical representation in conjunctions with the Cartesian Axes System to find lengths.	Building-with (synthetic-analysis) by simultaneously considering the sketch, the Cartesian Axes System, and a numerical representation of these, a relevant procedure was developed.
"Do both methods give the same answer?" "Does it always work?"	Simultaneous considering of operating with numbers in the Cartesian Axes System and measuring side lengths in graphical representation.	Evaluative-analysis: Synthetic-analysis for the purpose of making decisions about reasonableness, and comparability of methods.
"Is there an easier way?" "Can the process be curtailed?"	Saw the equivalence of attributes (side lengths and operations on x and y values in coordinates of points). Realised she no longer needed to diagram to find lengths.	Synthesis: Subsuming the side lengths into an algebraic formula using x values and y values in coordinates.
"Can this be used for anything else?"	As the length of the line segment between the two points is the hypotenuse of a right-angled triangle where the other two side lengths can be found, Pythagoras' Theorem can be used in conjunction with this new insight to find the length of the line segment.	Evaluation: Using the new insight for another purpose. Subsuming the hypotenuse in Pythagoras' Theorem into the slope triangle by 'seeing' the equivalence of the hypotenuse and the line segment between the two points and extending the numerical operations used to find line segments within the Cartesian Axes System (synthetic-analysis and synthesis nested within evaluation).

This involved simultaneous analysis of the sketch, and its placement in the axes system, (synthetic-analysis as part of building-with) to answer the question "Can it help me find those lengths I cannot find the other way?" Once she had recognised the Cartesian Axes System was relevant, she formulated appropriate numerical operations to find the lengths she could not measure. Crucial to Kerri developing insight was her activity during her homework that night. She compared answers she generated by the teacher's method with answers she generated by her own method and decided they were always the same (evaluative-analysis): "Do both methods give the same answer?" "Does it always work?" Her thinking crystallised at this stage (synthesis). She realised she had something that always worked that could be expressed generally through an algebraic representation. Kerri made judgments based on her simultaneous analysis of four representations (diagrammatic, Cartesian Axes System, numeric, and algebraic) (evaluative-analysis) by asking questions of the nature of: "Is there an easier way?" "Can the process be curtailed?" She subsumed the other representations into the algebraic representation, and 'realised really solidly' that she did not need the diagram (synthesis) because she recognised the equivalence of the line lengths, and the algebraic representations derived from her knowledge of the Cartesian Axes System.

Kerri's thinking was curtailed (Krutetskii, 1976) when she operated on the values in the coordinates without needing the diagram and was able to express this generally (synthesis as part of constructing). Kerri continued to think further once she had developed insight: "Can this be used for anything else?" She rapidly developed an additional insight: she recognised the relevance of Pythagoras' Theorem and subsumed line segment into the algebraic representation of the hypotenuse of the right-angled slope triangle because she 'saw' their equivalence.

Kerri Complexifies Her Thinking through Structuring Questions

Unlike the questions that Cifarelli (1999) identified that were specific to the problem at hand, most of the questions Kerri asked had broader applicability. They included:

a) What can I do instead?
b) What mathematics could help?
c) What does this tell me?
d) Will it always work?
e) Is there a simpler way?
f) Can I use what I have found for anything else?

Questions a) and b) elicit analysis of the context, Question c) elicits evaluative-analysis with synthetic-analysis nested within it, whilst Question e) elicits thinking about the connecting of ideas that could result in synthesis, and Question f) elicits evaluation. Task features that stimulated this constructing process included the absence of a resource used previously (graph paper), and the possibility to use the mathematical context differently by recognising other relevant mathematics (the

Cartesian Axes System). The hands on activity prior to the test supported Kerri's creative activity because she had become familiar with the mathematics involved with the context, and the representation she had worked in earlier provided opportunities to consider alternative pathways.

Narrative of Leon's Area of Triangles Task

Prior to Australian School 1, Lesson 12 in which Leon created the task under study, the class had found the areas of their hands by tracing them, then drawing and counting squares. In Lesson 12, the teacher:

– Placed three large coloured triangles on the board (see Figure 1)
– Allocated triangles to pairs of students
– Asked pairs to find the area of their triangles without using a rule.

The class did not know the rule for finding areas of triangles and all students except Leon focused on counting squares. This was probably because they had just completed such an activity. Leon and Pepe worked on Triangle 1 and although Pepe counted squares for the pair to produce their solution, Leon searched for a faster way to proceed. Once Pepe commenced work on the task Leon did not write or draw anything but instead focused idiosyncratically on the three triangles on the board asking himself: "which triangle is easiest [to find the area of]". This question elicited synthetic-analysis through simultaneously considering the triangles in Figure 1, and evaluative-analysis in making the judgement that Triangle 2 was the easiest. He then developed Method A:

– Juxtapose two right-angled triangles to form a rectangle
– Find its area
– Halve this to find the area of the triangle.

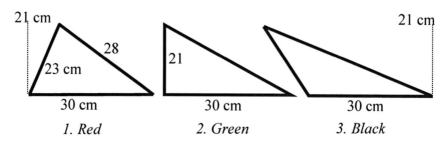

Figure 1. Triangles placed on the board in Leon's Class

Leon reconstructed his thinking about how to find the area of a right-angled triangle in his post-lesson interview: "Figure out what a rectangle is that has ... [that] length and width and ... then you can just halve it". He did not rely solely on visual images to justify the shapes formed: he considered the figures' properties as well.

To try to find the area of the acute-angled triangle (Method B), Leon drew upon one of the strategies he used in Method A (juxtaposing triangles). He:

- Juxtaposed two acute-angled triangles
- Recognised the shape was a parallelogram by its properties
- Sectioned the parallelogram into four right-angled triangles to find its area (Figure 2, top left-hand diagram)
- Used Method A four times to find the areas of the four rectangles made by juxtaposing right-angled triangles (see Figure 2)
- Total areas and halve result.

Figure 2 shows the parallelogram sectioned into four right-angled triangles as indicated by Leon's statement "figure out what it would be if it was four" and the rectangles formed by juxtaposition of another congruent right-angled triangle beside each (multiple use of Method A as part of Method B) to form four rectangles. He had not written or drawn anything whilst undertaking this activity. He was trying to find the area through multiple calculations of areas of rectangles, totalling them, "and then halve it".

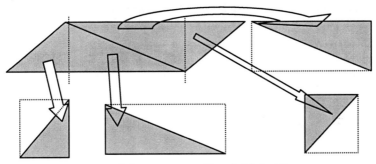

Figure 2. Interpretation of Leon's Method B

Leon expressed the fragility of his thinking about Method B in his interview: "I understood it – I didn't understand it then I understood it then I didn't understand it". The process had become difficult to retain in his head.

Before he had completed his calculations, he 'looked-in' on what was happening around him, and wondered: "Ooh! Maybe my method isn't the best". The term 'looking-in' (Williams, 2004) was used by Leon to describe his focusing on dynamic visual displays generated by others and extracting mathematical ideas implicit within them. It is an idiosyncratic student activity that can occur when a student does not possess appropriate 'cognitive artefacts' to progress their exploration. Leon described looking-in as a common part of his classroom activity:

```
Leon      When you look around the classroom and see how everyone
          else is doing it and you are doing it a completely
          different way- … and you think ooh! [soft] maybe my method
          isn't the best and … you think about everyone's ... and
```

> then you think about your own and they all sort of piece
> together and you just sort of go oh! and it pops into your
> head.

Leon described how he used dynamic visual displays visible around him in class in conjunction with the ideas he was developing himself to 'see' something new:

Leon   People were drawing the actual rectangles around it
            [triangles]- I don't know whether they knew they
            [triangles] were coming from rectangles … the way they were
            drawing it made it look like they did … made me think about
            it.

As other students drew grids across their triangles in preparation for counting squares, they formed rectangles during this process. Leon knew they probably had not realised what he saw when he looked-in. He was the only student identified using methods other than counting squares for the acute-angled triangle. As Leon 'looked-in' his goal changed from laboriously *finishing* the work to *understanding* the work. By looking-in, he extracted a big idea that he had not previously been aware of: "triangles come in rectangles" and wondered how he could use this.

Leon was excited by what he had found. He might no longer need to section a parallelogram and laboriously apply Method A four times, total areas, and halve. There could be a more 'elegant' way. Half way through Lesson 13, when the teacher held a large pink rectangle behind a red acute-angled triangle, Leon softly exclaimed "Oh!" He reconstructed his thinking in his interview:

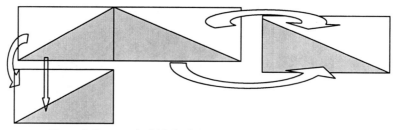

Figure 3. Leon applied Method A twice within his elegant Method

Leon   I sort of- sort of thought a little bit about why it was
            happening [triangle area half rectangle area] ... if you
            take one part out like a triangle that's set at an angle if
            you take both parts out and put them together it equals the
            rectangle. … I was sort of looking at them and then I just
            realised, like I (pause) sort of just in my head I pulled
            it apart and put them together so that they equalled the
            same (see Figure 3).

Figure 3 represents the mental images Leon generated. He mentally moved the two right-angled-triangle sections of the acute angled triangle (shaded parts) out of the larger rectangle. The triangles congruent to each of these shaded sections were then taken out of the initial diagram and juxtaposed with the appropriate shaded triangle to make two smaller rectangles: "if you take one part out like a triangle that's set at an angle if you take both parts out and put them together it equals the rectangle". He had simultaneously drawn upon what he knew from Method A and shifted pieces in his head to justify that the area of the acute angled triangle was always half the area of the enclosing rectangle.

Like Kerri, Leon realised almost immediately that his new insight could be used for something else. He clapped his hand against his cheek as he realised different shaped triangles had the same area if they were enclosed by rectangles of the same size. The following excerpt of whole class discussion captures Leon's justification:

Leon	That's [Triangle 1] half of the rectangle as well [as Triangle 2]
Leon	That would be three hundred and thirty centimetres squared
Teacher	Three hundred and thirty. Why?
Leon	It would be exactly the same as the first one [Triangle 2]
Teacher	Why?
Leon	Because the green one is half of the rectangle too [see Figure 3]

Leon explained that both Triangle 1 and Triangle 2 have areas that are half of equivalent rectangles so they must be the same size. The exercise set by the teacher towards the end of Lesson 13 involved finding areas of triangles in different orientations. The teacher found that (other than Leon) the class struggled to find areas of these triangles: "I *assumed* ... they knew ... base and height ... and how to recognise it ... [it's] *very obvious* ... they don't understand". The other students, including those with higher mathematical performances on class tests, knew the rule but not why it worked (Skemp, 1976) so were not able to 'see' the perpendicular height that Leon could recognise easily.

Wertheimer (1959) identified similar problems with students not recognising perpendicular heights in parallelograms. Leon knew more than the rule, he knew why it worked. Leon could do examples with triangles in any orientation because he could 'see' the perpendicular height of the triangle (even though he did not use this terminology). Leon had subsumed the attributes of the rectangle into equivalent attributes of triangles so he could operate with attributes of triangles instead, and not need to draw the enclosing rectangle. The questions Leon asked himself to structure the future parts of his exploration, and the more complex thinking that resulted are captured in Table 2.

Types of Questions Leon Asked

Unlike Kerri, whose synthetic-analysis involved considering the same attributes in graphical, diagrammatic, numerical, and algebraic representations, Leon's early synthetic-analysis focused on more than one diagrammatic representation arising from his question: "Which triangle is easiest?" Leon's quest for elegance led to his questioning whether there was an easier way (synthetic-analysis nested within evaluative-analysis) once his calculations in Method B became too messy to easily undertake in his head.

Table 2. Types of questions Leon posed and how they contributed to his developing understanding

Questions in Order Posed	What Was Involved in Answering Them?	Complexity of Thinking Involved in Answering this Question
"Which triangle is easiest?"	Analysed the three triangles on the board to find which was the easiest area to find.	Analysis: recognising that two right-angled triangles put together make a rectangle (knowing properties of rectangles).
"What maths could help?"	Recognised rule for finding areas of rectangles could be used and the answer halved to find the area of the right-angled triangle.	Analysis: Considering the use of previously known processes one after the other to find an answer (building-with but not yet synthetic-analysis because procedures occur one after another).
"Can I use similar strategies here?"	Recognised parallelogram was formed when two acute-angled triangles were juxtaposed but had not found the areas of parallelograms previously.	Building-with (synthetic-analysis) by simultaneously considering the acute angled triangles and the properties that showed a parallelogram was formed.
"What maths can I use to help?"	Recognised the previously developed process to find the area of a right-angled triangle could be used. Made four right-angled triangles within the parallelogram (drop perpendiculars from two vertices to opposite sides). Process became too messy to easily complete in his head.	Synthetic-analysis: Considered what had been previously developed that might be useful to this new situation. Analysis nested within: Considered the use of previously known process one after the other to find an answer
"Is there an easier way?"	Simultaneously considered ideas developed and diagrams produced by others to form grids for counting squares. Insight: Triangles always come in rectangles.	Synthesis: Knew right triangles were useful to him and that there was always a rectangle that could be made to enclose any triangle.
Can 'triangles always come in rectangles' help me to find the area of any rectangle?	Recognised two right-angled triangles are embedded in the diagram so knew how to find the area of each. In addition, the triangles needed for the juxtaposing process were also within this rectangle. Thus, the area of this rectangle can be halved to find the area of the triangle.	Synthesis: Insight that the rectangle is not needed to find the area of the acute angled triangle because there are attributes of this triangle that are equivalent to the length and width of the rectangle. Subsumed attributes (length, width) of one representation into another (base, perpendicular height).
"Can this be used to save work in finding the areas of the other triangles?"	Simultaneous considering another triangle with the same width and height and his new insight. As the two triangles had the same enclosing rectangle, they should have the same area.	Evaluation: Using the previously developed insight for another purpose

Although Leon did not use algebra to express what he had found, his generalised understanding was indicated by his insight that triangles enclosed by the same rectangle having the same area. Task features that stimulated Leon's creating of a conceptual task were: the display of three very different triangles with the same areas, the opportunity to look-in, knowing the answer but not the reason (from empirical explorations of others), and the teacher's juxtaposition of an acute angled triangle with its enclosing rectangle in sharply contrasting colours. As with Kerri, the task set by the teacher (that was not intended to elicit creative thinking) lead to the idiosyncratic formulating of a student-created conceptual task.

Leon Complexifies His Thinking through Structuring Questions

Table 2 shows the complexifying of thinking that was stimulated by the questions Leon asked himself. Again, as for Kerri, Leon subsumed some representations within others. In Leon's case he subsumed the attributes of the rectangle into the triangle and this occurred because the synthetic-analysis and evaluative-analysis he undertook brought him closer and closer to a realisation of this equivalence as he found the enclosing rectangle was useful for different types of triangles.

CONCLUSIONS

This chapter highlights student-formulated questions that elicit complex thinking that supports the development of new mathematical structures. It suggests pedagogical advantages to integrating these types of questions into tasks to scaffold student entry to idiosyncratic exploration. In these cases, students exploring self-created tasks developed deeper understandings than those who undertook the task as set by the teacher. The finding (Williams, 2005) that a student who struggled in mathematics could think creatively to develop a greater understanding than other students with higher performances on class tests (Williams, 2005) negates assumptions that only highly able students should be presented with rich explorations.

The process of evaluative-analysis appeared crucial to the process of subsuming representations to form new mathematical structures. Questions eliciting this type of thinking were focused around finding more elegant ways to proceed (Leon), and checking the reasonableness of mathematics generated (Kerri). This seemed to highlight the equivalence of attributes that was needed for the subsuming process (synthesis). The questions these students asked themselves could be built in to tasks to scaffold students who are not yet able to ask such questions for themselves. This should increase the likelihood that students undertake synthetic-analysis and evaluative analysis and this should support synthesis. Increasing looking-in opportunities could be achieved by structuring reporting sessions *during* a task, rather than only after the task (e.g., Williams, 2007b). Introducing these aspects into task design should increase opportunities for students to discovering mathematical complexities that were not evident to them at the start of the task and this could provide the impetus for student-created tasks. The following section uses these findings to suggest a possible task and the rationale for different features.

SPECULATING: A CONCEPTUAL TASK ABOUT AREAS OF TRIANGLES

A conceptual task could be built around the triangles in Figure 1 because they look so different yet their areas are the same so there is potential for surprise that could create the impetus to explore. Structuring a task that requires students to predict the areas, thus commit to a position, could create this element of surprise. For students of differing abilities to have a chance to access the task, it should be set prior to finding areas of:

- Irregular shapes by counting squares
- Triangles using the rule $A = bh$.

The background knowledge needed includes a conceptual rather than procedural understanding of area as the amount of space within the boundaries of a two-dimensional figure. The task could be undertaken with or without knowledge of how to find areas of rectangles because it is possible for students to find these areas without formal knowledge. Thus, the type of task suggested could be appropriate in late elementary school or early secondary school. The type of wording in the questions below is intentionally predominantly common language and tentative, rather than demanding and technical. This should increase the likelihood of informal exploration. Questions like the following could be embedded in the task to stimulate idiosyncratic thinking:

- Predict the areas of the three triangles giving reasons for your predications
- Find a way to find the areas using any method that you can explain
- Find a way to quickly check that your answers are reasonable (explain how you did this)
- Can you see any patterns? Describe them
- Can you add another triangle that fits this pattern? Explain and test
- Can you work out why this pattern works?
- Work out how to tell a friend what you have found as simply as possible.

This task includes the ideas behind the structuring questions that Leon and Kerri asked. The first dot point should elicit: "What can I use?" The second dot point: "What mathematics might help?" The third dot point stimulates evaluative-analysis through comparing of two methods to make a judgment. The fourth dot point elicits synthetic-analysis through the search for patterns by considering various aspects simultaneously. The fifth dot point involves making a judgment (evaluative-analysis) and the sixth dot point can elicit synthesis because knowing why involves developing a new mathematical structure. The seventh dot-point is intended to assist students to express what they know by asking them to focus on communicating their ideas to a friend. Some students are likely to create their own tasks earlier than others because the mathematics needed earlier in the task will be unfamiliar to some. Student-created tasks, elicited by this classroom task, might focus around topics including: constructing triangles, counting squares, approximating when counting squares, areas of composite shapes, juxtaposing shapes to find ways to find areas, recognising the significance of enclosing rectangles, areas of triangles, and areas of parallelograms. Even though the study upon which this chapter was based identified only eight student-created tasks, the diversity of the educational settings, pedagogical approaches, and student abilities adds strength to the usefulness of these student-formulated questions for task design in mainstream classes.

REFERENCES

Cifarelli, V. (1999). Abductive inference: Connections between problem posing and solving. In O. Zaslavsky (Ed.), *Proceedings of the 23rd Conference of the International Group for the Psychology of Mathematics Education, 23*(2), 217-224.

Clarke, D. J. (2006). The LPS research design. In D. J. Clarke, C. Keitel & Y. Shimizu (Eds.), *Mathematics classrooms in twelve countries: The insider's perspective*. (pp. 15-36). Rotterdam: Sense Publishers.

Cobb, P., Wood, T., Yackel, E., & McNeal, B. (1992). Characteristics of classroom mathematics traditions: An interaction analysis. *American Educational Research Journal, 29*(3), 573-604.

Dreyfus, T., Hershkowitz, R., & Schwarz, B. (2001a). Abstraction in context II: The case of peer interaction. *Cognitive Science Quarterly, 1*(3), 307-368.

Dreyfus, T., Hershkowitz, R., & Schwarz, B. (2001b). The construction of abstract knowledge in interaction. In M. van den Heuvel-Panhuizen (Ed.), *Proceedings of the 25th Conference of the International Group for the Psychology of Mathematics Education, 25*(2), 377-384.

Ericsson, K. A., & Simon, H. A. (1980). Verbal reports of data. *Psychological Review, 87*(3), 215-251.

Hershkowitz, R., Schwarz, B., & Dreyfus, T. (2001). Abstraction in context: Epistemic actions. *Journal for Research in Mathematics Education, 32*(2), 195-222.

Kieran, C., & Guzmàn, J. (2003). The spontaneous emergence of elementary number-theoretic concepts and techniques in interaction with computer technology. In P. Neil, A. Dougherty, & J. Zilliox (Eds.), *2003 Joint Meeting of the 27th conference of the International Group for the Psychology of Mathematics Education and the Group for the Psychology of Mathematics Education of North America* (Vol. 3, pp. 141-148). Honolulu, Hawaii: PME.

Krutetskii, V. (1976). *Psychology of mathematical abilities in school children*. (J. Kilpatrick, & I. Wirzup, Eds., J. Teller, Trans.). Chicago: University of Chicago Press. (Original work published in 1968.)

Lampert, M. (2001). *Teaching problems and the problems of teaching*. New Haven, CT: Yale University Press.

Skemp, R. (1976). Relational understanding and instrumental understanding. *Mathematics Teaching, 77,* 20-26.

Steffe, L., & Thompson, P. (2000). Teaching experiments methodology: Underlying principles and essential elements. In A. Kelly & R. Lesh (Eds.), *Handbook of research design in mathematics and science education* (pp. 267-306). Mahwah, NJ: Lawrence Erlbaum.

Tabach, M., Hershkowitz, R., & Schwarz, B. (2005). The construction and consolidation of mathematical knowledge within dyadic processes: A case study. Manuscript submitted for publication.

Thornton, S. (1999). Creating the conditions for cognitive change: The interaction between task structures and specific strategies. *Child Development, 70*(3), 588-603.

Treffers, A., & Goffree, F. (1985). Rational analysis of realistic mathematics education. In L. Streefland (Ed.), *Proceedings of the 9th Conference of the International Group for the Psychology of Mathematics Education, 9*(2), 97-123.

Vygotsky, L. S. (1978). *Mind and society: The development of higher psychological processes*. M. Cole, V. John-Steiner, S. Scribner, & E. Souberman, (Eds.), (J. Teller, Trans.). Cambridge, MA: Harvard University Press.

Wertheimer, M. (1945/1959). *Productive thinking*. New York: Harper.

Williams, G. (1996). *Unusual connections: Maths through investigation*. Brighton, Victoria: Gaye Williams Publications.

Williams, G. (2000a). Collaborative problem solving and discovered complexity. In J. Bana & A. Chapman (Eds.), *Mathematics education beyond 2000* (Vol. 2, pp. 656-663). Fremantle, Western Australia: Mathematics Education Research Group of Australasia.

Williams, G. (2000b). Collaborative problem solving in Mathematics: The nature and function of task complexity. Unpublished Masters Thesis, Department of Science and Mathematics Education, University of Melbourne, Melbourne, Victoria, Australia. Accessed at http://eprints.infodiv. unimelb.edu.au/archive/00002770/

Williams, G. (2002a). Associations between mathematically insightful collaborative behaviour and positive affect. In A. Cockburn & E. Nardi (Eds.), *Proceedings of the 26th Conference of the International Group for the Psychology of Mathematics Education, 26*(4), 402-409.

Williams, G. (2002b). Identifying tasks that promote creative thinking in Mathematics: A tool. In B. Barton, K. Irwin, M. Pfannkuch, & M. Thomas (Eds.), Mathematics Education in the South Pacific. *Proceedings of the 25th Annual Conference of the Mathematics Education Research Group of Australasia, 25*(2), 698-705.

Williams, G. (2004). The nature of spontaneity in high quality learning situations. In M. J. Hoines & A. B. Fuglestad (Eds.), *Proceedings of the 28th conference of the International Group for the Psychology of Mathematics Education, 28*(4), 433-440.

Williams, G. (2005). Improving intellectual and affective quality in mathematics lessons: How autonomy and spontaneity enable creative and insightful thinking. Unpublished doctoral dissertation, Department of Science and Mathematics Education, University of Melbourne, Melbourne, Australia. Accessed at http://eprints.infodiv.unimelb.edu.au/archive/00002533/

Williams, G. (2006). Autonomous looking-in to support creative mathematical thinking: Capitalising on activity in Australian LPS classrooms. In D. J. Clarke, C. Kietel, & Y. Shimizu (Eds.), *Mathematics classrooms in twelve countries: The insider's perspective* (pp. 221-236). Rotterdam: Sense Publishers.

Williams, G. (2007a). Abstracting in the context of spontaneous learning. In M. Mitchelmore & P. White (Eds.), *Abstraction, Special Edition, MERJ, 19*(2), 69-88.

Williams, G. (2007b). Classroom teaching experiment: Eliciting creative mathematical thinking. In J. H. Woo, H. C. Lew, K. S. Park, & D. Y. Seo (Eds.), *Proceedings of the 31st Conference of the International Group for the Psychology of Mathematics Education, 31*(4), 257-364.

Wood, T., Williams, G., & Mc Neal, B. (2006). Children's mathematical thinking in different classroom cultures. *Journal for Research in Mathematics Education, 37*(3), 222-252.

Gaye Williams
Faculty of Education, Deakin University

International Centre for Classroom Research
Melbourne Graduate School of Education, University of Melbourne
Australia

CARMEL MESITI AND DAVID CLARKE

CHAPTER TEN

*A Functional Analysis of Mathematical Tasks in China, Japan, Sweden,
Australia and the USA: Voice and Agency*

INTRODUCTION

In the mathematics classroom, the teacher, the student and the tasks provide the
key structural elements through which the classroom's social activity is constituted.
In the analysis reported in this chapter, we restrict our consideration of task to
activities that are recognizably mathematical. Marx and Walsh (1988) identified
three essential elements to any consideration of the role of 'academic tasks': the
conditions under which the tasks are set; the cognitive plans students use to
accomplish tasks; and the products that students create as a result of their task-
related efforts. This conception either ignores the role of teacher intentionality and
mediation, or it relegates this to just another element in the social context in which
the task is undertaken. Our conception of the teacher/student/task triad is much
more interconnected and accords significant agency to each in the determination of
the actions and outcomes that find their nexus in the social situation for which the
task is the pretext.

More recently, theories of learning have viewed cognitive activity as not simply
occurring in a social context, but as being constituted in and by social interaction
(Hutchins, 1995; Salomon, 1993). From this perspective, the activity that arises as
a consequence of a student's completion of a task is itself a constituent element of
the learning process and the artefacts (both conceptual and physical) employed in
the completion of the task serve simultaneous purposes as scaffolds for cognition,
repositories of distributed cognition and cognitive products. Task selection by
teachers represents the initiation of an instructional process that includes task
performance (collaboratively by teacher and student) and the interpretation of the
consequences of this enactment (again, by teacher and student).

In Simon's (1995) construct of the *hypothetical learning trajectory* (HLT),
mathematical tasks are seen as central to the promotion of student learning.
Baroody, Cibulskis, Lai and Li (2004) have drawn attention to the important
distinction between learning trajectories and other learning sequences, such as
Gagnè's learning hierarchies (e.g. Gagnè & Briggs, 1974). A key aspect of this

*Y. Shimizu, B. Kaur, R. Huang and D. J. Clarke (Eds.), Mathematical Tasks in Classrooms around the
World, pp. 185–216.*
© *2010 Sense Publishers. All rights reserved.*

distinction is the degree of prescription implicit in the learning sequence. Hypothetical learning trajectories maintain an emphasis on the hypothetical and incrementally adjusted nature of any posited learning trajectory for any student. Any investigation of the function of tasks in mathematics instruction/learning (viewed in this paper as a conjoint, co-constructed activity, see Clarke, 2001 and 2006a), must take into account intention, action, and interpretation (by both teacher and students) and view any hypothetical learning trajectories as subject to continual and incremental adjustment during the course of classroom task performance (Simon & Tzur, 2004).

In this chapter, we examine the function of mathematical tasks in classrooms in five countries. Utilising a three-camera method of video data generation (see Clarke, 2006b), supplemented by post-lesson video-stimulated reconstructive interviews with teacher and students, we can characterize the tasks employed in each classroom with respect to intention, action and interpretation and relate the instructional purpose that guided teacher task selection and use to student interpretation and action, and, ultimately, to the learning that post-lesson interviews encourage us to associate with each task.

Our analysis utilises the conception by Clarke and Lobato (2002) of 'function' as the combination of intention, action and interpretation to examine the functionality of mathematical tasks in classrooms in several countries. Of particular interest are differences in the function of mathematically similar tasks when employed by different teachers, in different classrooms, for different instructional purposes, with different students. The significance of differences between social, cultural and curricular settings, together with differences between participating classroom communities, challenges any reductionist attempts to characterize instructional tasks independent of these considerations. Of equal interest are differences in learning outcomes arising from the use of fundamentally different mathematical tasks, such as highly decontextualised or abstract tasks (in the Chinese classrooms, for example) in comparison with contextualised or so-called 'real world' tasks (for instance, in one Swedish classroom). In particular, student willingness and capacity to associate classroom mathematics with out-of-class activities was inconsistently associated with the explicitness of the teachers' goal of establishing (or not establishing) such connections.

Data Construction

In any classroom video study, the choice of classroom, the number of cameras used, who is kept in view continuously and who appears only given particular circumstances, all contribute to a process that might best be characterised as 'data construction' or 'data generation' rather than 'data reduction' (Miles & Huberman, 2004). Every decision to zoom in for a closer shot or to pull back for a wide angle view represents a purposeful act by the researcher to selectively construct a data set optimally amenable to the type of analysis anticipated and maximally aligned with the particular research questions of interest to the researcher. The process of data construction does not stop with the video record, since which statements (or whose voices) are transcribed, and which actions, objects or statements are coded, all constitute further decisions made by the researcher, more or less explicitly justified in terms of the project's conceptual framework or the focus of the researcher's interest. The researcher is the principle agent in this process of data construction. Data construction in the Learner's Perspective Study (LPS) used a three-camera approach (Teacher camera, Student camera, Whole Class camera) that included the onsite mixing of the Teacher and Student camera images into a picture-in-picture video record that was then used in post-lesson interviews to stimulate participant reconstructive accounts of classroom events (see Clarke, 2006b, for more detail). The analysis reported in this chapter was carried out on sequences of at least ten consecutive lessons occurring in the 'well-taught' eighth grade mathematics classrooms of teachers in Australia, China, Japan, Sweden and the U.S.A. This combination of countries gives useful representation to both Western and Asian educational traditions.

Each participating country used the same research design to collect videotaped classroom data for at least ten consecutive mathematics lessons and post-lesson video-stimulated interviews with at least twenty students in each of three participating 8th grade classrooms. The three mathematics teachers in each country were identified for their locally-defined 'teaching competence' and for their situation in demographically diverse government schools in major urban settings. Rather than attempt to apply the same definition of teaching competence across a dozen countries, which would have required teachers in Uppsala and Shanghai, for instance, to meet the same eligibility criteria, teacher selection was made by each local research group according to local criteria. These local criteria included such things as status within the profession, respect of peers or the school community, or visibility in presenting at teacher conferences or contributing to teacher professional development programs. As a result, the diverse enactment of teaching competence is one of the most interesting aspects of the project. In this chapter, this diversity was especially visible in the choice and performance of mathematical tasks.

In the key element of the post-lesson student interviews, in which a picture-in-picture video record was used as stimulus for student reconstructions of classroom events, students were given control of the video replay and asked to identify and comment upon classroom events of personal importance. In addition, the classroom video data (three independent video records plus the combined picture in picture record) and the post-lesson video-stimulated interview data were supplemented by additional data in the form of teacher questionnaires (before and after the lesson sequence and after each individual lesson), scanned written and text material used or generated by the focus students or the teacher, classroom test material and a test of student mathematical achievement administered after the completion of videotaping.

This data set provided an extensive pool of mathematical tasks, documented in use in classrooms around the world. From the combination of data described above, it is possible not only to describe the mathematical tasks employed, but by drawing on the complementary accounts provided by the teacher and the students, analysis of the function of tasks can include both intention and interpretation.

Analytical Approach

The key to our task selection for this paper was the identification of 'distinctive' tasks. For the purposes of this paper, 'distinctive' could mean either typical or unusual. While this may sound paradoxical, our primary purpose was to examine mathematics tasks in the classrooms of competent teachers around the world for the implications that these might have for instructional practice and theory. Given this goal, a task may be 'distinctive' because it represents something characteristic (typical) of the practices of a particular competent teacher, or a task may be distinctive because it is unusual. It is possible, of course, for a task to be both typical of a teacher's practice, and unusual in comparison with the practice of other teachers. In both cases, we have chosen tasks that the data suggest were instructionally effective.

Results

Each of the selected 'Distinctive tasks' is described below in terms of the Educational Context of the Task, the Social Performance of the Task, and the Intermediate and Consequent Artefacts arising from the social activity of performing the task. Our description of the Educational Context of each task includes the teacher's goals for the lesson, as described in the teacher interview data, teacher questionnaire data or when stated by the teacher in class.

We have chosen in this chapter to focus on nine distinctive tasks: one from each of the classrooms in Shanghai and Tokyo, plus one task from a classroom in Sweden, one from Australia, and one from the U.S.A. The last three tasks were chosen, in part, for the contrast they represented to the tasks employed in the LPS classrooms in China and Japan. In the tabular display of each task, the various contributions to the 'Social Performance of the Task' are displayed in chronological order down the page. Present tense is used in describing the Social Performance of the Task in order to provide a text account with a sense of immediacy comparable to that provided by the video record. The 'Interpretive Reflections' represent our interpretations of the video record of the task. The subsequent discussion examines similarities and differences across the selected tasks, particularly from the perspectives of the distribution of responsibility for the generation of new knowledge in the classroom and with respect to the distribution of voice and agency within the classroom performance of each task.

Our intention in this chapter was to represent the selected tasks in such a way as to facilitate their comparison. There are many comparative analyses that might be undertaken on the tasks as performed and as documented here, but our focus concerned the extent to which the task has served as a vehicle for the distribution of responsibility for knowledge generation. Specifically, our discussion of each task addresses the question of whether or not the teacher has accorded the students significant agency and/or voice in the development of new mathematical (in this case, algebraic) knowledge.

Task One: Japan School 1 – Lesson 1 (the Stairs Task)

Educational Context of the Task

This was the first lesson in a sequence of lessons concerned with functions, relations and patterns, where particular emphasis was placed on the special terms used in mathematics.
   The teacher identified her global aims for the entire lesson sequence of about sixteen lessons, as: i) identifying functions and their relationships to everyday life; and ii) understanding how to solve equations using a table, graph or formal solving techniques.
   This particular lesson was designed by the teacher to focus on: i) different variables and their relationships with one another; ii) understanding the form of a linear equation; and iii) understanding that the investigation of the nature and function of equations is of utmost importance.

Social Performance of the Task		
Teacher	*Mathematical Task as Stated*	*Student*
The teacher states her goal to the class, "I'd like to think about change using these figures."	The Stairs Task	(Students attentive)

The teacher asks students to work on drawing the next two figures in the sequence.	The first three figures have been drawn for you. Draw the next two figures by stacking one cm sided squares on top of each other.	------------------------------------
		Nou is invited to the board to draw the next two figures.
------------------------------------	-------------------------	
The teacher invites students to present ideas on identifying what aspect of the figures is changing.	What changes when the number of steps changes?	------------------------------------
		Jitsu immediately suggests, "the number of steps." Nobo and Nou add "size" and
The teacher invites students to work in small teams to identify as many aspects as they can.		"area" respectively. Taka adds "height."

CARMEL MESITI AND DAVID CLARKE

(The teacher roams the classroom and speaks with individual students) The teacher addresses the class and invites further suggestions on "what changes?" ------------------------------------- The teacher invites students to suggest how they might go about examining the relationship between the number of steps and the circumference. The teacher reiterates Mawa's mention of the use of a table and reminds students that mathematical expressions are also useful in examining relationships. She proceeds to draw up a table: 	number of steps	1	2	3	4	5
---	---	---	---	---	---
circumference (cm)					| She asks students to complete the table and to identify a mathematical relationship. (The teacher roams around the room assisting students) The teacher asks Yama to go to the board and trace the circumference of the staircase with four steps.		(Students working in small groups) Nii adds "number of sides" and "number of squares." Mika adds "circumference." Taka says, "shape." Nou responds with "the length of the base." Jitsu adds "the time it takes to draw the figures." Nobo adds "sum of the interior angle" and "the number of vertices." ------------------------------------- Some students suggest, "graphs." Mawa mentions "table." (Students work on the assigned task at their desks)

(middle column contains: -------------------------- Examine the relationship between the number of steps and the circumference.)

190

The teacher invites a student to fill out the table and another to write the relationship as an equation.		Yama assists the teacher by tracing the circumference of the figure with his finger.
		Ume volunteers :

number of steps	1	2	3	4	5
circumference (cm)	4	8	12	16	20

The teacher reviews the results in the table with the class and discusses the mathematical relationship represented by the table.		Taka writes $y = 4x$.
The teacher asks for other interpretations – other methods for getting the answer.		Most of the students agree that to find the circumference the number of steps is simply multiplied by four.
The teacher highlights this method graphically with Nobo's help: ------------------------------------ The teacher assigns the homework task:		Nii responds that you can add four to the previous answer, so that to get the circumference for six steps, one adds four to 20.
	-------------------------- Think about how to show that 'multiplying by four' works. Examine the relationship between the number of steps and another feature of the diagrams.	------------------------------------

---

Interpretive Reflection

The Stairs Task is well-known and used by mathematics teachers in many countries. The task was chosen for analysis because of its visual appeal and capacity to provide a focus for student attention. The teacher presented the problem and asked the students, *"What changes when the number of steps change?"* The teacher then took suggestions, and in doing so made clear the sort of responses she was expecting, and then gave the students the opportunity to work with one another on the task.

The task was presented with great care and appeared quite successful in meeting the teacher's objectives as stated in the questionnaire data. In particular, the students were able to identify a large number of differing variables. It was at this point in the lesson that the teacher narrowed the focus to the particular connection between the number of steps and the circumference and began to model a mathematical approach to defining this relationship. The teacher's focus on the students and the partnership she had formed with them in their learning was evidenced by students' contributions at the board: Nou drew steps four and five; Yama traced one of the figures with his finger to illustrate the concept of circumference; Ume completed the table, while Taka wrote the relationship in algebraic terms; and Nobo shared his various conjectures of relevant variables.

Once the relationship ($y = 4x$) was proposed, the teacher's attention turned to how to demonstrate the correctness of this equation, *"Think about how to show that multiplying by four works."* In her questionnaire responses, the teacher identified the goal of student recognition of the possible relationships between different variables and implemented this aim with the tasks she assigned and the questions she asked.

Task Two: Shanghai School 2 – Lesson 8 (the Numbers task)

Educational Context

The class was learning about the system of linear equations. The students have spent previous lessons working with inequalities, the relationship between the concept of linear equations in two unknowns and their solution, the transformation of equations and solution methods involving substitution and elimination.

This was the eighth lesson in this topic and one of the teacher's goals for this lesson was for students to learn to solve some special linear equations in three unknowns.

Social Performance of the Task		
Teacher	*Mathematical Task as Stated*	*Student*
The teacher presents the class with a task for all to consider. The teacher reads out the question. The teacher invites students to set up the equations.	There is a three digit number. The sum of the three digits is 12. The sum of the hundreds digit and the tens digit is greater than the ones digit by 2. Three times the hundreds digit equals the sum of the tens and the	(Students attentive)
------------------------------------		--------------------------------
The teacher invites a student to give her response.		
		Carry proposes, "x plus y plus z equals twelve."
The teacher confirms Carry's response is indeed correct.		
		Charlene states, "x plus y equals z plus two."
The teacher restates Charlene's		

	ones digits.	
response confirming its accuracy.		
	Let the hundreds digit be x, and the tens digit be y and the ones digit be z.	Cy adds, "y plus z equals three x."
------------------------------------ The teacher discusses the characteristics of this system of equations. $$\begin{cases} x+y+z = 12 \\ x+y = z+2 \\ y+z = 3x \end{cases}$$ This involves identifying which equations must be satisfied ("all of them") and using the exact terminology ("system of **linear** equations in **three** unknowns").		--------------------------------
	Set up the equations according to the question.	(Students verbally responding to teacher questions in unison)

Interpretive Reflection

We chose this task in part because of its function in introducing students to the underlying structure of algebraic representations and in assisting them to develop appropriate mathematical language. The strategic development of technical language has emerged from other analyses as a possible characteristic of mathematics teaching in China (Clarke & Xu, 2007). The task was presented to the class and three students were able to correctly provide the individual equations to form the entire system – indeed, it appeared they were able to do so quite effortlessly. It was at this point that the teacher spent some time identifying the exact nature and definitive characteristics of a system of linear equations in three unknowns.

The students were not encouraged to actually solve the equations, algebraically or by other means. The task consisted entirely of setting up the system of equations. Students were then presented with the following system to solve, understandably easier but perhaps not as enticing as the task that prompted the set of equations they had just constructed:

$$\begin{cases} x+y = 11 \\ y+z = 17 \\ x+z = 10 \end{cases}$$

Task Three: Sweden School 1 – Lesson 11 (the Graph Task)

Educational Context

This class had been working on the topic of proportionality. This involved an introduction to: the coordinate system; the construction of a graph; direct variation and non-proportionality.

This was the sixth lesson in this topic and the teacher's target content for this lesson included: calculating price per unit from a straight line graph; determining the equation of a

straight-line graph; gradient; and determining which equations best represented a particular graph.		
Social Performance of the Task		
Teacher	*Mathematical Task as Stated*	*Student*
The teacher projects the straight-line graph on a screen at the front of the class and asks students, "what can you tell me about this?"		(students seated and attentive)
--------------------------------------	What can you tell me about these two lines?	------------------------------- Martina responds "red and green and blue". Viktoria adds, "something is more expensive than the other." This point is debated. Beata points out there are no units.
In response to Beata the teacher adds to the diagram:		
The teacher amends the diagram in response to the students' comments:		A discussion ensues with students pointing out certain features that are absent from the diagram. These include: the labelling of the x and y axes, the origin and numerical values for the dashes along the axes.
The teacher states that the		

different lines now represent apples and pears. He asks the students whether they now have new information to add.		
		The students respond that it is now possible to find the cost of a single piece of fruit. Alva and Viktoria explain how to read the cost of a single fruit.
The teacher attempts, with a ruler, to read the cost of a single fruit but declares that it is rather difficult and that if they were to consider a larger quantity of fruit they would achieve a more accurate result.		
After attempts to indicate on the graph the cost of 5 pieces of fruit the teacher summarises their findings so far: o one is more expensive than the other o one is cheaper than the other o it has something to do with how the graph slopes		
(The task is momentarily abandoned as the subsequent discussion involves the problem 90×90 and the different ways of calculating this quantity)		
The teacher asks for a cost equation that summarises the information in the graph.		
		Annette suggests that it is, "the quantity times 15."
The teacher highlights the meaning of the x in the equation $K = 15x$. They then determine that the other cost equation is $K = 10x$.		
The teacher continues the conversation by asking the students to determine where		

$K = 2x$ would appear on the given graph. The teacher continues by drawing up a table:		

x	K	
0	0	(0,0)
1	2	(1,2)
5	10	(5,10)

and with the use of these points determines the graph of $K = 2x$.

Interpretive Reflection

The Graph Task was chosen for its strategy of 'creating' a real-world context for an abstract mathematical representation. The students became responsible for giving meaning to two lines on a graph and subsequently for determining the relationship in algebraic terms by identifying the value of the gradient. The problem was introduced quite conversationally and this relatively informal presentation reflects the classroom's social interactions. Students were encouraged to make observations about the two lines and the teacher responded to those comments that were of a mathematical nature. The teacher's selective acknowledgement of particular responses established him as the mathematical authority in an otherwise very casual classroom environment.

The character of this classroom and of the mathematical activity appeared to be dependent upon participants being willing to make verbal contributions. The teacher's strategy to maximise student interest and engagement appeared to be based on the conversion of an abstract mathematical situation into one that had a real-world context.

Task Four: Shanghai School 3 – Lesson 7 (the Train Task)

Educational Context

This topic was intended to promote learning about systems of linear equations in two unknowns. The students have spent previous lessons discussing the concept of linear equations in two unknowns, the rectangular coordinate plane and the graph of a linear equation, determining whether a given system satisfies the criteria to be classified as a system of linear equations in two unknowns and determining whether a particular ordered pair is a solution.

This was the seventh lesson in this topic and one of the teacher's goals for this lesson was to demonstrate how to solve a system of linear equations in two unknowns by elimination (using addition and subtraction).

Social Performance of the Task

Teacher	Mathematical Task as Stated	Student
The teacher presents the class with a task for all to consider. The teacher reads out the problem and invites students to calculate an answer mentally. ------------------------------------	Siu Ming's family intends to travel to Beijing by train	(Students attentive) --------------------------------

The teacher asks students to explain how to calculate the cost of the student ticket.	during the national holiday, so they have booked three adult tickets and one student ticket, totalling $560.	
		Dora responds by stating the student ticket costs $80. She further explains that the difference between the two amounts ($560 and $640) is the cost of one student ticket.
	After hearing this, Siu Ming's classmate Siu Wong would like to go to Beijing with them. As a result they buy three adult tickets and two student tickets for a total of $640.	
The teacher reiterates Dora's explanation and invites students to explain how one would calculate the cost of an adult ticket.		
		Eva responds that "$560 minus $80 for a student ticket is $480 and divided by 3 is $160."
The teacher highlights that this solution has been achieved by inspection. He then requests students to use their recent knowledge to form appropriate equations.	Can you calculate the cost of each adult and student ticket?	
		Felix contributes, "three x plus y equals five hundred and sixty," and then continues with, "three x plus two y equals six hundred and forty."

The teacher demonstration of the solution to this task involves: Confirming that the system of equations the students are working with is $\begin{cases} 3x + y = 560 \\ 3x + 2y = 640 \end{cases}$ Subtracting the first equation from the second gives $y = 80$. Substituting $y = 80$ into the first equation gives $3x + 80 = 560$, thus $x = 160$.		(Students taking notes)

Interpretive Reflection

The Train Task was chosen because of its integrated use of different representations. Students initially solved the word problem by inspection. Dora succinctly explained her thinking in identifying the cost of the student ticket and Eva was able to continue the calculation to find the cost of the adult ticket. The task was then represented as a pair of simultaneous equations that were then solved by the teacher, with the appropriate algebraic techniques.

> By removing the burden of finding a solution early on, the teacher was able to focus his students' attention on the algebraic representation and the technique of elimination and, perhaps, also reassure students, at the same time, of the legitimacy of abstract algebraic manipulation.

Task Five: Japan School 2 – Lesson 1 (the Equivalent Deformation task)

Educational Context
This classroom was studying the topic of geometric congruence and similarity. The first three lessons in this topic sequence focused on the skill of 'equivalent deformation.' The task of this lesson, the first lesson, involved learning and understanding the technique of converting a parallelogram to a triangle while keeping the area constant. The second and third lessons extended and consolidated this skill with a more difficult example – in this additional case the class converted one triangle to another triangle, again without changing the value of the area.

Social Performance of the Task		
Teacher	*Mathematical Task as Stated*	*Student*
The teacher identifies the theme for the day as 'equivalent deformation.' Some time is spent discussing the meaning of the phrase – it is concluded that students will learn how to change the shape of a given diagram keeping the area constant. He then invites students to solve the task. A few hints are given, including: drawing a quadrilateral, reminding students to keep the area constant; identifying the problem as a construction problem thereby asking students to use a ruler; reminding students to use parallel lines ---------------------------------- (The teacher offers individual assistance to students.) ---------------------------------- The teacher demonstrates the solution to the task: the quadrilateral is divided in two with a diagonal line	Consider parallelogram ABCD Change the quadrilateral to a triangle keeping the area constant.	 ---------------------------- (Students are solving the problem in their seats.) ----------------------------

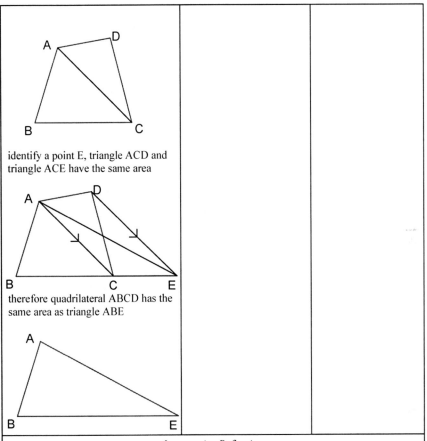

identify a point E, triangle ACD and
triangle ACE have the same area

therefore quadrilateral ABCD has the
same area as triangle ABE

Interpretive Reflection

The Equivalent Deformation task was chosen for its highly visual nature and because it allowed students to engage with a task that required diagrammatic manipulation, which was not a common feature of the tasks studied. We also considered it an unusual task and a challenging one; certainly this type of task was not commonly found in the classrooms we have studied.

The presentation of the task involved defining the term 'equivalent deformation' and students were then given various hints on how to perform the task. Much of the time dedicated to this task was spent by the teacher offering individual advice to students at their desks. This advice commonly took the form of encouraging them to talk about what they were trying to achieve. The public presentation of the solution, however, was entirely performed by the teacher, with each step clearly drawn and accompanied by lengthy explanations.

Task Six: Shanghai School 1 – Lesson 10 (the Coefficients Task)

Educational Context of the Task		
The class was learning about the system of linear equations in two unknowns. The students had spent previous lessons discussing the concept of solution sets, the relationship between the solution of a system and the solutions of the individual equations, the representations of linear equations on the Cartesian plane and the solution methods involving substitution and elimination. This was the tenth lesson in this topic and one of the teacher's goals for this lesson was to strengthen existing student knowledge of solution methods suitable for simultaneous equations.		

Social Performance of the Task		
Teacher	*Mathematical Task as Stated*	*Student*
The teacher presents the class with a task for all to consider. The teacher explains the question and invites students to suggest solution strategies. ------------------------------------	Students A and B try to solve a system of linear equations $$\begin{cases} ax + by = 2 \\ cx - 7y = 8 \end{cases}.$$	(Students attentive) -------------------------------- Bride suggests substituting both student solutions into the system of equations.
The teacher asks class whether Bride is correct. The teacher asks a third student what he thinks.	Student A finds the correct answer $$\begin{cases} x = 3 \\ y = -2 \end{cases},$$ however, Student B copies the wrong value of c, which resulted in the answer $\begin{cases} x = -2 \\ y = 2 \end{cases}.$	Bern suggests substituting both student solutions into equation $ax + by = 2$, in order to find the values of a and b. Bandson suggests substituting the correct values of x and y into the equation $cx - 7y = 8$. This will give the correct value of c.
The teacher announces that he will proceed by combining the suggestions of Bern and Bandson. ------------------------------------	Find the correct values of a, b and c. Find the incorrect value of c.	--------------------------------
The teacher demonstration of the solution to this task involves the following key steps: Substituting the correct values of x and y into the system of		(Students taking notes)

equations $\begin{cases} 3a - 2b = 2 \\ 3c + 14 = 8 \end{cases}$ to determine $c = -2$. Substituting the incorrect values of x and y into the first equation to create a third equation $-2a + 2b = 2$. Using the first and third equations $\begin{cases} 3a - 2b = 2 \\ -2a + 2b = 2 \end{cases}$ to determine $a = 4$ and $b = 5$. Substituting the incorrect values of x and y into the second equation to create a fourth equation $-2c - 14 = 8$, thus the incorrect value of c is -11.		

Interpretive Reflection

The Coefficients Task appeared to be an intellectually demanding exploration of the students' understanding of simultaneous equations. The task certainly required more than the replication or use of a standard procedure by requiring the students to treat the coefficients of the standard format as variables and the variables as knowns (by virtue of the stated solutions).

The teacher invited students to suggest possible solution strategies; three students dutifully responded. The teacher then demonstrated the solution to the problem step-by-step, utilising elements of the methods suggested by two of the students.

The extent to which responsibility for the development of this particular solution was intended to be devolved to the students is uncertain. However, the teacher has commented in interview that *"I stress on having students be the active agent in the class… the conclusion is not told by the teacher. It is through teacher's guidance, the students observe and operate… then they get the conclusion. It is like this."*

The complexity of the task and the evident complexity of the teachers' decision making warrant further investigation to establish the teacher's intentions at each stage in the performance of the task.

Task Seven: Japan School 3 – Lesson 1 (the Long Task)

Educational Context	
This class was learning about the system of linear equations in two unknowns. This was the first lesson in the topic and the teacher's goal for this lesson was to demonstrate how to solve a system of linear equations in two unknowns by elimination and substitution as well as to help students grasp the exact meaning of solving equations.	

Social Performance of the Task		
Teacher	*Mathematical Task as Stated*	*Student*
The teacher presents the class		

with a system of linear equations to solve.	$\begin{cases} 5x + 2y = 9 \\ -5x + 3y = 1 \end{cases}$	(Students attentive)
----------------------------------		--
The teacher invites Kori to the board to present his solution.		Kori writes: $$5x + 2y = 9$$ $$-(-5x + 3y = 1)$$ $$\overline{}$$ $$5x + 5x + 2y - 3y = 9 - 1$$ $$10x - y = 8$$ $$10x = 8 + y$$ $$x = \frac{8 + y}{10}$$ $$\overline{}$$ $$5x + 2y = 9$$ $$5\left(\frac{8 + y}{10}\right) + 2y = 9$$ $$8 + y + 4y = 18$$ $$y + 4y = 18 - 8$$ $$5y = 10$$ $$y = 2$$ $$\overline{}$$ $$5x + 2y = 9$$ $$5x + 4 = 9$$ $$5x = 5$$ $$x = 1$$
The teacher asks students what their thoughts are with respect to Kori's solution. He then invites Kori to explain his solution.		
----------------------------------		Kori's explanation involves describing each step.
The teacher once again questions students on their thoughts.		--
(While Suzu writes at the board the teacher conducts a discussion with the class about Kori's solution. His comments invite the students to reflect on the different solutions and how one may be an improvement on		Suzu responds that there may be a simpler equation and is subsequently invited to the board to present his solution: Suzu writes: $$5y = 10$$ $$y = 2$$ $$\overline{}$$ $$5x + 2 \times 2 = 9$$

the other.)		$5x + 4 = 9$ $5x = 9 - 4$ $5x = 5$ $x = 1$
---------------------------- (The teacher uses this time to wander around the class and question individual students on there understandings.) ---------------------------- The teacher asks Endo to reproduce his solution on the board. The class is invited to "check" the solution. The teacher proceeds to highlight the unusual 0=0 result and asks, "Why did this happen?" The bell rings so he adjourns the discussion to the following lesson.		-- (The students are given time to replicate both solutions in their notebooks and reflect on two solution processes.) -- Endo writes: $5x = 9 - 2y$ $x = \dfrac{9 - 2y}{5}$ (equation 3) $5\left(\dfrac{9 - 2y}{5}\right) + 2y = 9$ $9 - 2y + 2y = 9$ $-2y + 2y = 9 - 9$ $0 = 0$ $-5 \times \dfrac{9 - 2y}{5} + 3y = 1$ $-(9 - 2y) + 3y = 1$ $-9 + 2y + 3y = 1$ $2y + 3y = 1 + 9$ $5y = 10$ $y = 2$ -- $5x + 2 \times 2 = 9$ $5x + 4 = 9$ $5x = 5$ $x = 1$

Interpretive Reflection

In this task, the seemingly simple pair of simultaneous equations $\begin{cases} 5x + 2y = 9 \\ -5x + 3y = 1 \end{cases}$ engaged the class for a fifty-minute lesson (and indeed was the discussion point for the first fifteen minutes of the following lesson). A feature of the performance of this task was the extent to which student suggestions, responses and the articulation of their thinking were regarded as instruments for developing understanding.

The teacher, in an interview, when asked about his aim for this lesson responded, *"It's not that I just wanted them to just solve the problems but also, um, I wanted to teach them that there is a need to think about it a little – what solving equations is all about."*

Task Eight: Australia School 1 – Lesson 8 (the Coin Task)

Educational Context of the Task
This is the eighth lesson in a series of fifteen lessons concerned with perimeter and area and particular emphasis is placed on the use and definitions of mathematical terms.
The teacher identified her global aims for the entire lesson sequence, as representing mathematical activity as a real-life activity and demonstrating how it relates to real-life situations.
This particular lesson was designed to focus on: i) finding the perimeter of a semi circle and quarter circle; ii) developing rules for the perimeter of non-common shapes; and iii) using student understanding and knowledge of perimeter to solve a non-routine, challenging problem.

Social Performance of the Task		
Teacher	*Mathematical Task as Stated*	*Student*
The teacher sets up the task by stating, "Now, I've got another question I'd like you to do… I want you to discuss it with the person sitting next to you, and see what solution you come up with. She proceeds by drawing the following diagram: A verbal explanation of the problem follows with students asking questions and the teacher responding. Additional information is added to the diagram, namely that the side length of the square is 25cm (this follows that the perimeter of the square itself is 100cm) and that the radius of the circle is 2 cm. The explanation involves the use of a cardboard cut-out of a 'coin' with a hole in its centre	A coin of radius 2 cm is rolled around a square of side 25 cm, always being in contact with the edge of the square. Find the distance travelled by the centre of the coin when the coin has travelled once around the square. (diagram used in textbook from which this task was taken, but not used by the teacher)	(Some students copying previous worked example from the board, others attentive to the new task. At one point the teacher requests that all students place their pens down and focus on the explanation of the given task.) Students contributing comments and questions.

– the teacher uses this manipulative to indicate that along the side of the square as the "coin" rolls the centre's path is a straight line.		Marcus is invited to the board and draws some of the path, along the side of the square.
The teacher now writes, "Find the distance travelled by the centre of the coin when the coin has travelled once around the square."		
----------------------------------		----------------------------------
While the students work on the problem the teacher approaches each student in turn to see how they coped with their homework. This activity was interspersed with statements of advice to the whole class, examples include: "Have a look at how the centre of the circle moves as it goes round a corner. How would the centre of the circle move?" "The important thing to understand, or what you need to realise, is what happens when the circle goes around a corner." The teacher also invited students to use the manipulative at the board if they needed to.		Jessica approaches the board and adds to the initial drawing to indicate the path taken by the centre of the circle. Her workings result in the following diagram:

205

The teacher comments on Jessica's diagram to the whole class, "Jessica's come to the board, and from what I can tell, she's drawn how the circle travels… you're telling me the circle gets to the edge, and it keeps coming out, and then it drops down."		
Leon is invited to the board. His forearm is used to indicate the radius of the coin, while his fingertips indicate the path of the centre of the coin and his arm is rotated around the square's edge with the help of the teacher.		
		Leon responds that the path taken around the edge, by the centre of the coin, is a quarter circle. He amends Jessica's diagram to highlight this discovery:
The teacher continues to assist students at their desks with this task. A number of students are able to arrive at a correct solution. ---------------------------------- (following lesson) During the following lesson, after the students have attempted and corrected other problems related to perimeter the teacher gives a full solution of this task to the class.	----------------------------	----------------------------
		Adrian is invited to the board to assist in marking out the path of the coin and to discuss the exact calculation.

She concludes by highlighting that this is not a "perimeter" problem, but a task that requires the application of the mathematics learnt in relation to perimeter.		

Interpretive Reflection

The Coin task was chosen for its visual appeal, for the attempt at modelling the problem with a manipulative and for its non-routine nature. The teacher presented this problem as an 'additional' task – as it seemed that those students who hadn't completed their homework were to spend the time in the lesson doing 'both'. Having the students work on their homework and the coin task gave the teacher an opportunity to move around the room and to talk with each student to determine how they were coping with the work on perimeter.

Interestingly, the task was amended slightly from how it was presented in the textbook. The diagram in the textbook indicates the path of the coin's centre, and is clearly shown to be non-linear. The teacher chose to change the task slightly by not providing a visual cue for the path taken by the coin's centre around the corner of the square. The teacher tries to give verbal clues and tries to direct their attention to the path taken around the corner but it appears few students are able to determine this for themselves. Jessica's diagram gives the teacher an opportunity to address their misunderstandings.

In the end, Leon's use of his arm to model the movement undertaken by the coin successfully illustrated the curved nature of the coin centre's path. Some students still appeared to struggle with the actual calculation itself, while others appeared unwilling to record any steps in their books and made use solely of the calculator.

There are no summarising comments made at the end of the lesson. Indeed, it is unclear what is expected of the students, if anything, before next lesson. The teacher returns to this problem in the following lesson and gives a full, detailed explanation of the solution. Although this task was chosen for its non-routine characteristics, it appeared that the majority of the students of the class were not quite ready for the degree of sophistication of the task and had not yet mastered the mathematical skills required.

Task Nine: U.S.A. School 2 – Lesson 9 (the Compare and Contrast task – student presentations)

Educational Context
This was the ninth lesson in a series of lessons concerned with functions and relations. In the previous lesson, the students were asked to complete tabulations of corresponding x and y values, in which the x-values change (-2, -1, 0, 1, 2) for the functions $0x + 3y = 6$ and $2x + 0y = 6$. The teacher discussed the slope of the graph and introduced the term "undefined slope". She also led a discussion involving the similarities and differences between the two graphs. This discussion appeared to model the type of activity she was expecting from the Compare and Contrast task.   The teacher stated in the questionnaire data that this particular lesson was designed to focus on: i) extending the students' knowledge of linear and non-linear graphs; and ii) seeing how the structured vocabulary studied in the prior lessons "crystallised." She also expressed an additional purpose for the lesson: that is, *"to take a broad look at what algebra may be about (rates of change) before plugging in discrete, "small" understandings and procedures."*

	Social Performance of the Task	
Teacher	*Mathematical Task as Stated*	*Student*
The Compare and Contrast task was assigned in the previous lesson (lesson 8). In order for students' work to contribute to answering the question, "How are the following pairs of functions alike and different?" students were asked to complete one of the following a) draw up T-charts (tabulations of corresponding x and y values); b) draw the graph; c) find similarities; d) find differences; for one pair of functions on a small, portable whiteboard. ---------------------------------- (Lesson 9) The task is written up for reference on paper on another smaller board. She invites the students who worked on the first and second pair of functions to place their mini-whiteboards up against the main board for display. ---------------------------------- The students who worked on the third pair of equations are invited to the front. They hold their workings in front of them and the teacher asks them to, "Tell me about yours.... Tell me what you graphed." The teacher comments that	COMPARE / CONTRAST How are the following pairs of functions alike and different? i) $y = 3x + 2$ and $y = -3x - 2$ ii) $0x + 3y = 6$ and $2x + 0y = 6$ iii) $y = x^2$ and $y = \dfrac{1}{x}$ iv) $y = 1 - 2x$ and $y = 1 - x^2$ v) $2y = x$ and $y = 2x$	---------------------------------- (students waiting, attentive, some propping their work up against the board and then taking their seats) ---------------------------------- The student responds that he graphed $y = \dfrac{1}{x}$ and that it turns out to be a hyperbola.

the function produces a curve but does not appear to have the form of a graph involving squaring or a higher power of x.

Another student adds that his task involved drawing the parabola, $y = x^2$ and adds that it touches at the origin.

A third student contributes her "similarities" – both equations are non-linear, both are a type of 'bola' and both are functions.

The teacher explains the student's use of the term 'function' by adding that she could draw a single vertical line anywhere on the graph and it would never touch the graph in more than one place.

The teacher then asks them to explain why the graph
$y = \dfrac{1}{x}$ is discontinuous at
the origin. She then comments on the difficulty of determining the shape of a hyperbola with only a limited number of points.

Lastly, the students that worked on the fourth pair of functions are invited to discuss their findings.

A student responds that both are functions and both have the same y-intercept.

Another student responds that the differences include that one is linear, the other non-linear.

The teacher makes some additional comments on the graphs regarding slope, linear decay and refers to the parabola as negative.

Interpretive Reflection

The Compare and Contrast task was chosen because of the open-ended nature of some aspects of the task (that is, to list similarities and differences) and because the sharing of students' work was essential for a full discussion to take place. The task required a level of collaborative activity during the whole class discussion and, in carrying out this particular task, the teacher appeared to value written and oral contributions equally.

An interesting feature was that most of the written work had been completed in the previous lesson. The teacher had also modelled the sort of discussion she was hoping to achieve with another pair of functions in the previous lesson. Despite the well-prepared workings on the students' hand-held whiteboards, much of the discussion and contribution of knowledge during the presentations was undertaken by the teacher. Students' made short responses and the teacher accompanied these with much commentary. The task was distributed in the sense that all students needed to relate their workings to another's if they were to engage with the task. As performed, the extent of the distribution of responsibility for knowledge generation to the students was limited.

DISCUSSION

Our conception of the teacher/student/task triad accords significant agency to *each* in the determination of the actions and outcomes that find their nexus in the social situation for which the task is the pretext. It is useful to review some aspects of the tasks described in this paper, particularly from the perspectives of the distribution of agency and voice among the classroom community.

Task One: Japan School 1 – Lesson 1 (the Stairs Task)

The level of student involvement in the task was high and the activity was communal and collaborative in character. The emphasis was on the development of understanding and the entire lesson time was devoted to utilising the visual representation to generate the algebraic representation. The teacher's orchestration of the several student contributions provides a useful illustration of the sort of teacher-managed distribution of responsibility that problematises the simplistic dichotomisation of classrooms into teacher-centred and student-centred (Clarke, 2006b; Mok, 2006).

Task Two: Shanghai School 2 – Lesson 8 (the Numbers task)

The task's focus on the establishment of the equations without the need to actually solve them added emphasis to the teacher's prioritisation of the underlying structure of algebraic representations and the development of fluency in the use of technical language. In the performance of this task, the teacher's evaluative authority was clear and, despite the several student contributions, the actual devolution of agency to the students was quite limited.

Task Three: Sweden School 1 – Lesson 11 (the Graph Task)

It is not uncommon for a task to involve constructing a mathematical model of a real-world situation. In this task, the progressive elaboration of the graph generates a context for the initial abstraction. While the teacher remained the primary authority in the construction of the context, there was some attempt at devolution of responsibility towards the students. Further analysis of the teacher interviews was required to determine whether this devolution was intended or perceived as such. In the interview, the teacher explained this approach to classroom discussions:

> We did something called the understanding of what is asked in the problem. Then we solved stuff in groups. It was done mostly to get them to talk. And I am to blame for this a lot, they talk a lot but many of them talk really well [laughter] they discuss math and they figure it out in a good way together, so it is more fun for many of them especially the girls but many guys also but mostly the girls they help each other with solutions really well and I am very satisfied with their work.

Task Four: Shanghai School 3 – Lesson 7 (the Train Task)

The Train Task takes the more familiar route from real-world context to algebraic representation. To us, it appeared a novel feature of the task that the teacher chose not to emphasise the utility of the algebraic representation in solving a problem that the students could clearly answer by other means. Rather, the teacher emphasised that both the situation and the method of solution can be modelled algebraically. In relation to distributed agency and voice, it should be noted that the teacher's approach explicitly affirms the students' ability to generate a correct answer using non-algebraic methods and then asserts his curricular authority by interpreting the students' methods in algebraic terms. The legitimacy of the student's initial solution is not contested, and the teacher's subsequent solution should be seen as an act of re-interpretation rather than appropriation.

Task Five: Japan School 2 – Lesson 1 (the Equivalent Deformation task)

Both authors, influenced by our experience of Australian mathematics classes, found the deformation task novel. We have been assured that the problem of how to change the shape of a given geometric figure, while keeping the area constant is a standard procedure in the Japanese mathematics curriculum, and it may be elsewhere, although we found no evidence of any similar tasks in the data set. The social performance of the task involved a form of Kikan-Shido (Between Desks Instruction, see O'Keefe, Xu, & Clarke, 2006) in which the teacher elicited the students' thoughts and methods through dialogue with individual students. It was clear from the formality of the teacher's presentation of the solution that what was being taught was intended as a standard procedure rather than a novel investigation. The combination of distributed student and teacher performance (performed through Kikan-Shido) and teacher summative task performance is highly similar to the practices evident in many of the Australian lessons. There was little devolution of agency to the student and the emphasis of the lesson was on the correct implementation of a mathematical procedure.

Task Six: Shanghai School 1 – Lesson 10 (the Coefficients Task)

This task offers an interesting illustration of the use of a non-routine task to interrogate established procedures. The extent to which the responsibility for generating the complete solution might have been devolved to a greater extent to the students is a matter of speculation. The teacher's intentions and conscious decision-making could usefully be juxtaposed with the students' interpretations and consequent learning. This is a further level of analysis that we plan to carry out.

Task Seven: Japan School 3 – Lesson 1 (the Long Task)

Student performance 'out the front' has been discussed elsewhere (Jablonka, 2006). It is a common procedure in some countries (Japan and the Czech Republic, for example) and much less common in others. The extent to which such public performances represent a devolution of responsibility to the student, with an associated amplification of agency and voice, depends significantly on the teacher's self-positioning as the evaluative authority of what is produced by the students. In this task, significant evaluative responsibility remained in the hands of the class. The solutions being compared were, of course, entirely student-generated. It must be noted that this is the first lesson in the topic, rather than a summative lesson intended to review content already taught. The teacher's articulated goal of wanting to teach them "what solving equations is all about" was very evident in the documented task performance. The lesson is distinguished by the teacher's use of a relatively simple (and ultimately routine) mathematical task to facilitate class discussion of what it means to solve a pair of simultaneous linear equations.

Task Eight: Australia School 1 – Lesson 8 (the Coin Task)

The classroom performance of the coin task drew on several familiar classroom protocols. Certainly, the task was sufficiently challenging to be considered a non-routine problem for the students and there was a consequent need for student exploratory activity. The teacher made extensive use of Kikan-Shido (between desks instruction) during this exploratory activity and the manner in which this was performed was a signature characteristic of this teacher's practice. The teacher's decision not to use the illustration in the textbook placed an additional interpretive responsibility on the students that some were clearly unable to meet. However, it was the omission of this illustration that gave the task its problem-solving character. The role of visual imagery in the mathematical modelling of the task situation was a key feature and the lesson's dependence on a key contribution from one student (Leon) represented a meaningful devolution of responsibility from the teacher.

Task Nine: U.S.A. School 2 – Lesson 9 (the Compare and Contrast Task – student presentations)

This task delegated some responsibility to the students to construct distinctions between equation types and also gave significant opportunity for student voice in the articulation of the constructed differences. Given the level of preparatory modelling by the teacher during the previous lesson, the actual devolution of responsibility for knowledge generation was lower than might be thought from an examination of the task as performed in this one lesson. However, notwithstanding the level of preparation, it was clearly the teacher's intention that the students should exercise significant agency in the construction of the differences between their assigned pairs of equations and that they should then articulate these differences in mathematically appropriate language.

While the classrooms studied both in Australia and the U.S.A. used a variety of task types, the most common form of communal task performance (involving both teacher and students) resembled either Task Five (distributed student performance followed by teacher summative performance) or an emphasis on procedural fluency. Having said this, the practices of the Australian and U.S.A. classrooms gave significant emphasis to student voice, without, however, according students significant responsibility or agency in the social development of new knowledge (cf. Sekiguchi, 2008).

It must be acknowledged that the selection of 'distinctive tasks' for discussion in this paper was inevitably a culturally-situated selection, carried out primarily by one of the authors (Mesiti). Nonetheless, we feel that the classroom task performances documented in this paper offer some interesting insights into the distribution of voice and agency in the classrooms of competent teachers and into the manner in which the task constrains and affords certain performances. What is clear is that classroom task performance is significantly influenced by teacher intention. This seemingly superficial observation is worth noting. The availability of 'good tasks' (and we would suggest that the tasks cited here have at least the potential to be good tasks, likely to promote student learning effectively) does not prescribe classroom task performance, which is a social consequence of many elements. There is no doubt that Task One (the Stairs Task), for example, would have been performed differently in the hands of a different teacher with different students.

CONCLUSIONS

Tasks have long been recognised as crucial mediators between mathematical content and the mathematics learner. In a very real sense, the tasks employed in the mathematics classroom represent a model of mathematics as it is performed in that classroom. The activity that arises as a consequence of a student's completion of a task is itself a constituent element of the learning process and the artefacts (both conceptual and physical) employed in the completion of the task serve simultaneous purposes as scaffolds for cognition, as repositories of distributed cognition, and as cognitive products. Task selection by teachers represents the initiation of an instructional process that includes task enactment (collaboratively by teacher and student) and the interpretation of the consequences of this enactment (again, by teacher and student). In this chapter, we have examined the function of nine mathematical tasks taken from classrooms in five countries. The tasks to be analysed were selected either because they appear to be typical of the mathematical activity of that classroom or because they offered a distinctive (and possibly unusual) model of mathematics, not evident in other classrooms.

We have characterised the tasks selected in each classroom with respect to intention, action and interpretation. The significance of differences between social, cultural and curricular settings, together with differences between participating classroom communities, challenges any reductionist attempts to characterize instructional tasks independent of these considerations. Rather than aiming to characterize the typical task used in any classroom, we have employed 'distinctive tasks' as our entry point in an investigation of what characteristics of distributed responsibility and of voice and agency are evident in the use of each particular task.

Of particular interest in our analysis were differences in the function of mathematically similar tasks, dealing with similar mathematical content (those relating to systems of linear equations), when employed by different teachers, in different classrooms, for different instructional purposes, with different students. An essential tool for our analysis is a tabulation of the details related to the social performance of the task. Using these tables, our analysis drew on the video-stimulated, post-lesson interview data to identify intention and interpretation and relate both to social performance of the task.

If, as has been suggested in the last section, the classroom performance of a task is ultimately a unique synthesis of task, teacher, students and situation, then what can be learned from the analysis of such idiosyncratic social performances? As Umberto Eco is reputed to have said, "Only the ephemeral is of lasting value" and it is the transient, fleeting and not-to-be-repeated social performances that constitute the daily occurrence of the mathematics classrooms of competent teachers. We would argue that the conception that the community-at-large holds of the mathematics classroom is intrinsically bound up in the type of tasks that characterise such settings. And this conception is not in error. Mathematical tasks are the embodiment of the curricular pretext that brings each particular set of individuals together in every mathematics classroom. In other contexts, individuals come together to engage in musical performances or dramatic performances. The performances of the mathematics classroom are largely the performance of mathematical tasks and if we are to understand and facilitate the learning that is the ostensible purpose of such settings then we must understand the nature of the performances that we find there.

214

We contend that insight into the nature of such performances may be most evident in the comparison of the classroom performances of distinctive mathematical tasks, since the very distinctiveness (as we have defined it) of the tasks and the associated performances is likely to throw into sharp relief the social dimensions (intentions, actions, interpretations, and consequences) that characterise and distinguish effective and less effective practice. While we are convinced that post-lesson interview data demonstrate the effectiveness of the documented task performances by any conventional standards, differences in the nature of the resultant student learning outcomes arising from the different task performances could be profound. A later analysis will explore these differences.

The thread that we have pursued through the examples discussed has been that of the social distribution of responsibility, agency and voice. We commenced our analysis disposed from other studies to believe that these issues were important. Our exploration of responsibility, agency and voice in the context of the classroom performance of mathematical tasks suggests to us that competent teachers of mathematics (within the constraints of culture and curriculum) share a belief in the importance of these elements. Analysis of the classroom performance of distinctive tasks offers insights into what constitutes valued performance in that classroom. This valuing could relate to the pedagogical value accorded to particular types of classroom activity or to the mathematical value of particular activities. The valuing of agency and voice is evident in the task performances in the classrooms of these teachers, rather than in any explicit articulation by them in classroom video data or in interview.

If we are to find pattern and structure in the profound diversity of 'well-taught' mathematics classrooms around the world, then the attention given by competent teachers to student voice and student agency, and the mathematical tasks that they employ to catalyse that voice and agency, may represent a useful entry point for analysis.

REFERENCES

Baroody, A. J., Cibulskis, M., Lai, M.-L., & Li X. (2004). Comments on the use of learning trajectories in curriculum development and research. *Mathematical Thinking and Learning, 6*(2), 227-260.

Clarke, D. J. (2001). Teaching/Learning. In D. J. Clarke (Ed.), *Perspectives on practice and meaning in mathematics and science classrooms* (pp. 291-320). Dordrecht: Kluwer Academic Publishers.

Clarke, D. J. (2006a). Using international comparative research to contest prevalent oppositional dichotomies. *Zentralblatt für Didaktik der Mathematik, 38*(5), 376-387.

Clarke, D. J. (2006b). The LPS research design. In D. J. Clarke, C. Keitel, & Y. Shimizu (Eds.), *Mathematics classrooms in twelve countries: The insider's perspective* (pp. 15-37). Rotterdam: Sense Publishers.

Clarke, D. J., & Lobato, J. (2002). To tell or not to tell: A reformulation of telling and the development of an initiating/eliciting model of teaching. In C. Malcolm & C. Lubisi (Eds.), *Proceedings of the Tenth Annual Meeting of the Southern African Association for Research in Mathematics, Science and Technology Education* (pp. 15-22).

Clarke, D. J., & Xu, L. H. (2007, August). *Distinguishing between mathematics classrooms in Australia, the USA, China, Japan and Korea through the lens of the distribution of responsibility for knowledge generation*. Paper presented at the annual conference of the European Association for Research in Learning and Instruction, Budapest.

Gagnè, R. M., & Briggs, L. J. (1974). *Principles of instructional design*. New York: Holt, Rinehart & Winston.

Hutchins, E. (1995). *Cognition in the wild*. Cambridge, MA: MIT Press.

Jablonka, E. (2006). Student(s) at the front: Forms and function in six classrooms from Germany, Hong Kong and the United States. In D. J. Clarke, J. Emanuelsson, E. Jablonka, & I. A. C. Mok (Eds.), *Making connections: Comparing mathematics classrooms around the world* (pp. 107-126). Rotterdam: Sense Publishers.

Miles, M. B., & Huberman, A. M. (2004). *Qualitative data analysis* (2nd edition). Thousand Oaks, CA: Sage Publications.

O'Keefe, C., Xu, L. H., & Clarke, D. J. (2006). Kikan-Shido: Between desks instruction. In D. J. Clarke, J. Emanuelsson, E. Jablonka, & I. A. C. Mok (Eds.), *Making connections: Comparing mathematics classrooms around the world* (pp. 73-106). Rotterdam: Sense Publishers.

Salomon, G. (1993). *Distributed cognitions: Psychological and educational considerations*. New York: Cambridge University Press.

Sekiguchi, Y. (2008). Classroom mathematical norms in Australian lessons: Comparison with Japanese lessons. In O. Figueras, J. L. Cortina, S. Alatorre, T. Rojano, & A. Sepulveda (Eds.), *Proceedings of the Joint Meeting of PME 32 and PME-NA*, *32*(4), 241-248.

Simon, M. A. (1995). Reconstructing mathematics pedagogy from a constructivist perspective. *Journal for Research in Mathematics Education, 26*(2), 114-145.

Simon, M. A., & Tzur, R. (2004). Explicating the role of mathematical tasks in conceptual learning: An elaboration of the hypothetical learning trajectory. *Mathematical Thinking and Learning, 6*(2), 91-104.

Carmel Mesiti
International Centre for Classroom Research
Melbourne Graduate School of Education
University of Melbourne
Australia

David Clarke
International Centre for Classroom Research
Melbourne Graduate School of Education
University of Melbourne
Australia

DAVID CLARKE

APPENDIX A

The LPS Research Design

INTRODUCTION

The originators of the LPS project, Clarke, Keitel and Shimizu, felt that the methodology developed by Clarke and known as complementary accounts (Clarke, 1998), which had already demonstrated its efficacy in a large-scale classroom study (subsequently reported in Clarke, 2001) could be adapted to meet the needs of the Learner's Perspective Study. These needs centered on the recognition that only by seeing classroom situations from the perspectives of all participants can we come to an understanding of the motivations and meanings that underlie their participation. In terms of techniques of data generation, this translated into three key requirements: (i) the recording of interpersonal conversations between focus students during the lesson; (ii) the documentation of sequences of lessons, ideally of an entire mathematics topic; and, (iii) the identification of the intentions and interpretations underlying the participants' statements and actions during the lesson.

Miles and Huberman's classic text on qualitative data analysis (Miles & Huberman, 1994) focused attention on 'data reduction.'

> Even before data are collected ... anticipatory data reduction is occurring as the researcher decides (often without full awareness) which conceptual framework, which cases, which research questions, and which data approaches to use. As data collection proceeds, further episodes of data reduction occur. (Miles & Huberman, 2004, p. 10)

This process of data reduction pervades any classroom video study. The choice of classroom, the number of cameras used, who is kept in view continuously and who appears only given particular circumstances, all contribute to a process that might better be called 'data construction' or 'data generation' than 'data reduction.' Every decision to zoom in for a closer shot or to pull back for a wide angle view represents a purposeful act by the researcher to selectively construct a data set optimally amenable to the type of analysis anticipated and maximally aligned with the particular research questions of interest to the researcher. The process of data

Y. Shimizu, B. Kaur, R. Huang and D. J. Clarke (Eds.), Mathematical Tasks in Classrooms around the World, pp. 217–231.

construction does not stop with the video record, since which statements (or whose voices) are transcribed, and which actions, objects or statements are coded, all constitute further decisions made by the researcher, more or less explicitly justified in terms of the project's conceptual framework or the focus of the researcher's interest. The researcher is the principle agent in this process of data construction. As such, the researcher must accept responsibility for decisions made and data constructed, and place on public record a transparent account of the decisions made in the process of data generation and analysis.

In the case of the Learner's Perspective Study: Research guided by a theory of learning that accords significance to both individual subjectivities and to the constraints of setting and community practice must frame its conclusions (and collect its data) accordingly. Such a theory must accommodate complementarity rather than require convergence and accord both subjectivity and agency to individuals not just to participate in social practice but to shape that practice. The assumption that each social situation is constituted through (and in) the multiple lived realities of the participants in that situation aligns the Learner's Perspective Study with the broad field of interpretivist research.

DATA GENERATION IN THE LEARNER'S PERSPECTIVE STUDY

Data generation in the Learner's Perspective Study (LPS) used a three-camera approach (Teacher camera, Student camera, Whole Class camera) that included the onsite mixing of the Teacher and Student camera images into a picture-in-picture video record (see Figure 1, teacher in top right-hand corner) that was then used in post-lesson interviews to stimulate participant reconstructive accounts of classroom events. These data were generated for sequences of at least ten consecutive lessons occurring in the "well-taught" eighth grade mathematics classrooms of teachers in Australia, the Czech Republic, Germany, Hong Kong and mainland China, Israel, Japan, Korea, The Philippines, Singapore, South Africa, Sweden and the USA. This combination of countries gives good representation to European and Asian educational traditions, affluent and less affluent school systems, and mono-cultural and multi-cultural societies.

Each participating country used the same research design to generate videotaped classroom data for at least ten consecutive math lessons and post-lesson video-stimulated interviews with at least twenty students in each of three participating 8th grade classrooms. The three mathematics teachers in each country were identified for their locally-defined 'teaching competence' and for their situation in demographically diverse government schools in major urban settings. Rather than attempt to apply the same definition of teaching competence across a dozen countries, which would have required teachers in Uppsala and Shanghai, for instance, to meet the same eligibility criteria, teacher selection was made by each local research group according to local criteria. These local criteria included such things as status within the profession, respect of peers or the school community, or visibility in presenting at teacher conferences or contributing to teacher professional development programs. As a result, the diverse enactment of teaching competence is one of the most interesting aspects of the project.

In most countries, the three lesson sequences were spread across the academic year in order to gain maximum diversity within local curricular content. In Sweden, China and Korea, it was decided to focus specifically on algebra, reflecting the anticipated analytical emphases of those three research groups. Algebra forms a significant part of the 8th grade mathematics curriculum in most participating LPS countries, with some variation regarding the sophistication of the content dealt with at 8th grade. As a result, the data set from most of the LPS countries included at least one algebra lesson sequence.

In the key element of the post-lesson student interviews, in which a picture-in-picture video record was used as stimulus for student reconstructions of classroom events (see Figure 1), students were given control of the video replay and asked to identify and comment upon classroom events of personal importance. The post-lesson student interviews were conducted as individual interviews in all countries except Germany, Israel and South Africa, where student preference for group interviews was sufficiently strong to make that approach essential. Each teacher was interviewed at least three times using a similar protocol.

Figure 1. Picture-in-picture video display

With regard to both classroom videotaping and the post-lesson interviews, the principles governing data generation were the minimisation of atypical classroom activity (caused by the data generation activity) and the maximisation of respondent control in the interview context. To achieve this, each videotaped lesson sequence was preceded by a one-week familiarisation period in which all aspects of data generation were conducted until the teacher indicated that the class was functioning as normally as might reasonably be expected.

In interviews, the location of control of the video player with the student ensured that the reconstructive accounts focused primarily on the student's parsing of the lesson. Only after the student's selection of significant events had been exhausted did the interviewer ask for reconstructive accounts of other events of interest to the research team. Documentation of the participant's perspective (learner or teacher) remained the priority.

In every facet of this data generation, technical quality was a priority. The technical capacity to visually juxtapose the teacher's actions with the physical and oral responses of the children was matched by the capacity to replay both the public statements by teacher or student and the private conversations of students as they struggled to construct meaning. Students could be confronted, immediately after the lesson, with a video record of their actions and the actions of their classmates.

In the picture-in-picture video record generated on-site in the classroom (Figure 1), students could see both their actions and the actions of those students around them, and, in the inset (top right-hand corner), the actions of the teacher at that time. This combined video record captured the classroom world of the student. The video record captured through the whole-class camera allowed the actions of the focus students to be seen in relation to the actions of the rest of the class.

CLASSROOM DATA GENERATION

Camera Configuration

Data generation employed three cameras in the classroom – a "Teacher Camera", a "Student Camera" and a "Whole Class Camera". The protocol below was written primarily for a single research assistant/videographer, but brief notes were provided suggesting variations possible if a second videographer was available. In order to ensure consistency of data generation across all schools in several countries, the protocol was written as a low inference protocol, requiring as few decisions by the videographer as possible. One or two possible anomalous cases were specifically discussed – such as when a student presents to the entire class. However, the general principles were constant for each camera: The Teacher Camera maintained a continuous record of the teacher's statements and actions. The Student Camera maintained a continuous record of the statements and actions of a group of four students. The Whole Class Camera was set up in the front of the classroom to capture, as far as was possible, the actions of every student – that is, of the "Whole Class." The Whole Class Camera can also be thought of as the "Teacher View Camera." While no teacher can see exactly what every individual student is doing, the teacher will have a sense of the general level of activity and types of behaviors of the whole class at any time – this is what was intended to be captured on the Whole Class Camera.

Camera One: The Teacher Camera

The "Teacher Camera" maintained the teacher in centre screen as large as possible *provided that all gestures and all tools or equipment used could be seen* – if overhead transparencies or boardwork or other visual aids were used then these had to be captured fully at the point at which they were generated or employed in the first instance or subsequently amended – but did not need to be kept in view at the expense of keeping the teacher in frame (provided at least one full image was recorded, this could be retrieved for later analysis – the priority was to keep the teacher in view). The *sole exception* to this protocol occurred when a student worked at the board or presented to the whole class. In this case, the Teacher Camera focused on the "student as teacher." The actions of the Teacher during such occasions should have been recorded by the Whole Class Camera. If the teacher was positioned out of view of the Whole Class Camera (eg front of classroom, at the side), then the Teacher Camera might "zoom out" to keep both the student and teacher on view, but documentation of the gestures, statements, and any written or drawn work by the student at the board should be kept clearly visible. Note: Although the teacher was radio-miked, in the simulated situations we trialled it was not necessary for the teacher to hand the lapel microphone to the student. The student's public statements to the class could be adequately captured on the student microphone connected to the Student Camera. The first few lessons in a particular classroom (during the familiarisation period) provided an opportunity to learn to "read" the teacher's teaching style, level of mobility, types of whole class discussion employed, and so on. A variety of practical decisions about the optimal camera locations could be made during the familiarisation period and as events dictated during videotaping.

Camera Two: The Student Camera

Where only a single videographer was used, the "Student Camera" was set up prior to the commencement of the lesson to include at least two adjacent students and was re-focussed in the first two minutes of the lesson during the teacher's introductory comments – during this time the Teacher Camera could be set up to record a sufficiently wide image to include most likely positions of the teacher during these opening minutes. Once the Student Camera was adequately focused on the focus students for that lesson, it remained fixed unless student movement necessitated its realignment. After aligning the Student Camera, the videographer returned to the Teacher Camera and maintained focus on the teacher, subject to the above guidelines.

If two research assistants ("videographers") were available (and this was frequently the case), then it became possible for the Student Camera to "zoom in" on each student's written work every five minutes or so, to maintain an on-going record of the student's progress on any written tasks. This "zooming in" was done sufficiently briefly to provide visual cues as to the progress of the student's written work, but any such zooming in had to be done without losing the continuity of the video record of all focus students, since that would be needed for the subsequent interviews. Since it was Learner Practices that were the priority in this study, the continuous documentation of the actions of the focus students and their interactions (including non-verbal interactions) was most important. A copy of the students' written work was obtained at the end of the lesson. The video record generated by this camera served to display each student's activities in relation to the teacher's actions, the tasks assigned, and the activities of their nearby classmates.

Camera Three: The Whole Class Camera

The "Whole Class (or Teacher-View) Camera" was set up to one side of whichever part of the room the teacher spoke from (typically, to one side at the "front" of the classroom). All students should be within the field of view of this camera (it is necessary to use a wide-angle lens). Apart from capturing the "corporate" behavior of the class, this camera provided an approximation to a "teacher's-eye view" of the class. It was also this camera that documented teacher actions during any periods when a student was working at the board or making a presentation to the entire class.

Microphone Position

The teacher was radio-miked to the Teacher Camera. The focus student group was recorded with a microphone placed as centrally as possible in relation to the focus students and recorded through the Student Camera (use of a radio microphone minimised intrusive cables). The Whole Class Camera audio was recorded through that camera's internal microphone.

Fieldnotes

Depending on the available research personnel, fieldnotes were maintained to record the time and type of all *changes* in instructional activity. Such field notes could be very simple, for example:
00:00 Teacher Introduction
09:50 Students do Chalkboard Problem
17:45 Whole Class Discussion
24:30 Individual Textbook Work
41:45 Teacher Summation
Specific events of interest to the researcher could be included as annotations to such field notes.

Where a third researcher was available, in addition to the operators of the Teacher and Student cameras, this person was able to take more detailed field notes, including detail of possible moments of significance for the progress of the lesson (eg public or private negotiations of meaning). In such cases, the field notes became a useful aid in the post-lesson interview, and the interviewee could be asked to comment on particular events, if these had not been already identified by the interviewee earlier in the interview.

Student Written Work

All written work produced by the focus students "in camera" during any lesson was photocopied together with any text materials or handouts used during the lesson. Students brought with them to the interview their textbook and all written material produced in class. This material (textbook pages, worksheets, and student written work) was photocopied immediately after the interview and returned to the student.

INTERVIEWS

In this study, students were interviewed after each lesson using the video record as stimulus for their reconstructions of classroom events. It is a feature of this study that students were given control of the video replay and asked to identify and comment upon classroom events of personal importance. Because of the significance of interviews within the study, the validity of students' and teachers' verbal reconstructions of their motivations, feelings and thoughts was given significant thought. The circumstances under which such verbal accounts may provide legitimate data have been detailed in two seminal papers (Ericsson & Simon, 1980; Nisbett & Wilson, 1977).

It is our contention that videotapes of classroom interactions constitute salient stimuli for interviewing purposes, and that individuals' verbal reports of their thoughts and feelings during classroom interactions, when prompted by videos of the particular associated events, can provide useful insights into those individuals' learning behaviour. Videotapes provide a specific and immediate stimulus that optimizes the conditions for effective recall of associated feelings and thoughts. Nonetheless, an individual's video-stimulated account will be prone to the same potential for unintentional misrepresentation and deliberate distortion that apply in any social situation in which individuals are obliged to explain their actions. A significant part of the power of video-stimulated recall resides in the juxtaposition of the interviewee's account and the video record to which it is related. Any apparent discrepancies revealed by such a comparison warrant particular scrutiny and careful interpretation by the researcher. Having relinquished the positivist commitment to identifying 'what really happened,' both correspondence and contradiction can be exploited. The interview protocols for student and teacher interviews were prescribed in the LPS Research Design and are reproduced below.

Individual student interviews

Prompt One: Please tell me what you think that lesson was about (lesson content/lesson purpose).
Prompt Two: How, do you think, you best learn something like that?
Prompt Three: What were your personal goals for that lesson? What did you hope to achieve? Do you have similar goals for every lesson?
Prompt Four: Here is the remote control for the videoplayer. Do you understand how it works? (Allow time for a short familiarisation with the

control). I would like you to comment on the videotape for me. You do not need to comment on all of the lesson. Fast forward the videotape until you find sections of the lesson that you think were important. Play these sections at normal speed and describe for me what you were doing, thinking and feeling during each of these videotape sequences. You can comment while the videotape is playing, but pause the tape if there is something that you want to talk about in detail.

Prompt Five: After watching the videotape, is there anything you would like to add to your description of what the lesson was about?

Prompt Six: What did you learn during that lesson?
[Whenever a claim is made to new mathematical knowledge, this should be probed. Suitable probing cues would be a request for examples of tasks or methods of solution that are now understood or the posing by the interviewer of succinct probing questions related to common misconceptions in the content domain.]

Prompt Seven: Would you describe that lesson as a good* one for you? What has to happen for you to feel that a lesson was a "good" lesson? Did you achieve your goals? What are the important things you should learn in a mathematics lesson?
[*"Good" may be not be a sufficiently neutral prompt in some countries – the specific term used should be chosen to be as neutral as possible in order to obtain data on those outcomes of the lesson which the student values. It is possible that these valued outcomes may have little connection to "knowing", "learning" or "understanding", and that students may have very localised or personal ways to describe lesson outcomes. These personalised and possibly culturally-specific conceptions of lesson outcomes constitute important data.]

Prompt Eight: Was this lesson a typical [geometry, algebra, etc] lesson? What was not typical about it?

Prompt Nine: How would you generally assess your own achievement in mathematics?

Prompt Ten: Do you enjoy mathematics and mathematics classes?

Prompt Eleven: Why do you think you are good [or not so good] at mathematics?

Prompt Twelve: Do you do very much mathematical work at home? Have you ever had private tutoring in mathematics or attended additional mathematics classes outside normal school hours?

Prompts 9 through 12 could be covered in a student questionnaire – the choice of method may be made locally, provided the data is collected.

Student Group Interviews

Prompt One: Please tell me what you think that lesson was about (lesson content/lesson purpose) (Discuss with the group – identify points of agreement and disagreement – there is NO need to achieve consensus).

Prompt Two: Here is the remote control for the videoplayer. I would like you to comment on the videotape for me. You do not need to comment on all of the lesson. I will fast forward the videotape until anyone tells me to stop. I want you to find sections of the lesson that you think were important. We will play these sections at normal speed and I would like each of you to describe for me what you were doing, thinking and feeling during each of these videotape sequences. You can comment while the videotape is playing, but tell me to pause the tape if there is something that you want to talk about in detail.

Prompt Three: After watching the videotape, is there anything anyone would like to add to the description of what the lesson was about?

Prompt Four: What did you learn during that lesson? (Discuss)
[As for the individual interview protocol, all claims to new mathematical knowledge should be probed. BUT, before probing an individual's responses directly, the interviewer should ask other members of the group to comment.]

Prompt Five: Would you describe that lesson as a good* one for you? (Discuss) What has to happen for you to feel that a lesson was a "good" lesson? (Discuss) What are the important things you should learn in a mathematics lesson?
[*As for the student individual interviews, "good" may be not be a sufficiently neutral prompt in some countries – the specific term used should be chosen to be as neutral as possible in order to obtain data on those outcomes of the lesson which the student values].

Prompt Six: Was this lesson a typical [geometry, algebra, etc] lesson? What was not typical about it?

The Teacher Interview

The goal was to complete one interview per week, according to teacher availability. The Whole Class Camera image was used as the stimulus. In selecting the lesson about which to seek teacher comment, choose either (1) the lesson with the greatest diversity of classroom activities, or (2) the lesson with the most evident student interactions. Should the teacher express a strong preference to discuss a particular lesson, then this lesson should take priority. Tapes of the other lessons should be available in the interview, in case the teacher should indicate an interest in any aspect of a particular lesson.

Prompt One: Please tell me what were your goals in that lesson (lesson content/lesson purpose).

Prompt Two: In relation to your content goal(s), why do you think this content is important for students to learn?
What do you think your students might have answered to this question?

Prompt Three: Here is the remote control for the videoplayer. Do you understand how it works? (Allow time for a short familiarisation with the control). I would like you to comment on the videotape for me. You do not need to comment on all of the lesson. Fast forward the videotape until you find sections of the lesson that you think were important. Play these sections at normal speed and describe for me what you were doing, thinking and feeling during each of these videotape sequences. You can comment while the videotape is playing, but pause the tape if there is something that you want to talk about in detail.

In particular, I would like you to comment on:

(a) Why you said or did a particular thing (for example, conducting a particular activity, using a particular example, asking a question, or making a statement).

(b) What you were thinking at key points during each video excerpt (for example, I was confused, I was wondering what to do next, I was trying to think of a good example).

(c) How you were feeling? (for example, I was worried that we would not cover all the content)

(d) Students' actions or statements that you consider to be significant and explain why you feel the action or statement was significant.

(e) How typical that lesson was of the sort of lesson you would normally teach? What do you see as the features of that lesson that are most typical of the way you teach? Were there any aspects of your behavior or the students' behavior that were unusual?

Prompt Four: Would you describe that lesson as a good lesson for you? What has to happen for you to feel that a lesson is a "good" lesson?

Prompt Five: Do your students work a lot at home? Do they have private tutors?

OTHER SOURCES OF DATA

Student tests were used to situate each student group and each student in relation to student performance on eighth-grade mathematics tasks. Student mathematics achievement was assessed in three ways:

Student written work in class. Analyses of student written work were undertaken both during and after the period of videotaping. For this purpose, the written work of all "focus students" in each lesson was photocopied, clearly labelled with the student's name, the class, and the date, and filed. Additional data on student achievement was also collected, where this was available. In particular, student scores were obtained on any topic tests administered by the teacher, in relation to mathematical content dealt with in the videotaped lesson sequence.

Student performance to place the class in relation to the national 8th grade population. In Australia, Japan, Korea, China and the USA, this was done by using the International Benchmark Test for Mathematics (administered immediately after the completion of videotaping). The International Benchmark Test (IBT) was developed by the Australian Council for Educational Research (ACER) by combining a selection of items from the TIMSS Student Achievement test. In the case of this project, the test for Population Two was used, since this was in closest correspondence with the grade level of the students taking part in the LPS project. In administering the IBT, the local research group in each country constructed an equivalent test using the corresponding version of each of the TIMSS items, as administered in that country. In some countries, where this was not possible (Germany, for example), the typical school performance was characterised in relation to other schools by comparison of the senior secondary mathematics performance with national norms.

Student performance in relation to other students in that class. Since student-student interactions may be influenced by perceptions of peer competence, it was advantageous to collect recent performance data on all students in the class. Two forms of student mathematics achievement at class level were accessed, where available: (a) student scores from recent mathematics tests administered by the teacher, and (b) brief annotated comments by the teacher on a list of all students in the class – commenting on the mathematics achievement and competence of each student.

Teacher Goals and Perceptions

Teacher questionnaires were used to establish teacher beliefs and purposes related to the lesson sequence studied. Three questionnaires were administered to each participating teacher:
- A *preliminary* teacher questionnaire about each teacher's goals in the teaching of mathematics (TQ1);
- A *post-lesson* questionnaire (TQ2 – either the short TQ2S or the long TQ2L version – if the short version was used, the researcher's field notes provided as much as possible of the additional detail sought in the long version);
- A *post-videotaping* questionnaire (TQ3) (also employed by some research groups as the basis of a final teacher interview).

DATA CONFIGURATION AND STORAGE

Transcription and Translation

A detailed Technical Guide was developed to provide guidelines for the transcription and translation of classroom and interview, video and audiotape data. It was essential that all research groups transcribe their own data. Local language variants (e.g. the Berliner dialect) required a "local ear" for accurate transcription.

Translation into English was also the responsibility of the local research group. The Technical Guide specified both transcription conventions, such as how to represent pauses or overlapping statements, and translation conventions, such as how to represent colloquialisms. In the case of local colloquial expressions in a language other than English, the translator was presented with a major challenge. A literal English translation of the colloquialism may convey no meaning at all to a reader from another country, while the replacement of the colloquialism by a similar English colloquialism may capture the essence and spirit of the expression, but sacrifice the semantic connotations of the particular words used. And there is a third problem: If no precise English equivalent can be found, then the translation inevitably misrepresents the communicative exchange. In such instances, the original language, as transcribed, was included together with its literal English translation. Any researcher experiencing difficulties of interpretation in analysing the data could contact a member of the research group responsible for the generation of those data and request additional detail.

Data Storage

To carry out serious systematic empirical work in classroom research, there is a need for both close and detailed analysis of selected event sequences, and for more general descriptions of the material from within which the analysed sample has been chosen. To be able to perform this work with good-quality multiple-source video and audio data, video and audio materials have to be compressed and stored in a form accessible by desktop computers. Software tools such as *Final Cut Pro* are essential for the efficient and economical storage of the very large video data files. Compression decisions are dictated by current storage and back-up alternatives and change as these change. For example, when the Learner's Perspective Study was established in 1999, it was anticipated that data would be exchanged between research teams by CD-ROM and compression ratios were set at 20:1 in order to get maximum data quality within a file size that would allow one video record of one lesson to be stored on a single CD. As a result, the complete US data set in 2001 took the form of a set of over fifty separate CDs. Later, it was possible to store all the data related to a single lesson (including four compressed video records) on a single DVD. The contemporary availability of pocket drives with capacities of 60 gigabytes and higher, has made data sharing both more efficient and cheaper. It is possible to store all the data from a single school in compressed form on such a pocket drive, making secure data transfer between international research groups much more cost-effective.

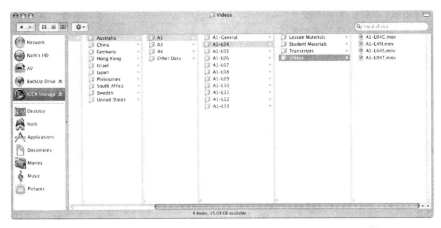

Figure 2. Structure of the LPS database at the ICCR circa 2004

The materials on the database have to be represented in a searchable fashion. In Figure 2, the configuration of the LPS database is displayed as a stratified hierarchy of: Country (column 1), school (column 2), lesson (column 3), data source (column 4), specific file (column 5). Any particular file, such as the teacher camera view of lesson 4 at school 2 in Japan, can then be uniquely located.

Setting up data in this way enables researchers to move between different layers of data, without losing sight of the way they are related to each other. Further, data can be made accessible to other researchers. This is a sharp contrast to more traditional ways of storing video data on tapes, with little or no searchable record available, and with data access limited to very small numbers of people. At the International Centre for Classroom Research (ICCR) at the University of Melbourne, for example, several researchers can simultaneously access the full range of classroom data. This capacity for the simultaneous analysis of a common body of classroom data is the technical realisation of the methodological and theoretical commitment to complementary analyses proposed by Clarke (1998, 2001) as essential to any research attempting to characterise social phenomena as complex as those found in classrooms.

ANALYTICAL TOOLS CAPABLE OF SUPPORTING SOPHISTICATED ANALYSES OF SUCH COMPLEX DATABASES

Research along the lines argued for above requires the development of software tools for analysing video efficiently. The reasons for this are, in short, that video editing software (such as *Final Cut Pro*) is not analytically resourceful enough, whereas qualitative analysis software (such as *Nudist* or *nVivo*) is not well enough adapted to video and audio work. Early examples of video analysis software (such as *vPrism*) have been hampered by problems arising from their project-specific origins, leading to a lack of flexibility in customising the analysis to the demands of each particular project or research focus.

Collaboration with the Australian software company, Sportstec, was carried out to adapt the video analysis software *Studiocode* for use with classroom video data. These adaptations were driven by specific methodological, theoretical and practical needs. For example, the commitment to the capturing and juxtaposition of multiple perspectives on classroom events was partially addressed with the onsite capture of the picture-in-picture display shown in Figure 1, but the need to 'calibrate' the actions of the focus students against the actions of the rest of the class required multiple viewing windows.

Figure 3 displays the key analytical elements provided within *Studiocode*: video window, time-line, transcript window, and coding scheme. The researcher has the option of analysing and coding the events shown in the video window, or the utterances shown in the transcript window, or both. The resultant codes can be displayed in timelines (as shown in Figure 3) or in frequency tables. Once coded, single lessons, events within single lessons, or combinations of lessons can be merged into a single analysis.

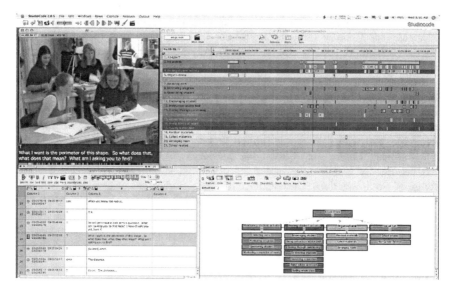

Figure 3. Sample analytical display (Studiocode) – video window (top left), time-line (top right), transcript window (bottom-left) and coding facility (bottom-right)

The continual addition of new countries to the Learner's Perspective Study community required that video data already coded should not need to be recoded when additional data (eg from a different country) were incrementally added to the database. Only the new data should require coding and the newly-coded data should be accessible for analysis as part of the growing pool of classroom data. This flexibility is ideally suited to a project such as the Learner's Perspective Study, with many collaborating researchers adopting a wide range of different analytical approaches to a commonly held body of classroom data.

The *Studiocode* software described above is only one of the many analytical tools available to the classroom researcher. Increasingly sophisticated public access software tools are being developed continually. Most of the chapters in this book and in the companion volume (Clarke, Keitel, & Shimizu, 2006) report specific analyses of different subsets of the large body of LPS classroom data. Each analysis is distinctive and interrogates and interprets the data consistent with the purpose of the authoring researcher(s). Analytical tools such as *nVivo* and *Studiocode* can support the researcher's analysis but ideally should not constrain the consequent interpretation of the data. In reality, all such tools, including statistical procedures, constrain the researcher's possible interpretations by limiting the type of data compatible with the analytical tool being used, by restricting the variety of codes, categories or values that can be managed, and by constraining the range of possible results able to be generated by the particular analytical tool.

REFERENCES

Clarke, D. J. (1998). Studying the classroom negotiation of meaning: Complementary accounts methodology. In A. Teppo (Ed.), *Qualitative research methods in mathematics education,* monograph number 9 of the *Journal for Research in Mathematics Education* (pp. 98-111). Reston, VA: NCTM.

Clarke, D. J. (Ed.). (2001). *Perspectives on practice and meaning in mathematics and science classrooms.* Dordrecht: Kluwer Academic Publishers.

Clarke, D. J., Keitel, C., & Shimizu, Y. (Eds.). (2006). *Mathematics classrooms in twelve countries: The insider's perspective.* Rotterdam: Sense Publishers.

Ericsson, K. A., & Simon, H. A. (1980). Verbal reports as data. *Psychological Review, 87*(3), 215-251.

Miles, M. B., & Huberman, A. M. (2004). *Qualitative data analysis* (2nd edition). Thousand Oaks, CA: Sage Publications.

Nisbett, R. E., & Wilson, T. D. (1977). Telling more than we can know: Verbal reports on mental processes. *Psychological Review, 84*(3), 231-259.

David Clarke
International Centre for Classroom Research,
Faculty of Education,
University of Melbourne,
Australia

AUTHOR INDEX

SUBJECT INDEX

LaVergne, TN USA
16 June 2010

186315LV00001B/53/P